The Official Illustrated History
of the
FA Cup

Also by Bryon Butler

The Official History of the Football Association
The Official Illustrated History of the Football League 1888–1988
The Giant Killers
Soccer Choice
Sports Report – 40 Years of the Best (Editor)

The Official Illustrated History
of the
FA Cup

Bryon Butler

HEADLINE

First published in 1996
by HEADLINE BOOK PUBLISHING

10 9 8 7 6 5 4 3 2 1

British Library Cataloguing in Publication Data

Butler, Bryon
  The official illustrated history of the F.A. Cup
  1.F.A. Cup - History 2.Soccer - Tournaments - England -
  History
  I.Title
  796.3'3464'0942

ISBN 0 7472 1781 5

Design, black and white origination: Clive Dorman & Co.
Printed and bound in Italy by Canale & C. S.p.A.

HEADLINE BOOK PUBLISHING
A division of Hodder Headline PLC
338 Euston Road
London NW1 3BH

Contents

Acknowledgements

To old and new friends for their patience, generosity and expertise –
especially, in absolutely random order, Graham Smith, David
Barber, Audrey Adams, Gordon Wallis, Chris Harte, Councillor Mrs
Ruby Hunt OBE, Andy Mitchell, Paul Macnamara, Richard Cohen,
Bernard Gallagher, Robert Pratten, Ian Rigby, Gareth Davies,
Dennis Marshall, Malcolm Graham, Tony Bentley, Ted Wilding,
David Frith, Clive Dorman, Francis Cartwright, Tracey Horn, Dave
Smith and Duncan Bond – as well as Marc, Elaine, Alison, Terry,
Mick, Andy, Andrew and Paul among the many who lit the way into
the darker corners of libraries and archives. Gratitude, and
admiration, to Lorraine Jerram, Nic Jones and
Ian Marshall of Headline.

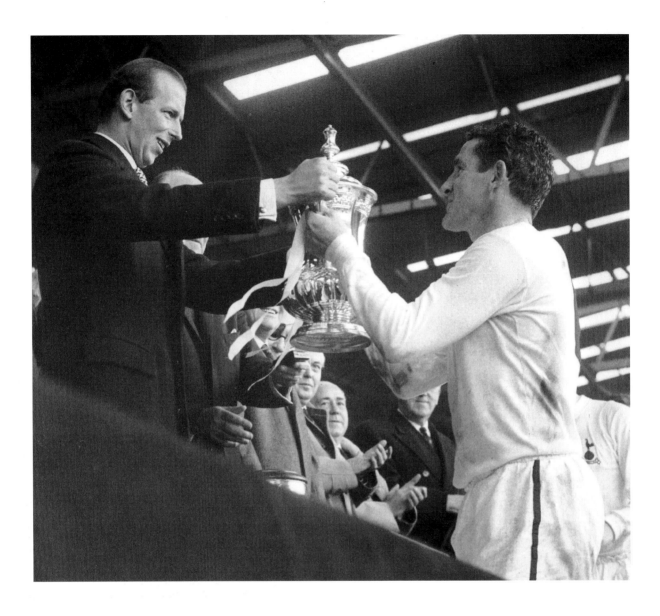

Above The Duke of Kent present-
ing the FA Cup for the first time,
Tottenham Hotspur v Chelsea 1967.
Dave Mackay is the happy recipient
and Prime Minister Harold Wilson is
in the background.

Foreword

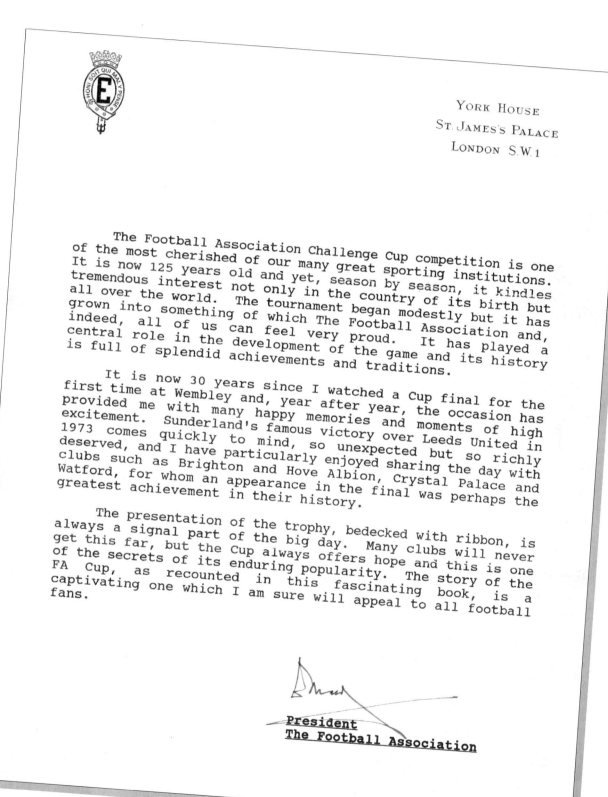

YORK HOUSE
ST. JAMES'S PALACE
LONDON S.W.1

The Football Association Challenge Cup competition is one of the most cherished of our many great sporting institutions. It is now 125 years old and yet, season by season, it kindles tremendous interest not only in the country of its birth but all over the world. The tournament began modestly but it has grown into something of which The Football Association and, indeed, all of us can feel very proud. It has played a central role in the development of the game and its history is full of splendid achievements and traditions.

It is now 30 years since I watched a Cup final for the first time at Wembley and, year after year, the occasion has provided me with many happy memories and moments of high excitement. Sunderland's famous victory over Leeds United in 1973 comes quickly to mind, so unexpected but so richly deserved, and I have particularly enjoyed sharing the day with clubs such as Brighton and Hove Albion, Crystal Palace and Watford, for whom an appearance in the final was perhaps the greatest achievement in their history.

The presentation of the trophy, bedecked with ribbon, is always a signal part of the big day. Many clubs will never get this far, but the Cup always offers hope and this is one of the secrets of its enduring popularity. The story of the FA Cup, as recounted in this fascinating book, is a captivating one which I am sure will appeal to all football fans.

President
The Football Association

'His name is symbolic of the beauty of the game,

his fame timeless and international,

his sportsmanship and modesty universally acclaimed.

A magical player, of the people, for the people.'

The inscription below the statue of Sir Stanley Matthews by Colin Melbourne which was unveiled in Hanley, his birthplace, on 21 October 1987.

Preface

More than sixty years have passed since I played in my first FA Cup game with Stoke City, but the battle for the dear old trophy still excites and fascinates me as much as ever. Its marvellous traditions, and the drama and surprises it provides every year, are part of all of us. The tingle is always there. I can't imagine football without it.

I had two big ambitions when I started. The first was a Cup-winner's medal and the second was to play for my country. I managed both but my first England cap came nearly twenty years before that precious medal. I only wish I could do justice to my feelings after Blackpool's win over Bolton in the 1953 final. I know exactly how disappointed I was after losing at Wembley to Manchester United in 1948 and Newcastle in 1951; but that win of ours in Coronation year, with not a lot to spare, left me feeling absolutely numb. People are generous enough to refer to it as the 'Stanley Matthews final' – but how can that be when Stan Mortensen got a hat-trick?

My playing career, the record books assure me, lasted thirty-three years and took me past my fiftieth birthday and well into the 1960s. It has left me with so many memories, so many friends and so many tributes and kindnesses to be grateful for, that I sometimes think I've imagined it all. Herbert Chapman's Arsenal ruled the land when I started and players such as Alex James, David Jack and the great Dixie Dean of Everton were making the headlines. Times change and so has the game, for better and worse, but I am very certain about one thing. I would love to be playing now – and having another crack at the FA Cup.

Introduction

Its old bones tell a wonderful story: 50,000 or so games played by 3,000 or so clubs in 115 tournaments over 125 years. It is a pageant which has sprinkled stardust through the drip and chill of English winters ever since the year in which Stanley found Livingstone, Rasputin was born, Verdi's *Aïda* was first heard and Gladstone introduced Bank Holidays.

Only World Wars have interrupted it and custom has never staled its infinite variety. Every season it touches, directly, the heart of hundreds of cities, towns and assorted dots on the map; and it enchants scores of millions, all over the globe, by way of television and radio. It offers fantasy, passion, democracy, warfare, tradition, ritual, instant fame and handy profit in one big and irresistible package. It is a band of gold in the fabric of a sporting nation. It is, of course, the Football Association Challenge Cup ... the FA Cup ... the Cup. It is the daddy of them all.

The Cup was football's fountain of life. It gave new status and authority to a young Football Association in London, nourished the game's laws, helped football take a firm foothold in the North and Midlands, paved the way for professionalism and the founding of the Football League and provided a simple game with a forceful push at the beginning of its journey around the earth. The World Cup? It is just a grandchild of *The* Cup.

Fifteen clubs entered the first skirmish in 1871–72 but, pruned by withdrawals and byes, only twelve clubs played and only thirteen games were involved. Now it is a campaign that takes thirteen rounds, nine months and nearly 700 matches to reduce 500 and more entrants to a winner. Two thousand spectators paid a total of £100 to watch the first final at Kennington Oval. Now 80,000 pay around £2.5 million to witness the modern version and the best seats at Wembley cost £115 each. The Cup began as a manly and innocent diversion for the privileged. Now it is a cosmic business.

The Cup's trail through the four seasons of the year is wide and vivid. It is a road full of potholes and tripwires; but it is a road, too, which is awash with starry dreams and deeds of derring-do. It begins in late summer with hundreds of cock-eyed optimists pounding their chests in a preliminary round. The elimination process, every tie a matter of life or death, continues quickly through four qualifying rounds, and then moves on to the arterial road to Wembley with six rounds proper and the semi-finals. The humbler Football League clubs enter the lists in the first of these and are joined, graciously, by the Bigtime Uniteds and Fancy Cities in the third. Four months later there are only two survivors – and one last game, a national spectacle in May beneath the twin towers of Wembley, is left to produce a victor.

It is summer again and the Cup puts on a show. Outside, before the final, there is a pilgrims' progress of chatter and chants, mingled vowels, fancy favours, kitchen smells and furtive touts. Inside, as kick-off draws nearer, Her Majesty's Guardsmen strut and puff with scarlet tunics and scarlet faces, and soon the old fortress will fill with the rumble of 'Abide With Me', a moment of reverence (boneheads permitting), before the battle to come. And then, at last, the teams appear, clattering out of their grey tunnel and passing through what Jack Charlton called 'a curtain of light'. There are Royal handshakes – and so to the football.

The strong arm and mighty spear usually prevail in the end, the big warrior clubs forming an orderly queue as they wait their turn for glory, but they are no more important to the story of the Cup than the little people who never make it past the foothills of the tournament. What can be wrong with a world-famous rodeo which has found room for such worthies as Rhoslianerchrugog (Clwyd), Wrockwardine Wood (Shropshire) and Jump Home Guard (Barnsley) at different times in its history?

The Cup would never claim to be perfect. It is a charming old romancer which seduces the socks off everyone; but it is also a perverse teaser, a cunning manipulator and a roguish match-maker that takes great pleasure in confounding us all. And we love it all the more for doing so.

Sometimes the Cup's annual plot is so well scripted that we may even feel a Higher Authority has had a hand in it. Sometimes, too, we suspect that the winner of the trophy is chosen, again up above, before a ball is kicked in earnest; and that this decision, once taken, is immutable. The chosen ones may play like a high-kick of chorus girls, be smitten by injuries and ambushed by better teams, but the force will be with them. They will have inspiration on one shoulder, good luck on the other and the hard boot of providence just behind them. But we can never be sure. The Cup is full of fancy theories and giddy illusions.

There are wisps of cloud in the sky. The requirements of television, moving ties to various days of the week, has reduced the impact of the old Cup Saturday. There is also a growing gap in resources and strength between the best and the rest which might just mean that, at the sharp end of the tournament, surprises become even more surprising. Not even the Cup can stand aside from modern notions of progress and, in any case, it has always had the good grace and flexibility to accommodate change. But we must be careful.

The Cup is old and forever new. No history of it is just an exercise in fluffing up memories because its past is a muscular part of its present. The Cup is the sum of all its yesterdays. The aim of this history, a celebration written and assembled with love, is to cherish the Cup's magic, to revel in its drama and traditions, its humour and tears, and to do some small justice to one of the most enthralling of all our sporting institutions. It is more about the heart and soul of the tournament than its statistics which are admirably covered in many other publications.

There is only one holder of the Cup; but we are all joint owners.

Bryon Butler

Guildford 1996

Sunderland v Aston Villa in the FA Cup. From the painting by Thomas M. Hemy (1893).

Chapter One

One Small Idea
1871–1882

'The Cup ties stir the blood of the footballer as no other competition does. When the first half of the season has come and gone and dark December drags its weary way, there is a beacon light ahead that fills the enthusiast with hope and joy. That light is the Cup, and all the glory and glamour that surrounds this wondrous bauble. The heart of the footballer leaps at the name of the Cup. The winter of our discontent is made glorious summer by the dawning of the Cup ties. It is safe to say that no single event in history causes more popular enthusiasm than the simple struggle for the Blue Ribbon of the football world.'

Association Football And The Men Who Made It
by Alfred Gibson and William Pickford.

No graphic first-hand account seems to exist of the meeting on 20 July 1871 at which the Football Association breathed life into its Challenge Cup. No trace is left of its birthplace, the offices of the old *Sportsman* newspaper, in Boy Court, just off the bottom of Ludgate Hill in the London parish of St Bride. The site is now covered by the concrete of commerce.

Even in the first minute book of the FA, the most precious football book in the world, the meeting is recorded with severe formality in fifty-three words. *The Sportsman* itself, which boasted 'the most efficient staff of contributors', was underwhelmed by the occasion, and so was every other newspaper. It may be added that Charles Alcock, secretary of the FA and the 'father' of the Cup, was a journalist who wrote regularly for *The Sportsman* and *The Field*.

Geoffrey Green, in his *Official History of the FA Cup* (1949), and Tony Pawson, in his centenary history, *100 Years of the FA Cup* (1972), allowed themselves a little licence. They pictured the birth of football's first national tournament in the same way: 'The scene was a small, oak-panelled room at the *Sportsman* office. There sat seven men, dressed in the height of fashion as befitted their place in society. The talk was of the events of the day – the Siege of Paris by the troops from Versailles; the proposal before Parliament to abolish the system of purchasing commissions in the Army; the serious illness of Edward, Prince of Wales; the decision of King William of Prussia to assume the title of German Emperor. Soon their conversation drifted to the exploits of their football clubs, for each was a member of one or other of the best known teams of that period.

'After the formal business had been dealt with, C. W. Alcock proposed: "That it is desirable that a Challenge Cup should be established in connection with the Association, for which all clubs belonging to the Association should be invited to compete."

'The idea was received at once with general favour, and at a subsequent meeting held on October 16th 1871 the rules were drafted, the entries were received and history took a deep breath and prepared for the plunge.'

This, perhaps, was the way it was; but, then again, it is just possible that these pioneers talked about other sporting matters. Shooting, billiards, hunting, racing, angling and various forms of unarmed combat were all very popular – and Alcock, soon to become secretary of Surrey County Cricket Club as well, was always ready to chat about his friend, W. G. Grace, who was enjoying the best summer of his Himalayan career.

The FA's first minute book, now with a hint of gold in its paling ink, records that the proposal was approved unanimously. But did no one suggest that the tournament might lead to excessive rivalry, attract undesirable elements and even undermine the true spirit of the game? They were criticisms made by many once the plan to launch a Challenge Cup became common knowledge.

It can be said with some certainty that there was no feeling of high destiny at the meeting. History may have been beckoning, but those seven men would not have foreseen a day when their competition would be one of the best loved of all England's sporting institutions. Nor a day when the FA Cup final would be watched by a global audience of millions by way of a marvel called television. Nor would they have imagined that their idea would be the seed from which would spring a World Cup embracing nearly 200 countries. Yet Alcock and his colleagues did have an aim in mind. The Football Association was eight years old and had partly succeeded in providing football with shape, direction and momentum. They had fashioned some sort of order out of chaos – but it now needed a push of a different kind. The Cup, they felt, might provide it.

Only a generation before the formation of the Football Association in 1863, the game had been a traditional but violent thing of the streets, market places and open countryside, an excuse for a riot which divided towns, set village against village and sometimes involved hundreds of players. But then England's ruling and professional classes adopted it, as new attitudes developed towards manly decorum and a proper balance between work and play. The value of organised team games was recognised by the public schools – and football fitted the bill perfectly.

Each school, however, developed its own style. Variations at Harrow, Eton, Winchester, Charterhouse and their like were extensive, and technical slang (hacking, piggling, shinning and tagging) muddled things further. The confusion became even more apparent when players of different creeds mixed at university or in the services. Slowly, though, two codes became distinguishable – football and rugby, dribblers and handlers – and the formation of the FA helped to establish a clear line between the two.

The FA gave a splintered game a new life force, but its early influence was not dramatic. Although football was essentially a game for gentlemen, the Association's authority and laws were regularly challenged and its field of influence was small. Its original membership was eleven clubs from the London area; two years later it had acquired only one provincial member, Sheffield; and by 1871 it had grown slowly to fifty.

The game needed a stimulus; and Alcock found the answer in his schoolboy memories. He recalled playing in an inter-house knockout tournament at Harrow, and, with a visionary's eye, saw it as a formula which might work on a bigger scale. Indeed it would.

A stubby, heavily embossed silver cup was bought for around £20 and fifteen clubs entered the first competition: Barnes, Civil Service, Clapham Rovers, Crystal Palace (no connection with the modern League club), Hampstead Heathens, Harrow Chequers, Hitchin, Maidenhead, Marlow, Reigate Priory, Royal Engineers, Upton Park, the Wanderers and two clubs from the North – Queen's Park of Glasgow, the illustrious heralds of Scottish football, and Donington School in south Lincolnshire. Queen's Park, annual income about £6, even contributed a guinea towards the cost of the trophy.

The first tournament was an erratic, loosely woven affair from which Harrow

Chequers, Reigate Priory and Donington School scratched without playing and Queen's Park were exempted up to the semi-finals because of distance and cost. Sides which drew were also allowed to move to the next round. Public donations enabled Queen's Park to make it to Kennington Oval, London's main sporting theatre, for their semi-final with the Wanderers. The Scottish pioneers held their redoubtable opponents, a mix of public school old boys, to a draw – and when lack of funds ruled out a replay at the Oval, they returned home with dignity.

This left the Wanderers to face the Royal Engineers, a team of officers from Chatham, in the final at the Oval on 16 March 1872. What a precious moment in history! Two thousand spectators paid a shilling apiece (when the average weekly wage was under £1) and they saw a 'most pleasant contest' (*Sporting Life*) on a day that was 'remarkably fine, too hot for the winter game' (*Bell's Life*). But it was not a game with which the modern fan would identify.

Shirt numbers were not even imagined then and knickerbockered players were distinguished by the colour of their caps or stockings. The crossbar was a length of tape or rope. Ends were changed when a goal was scored. There was little or no heading of the ball. The throw-in was one-handed and taken by the side which touched the ball first (hence the term touchline). And inside the touchlines the field was unmarked. The game was based on robust dribbling, with most of the rest of the team backing up the man in possession. Defence was a largely unconsidered art. The passing game, however, was developing in Scotland (as Queen's Park had shown in their semi-final with the Wanderers) and a few sides in the north of England had also moved towards combined 'team' football.

The Sappers from Chatham were firm favourites to win the first final, but the Cup made it clear from the start that it was never going to be predictable. One of the Royal Engineers, Lieutenant Edmund Cresswell, broke his collar-bone only ten minutes after the start and, although he remained on the pitch, the Wanderers made telling use of their advantage.

The Wanderers' winning goal was scored by Morton Peto Betts of West Kent and the Old Harrovians, a member of the FA committee that had approved the birth of the tournament, who played under the name of A. H. Chequer. It was a simple deceit which had much to do with the fact that the Wanderers were drawn against Harrow Chequers in the first round. The Chequers (including Betts) scratched – and Betts ('A Harrovian Chequer') duly re-emerged in the Wanderers' colours. Clearly all was above board, because the Wanderers were captained by none other than Charles Alcock, secretary of the FA.

The first twelve years of the 'little tin idol' were dominated by four clubs above all: the Wanderers (winners five times in the first seven seasons), Old Etonians (six finals, two wins), the Royal Engineers and Oxford University (each four finals, one win). It was, after all, *their* game – a diversion born of love and fun. The notion of playing for money never entered their heads.

Above Ebenezer Cobb Morley, president of the Football Association (1867–74) and the first man to present the FA Cup, rides beside the Thames near his home at Barnes. But he did not make the presentation after the final at Kennington Oval: he handed over the trophy nearly four weeks later at the Wanderers' annual dinner at the Pall Mall Restaurant, Charing Cross. Morley had been the first secretary of the FA (1863–66) and died at the age of ninety-three in 1924, a year after the opening of Wembley.

Right The resolution which launched the Challenge Cup in the Football Association's first minute book. The seven-man committee included the two captains in the first final, Charles Alcock and Francis Marindin, the scorer of its one goal, Morton Peto Betts, and its referee, Alfred Stair, who also took charge of the next two finals. It was a small world.

1872

16 March at Oval   Attendance 2,000
The Wanderers 1 (Betts)
Royal Engineers 0
The Wanderers: Alcock, Betts, Bonsor, Bowen, Crake, Hooman, Lubbock, Thompson, Vidal, Welch, Wollaston. (In alphabetical order.)
Royal Engineers: Marindin, Merriman, Addison, Cresswell, Mitchell, Renny-Tailyour, Rich, Goodwyn, Muirhead, Cotter, Bogle.
Referee: A. Stair

Left The first FA Challenge Cup, designed and made in silver by Martin, Hall and Company at a cost of £20. The 'little tin idol', eighteen inches high, capacity one quart, served for twenty-four years – and was then stolen.

Committee Meeting held at the Sportsman Office on 20 July, 1871.

Present. C. W. Alcock, C. W. Stephenson, J. H. Giffard, M. P. Betts, D. Allport, Capt. Marindin, & A. Stair.

Resolved unanimously "That it is desirable that a Challenge Cup should be established in connection with the Association for which all clubs belonging to the Association should be invited to compete.
The Secretary was instructed to communicate

Above Donington School, near Spalding in south Lincolnshire, at around the time they entered the first tournament. The grammar school received a bye in the first round and scratched before playing in the second because of the prohibitive cost of travelling to Glasgow to meet the redoubtable Queen's Park. They never entered the tournament again. Headmaster W. J. R. Constable towers over his pupils and, just discernible on the right, is the drill master who was appointed at three shillings a week to improve the athletic prowess of the boys. A hundred years later, for old times' sake, Donington School did make the journey to Glasgow to play Queen's Park. They lost.

Left Morton Peto Betts of the Wanderers, scorer of the only goal in the first final. Contemporary reports indicated that A. H. Chequer won the game with 'a well directed kick under the tape' – but this was Betts, who was using a pseudonym because he had begun the tournament as a Harrow Chequer. They scratched without playing (giving the Wanderers a walkover) and Betts surfaced again wearing the orange, violet and black of the Wanderers. He was a member of the Cup's founding committee, played once for England (1877) and was a useful cricketer who made a few appearances for Middlesex and Kent. This picture was discovered in the pavilion of Bickley Park Cricket Club in Kent.

1873

29 March at Lillie Bridge   Att 3,000

The Wanderers 2 (Wollaston,
  Kinnaird)

Oxford University 0

The Wanderers: Bowen, Thompson,
  Welch, Kinnaird, Howell,
  Wollaston, Sturgis, Stewart,
  Kenyon-Slaney, Kingsford, Bonsor.

Oxford University: Kirke-Smith,
  Leach, Mackarness, Birley,
  Longman, Chappell-Maddison,
  Dixon, Paton, Vidal, Sumner,
  Ottaway.

Referee: A. Stair

Above The Rt Hon. Arthur Fitzgerald Kinnaird, later 11th Baron Kinnaird of Inchture and football's first superstar. He was, according to Charles Alcock in *The Football Annual* of 1873, 'without exception the best player of the day; capable of taking any place in the field; is very fast and never loses sight of the ball; an excellent captain'. Kinnaird led the Wanderers to victory, scoring their second goal, in the 1873 final – the first of his nine finals (five won) for the Wanderers or the Old Etonians. He became an FA councillor in 1869 at the age of twenty-two and was an administrator and leader for fifty-four years, thirty-three as president, until his death just four months before the first final at Wembley in 1923. He had a full auburn beard and was a fearless, earthy, exuberant character with a huge appetite for football and life.

Stories about him abound. At one Etonian meeting, Lady Alma Kinnaird implored William Kenyon-Slaney, a fellow Wanderer, to persuade her husband to give up playing. 'If he goes on,' she said, 'you know it will end in a broken leg, won't it?' 'Yes,' said Kenyon-Slaney, 'but the leg won't be his own.' Kinnaird celebrated the Old Etonians' Cup win in 1882 by standing on his head in front of the Oval pavilion; on the way to another final, a crowd removed the horses from his carriage and pulled it themselves. He was one of the umpires for the 1889 final (in which Preston completed the double) and, according to the *Pall Mall Budget*: 'Lord Kinnaird was as much on the hop as if he had been in the Alhambra ballet, running here, throwing in the ball, waving that little flag of his, and whistling like the East wind.'

Kinnaird, who played for Scotland against England in the second official international in 1873, became president of the YMCA of Scotland and Lord High Commissioner to the Church of Scotland.

The *Sporting Life* reported that the Wanderers' victory over Oxford University in 1873 was 'in great measure due to the extremely brilliant play of their captain'. It was the only time that the holders, the Wanderers, did not take part until the final – hence 'Challenge Cup' – and there was a morning kick-off at Lillie Bridge, near the Thames, to allow the players to see the Boat Race.

Above William Kenyon-Slaney, outstanding footballer, gallant soldier and Member of Parliament, who helped the Wanderers win the Cup in 1873 and played for the Old Etonians in the finals of 1875 and 1876. Captain Kenyon-Slaney of the Household Brigade scored the first official international goal of all – for England against Scotland at the Oval in 1873 – just a minute after the start. He also scored England's third (4–2 after a goalless draw the year before) against Kinnaird's Scotland. *Bell's Life* observed: 'Capt. Kenyon-Slaney was of the greatest service for England.' He attained the rank of colonel and was later MP for Newport, Salop (1886–1908) and a Privy Councillor.

Above Sheffield Football Club, the oldest of all existing clubs, pictured in 1874, the year in which they took part in the FA Cup for the first time. They played Shropshire Wanderers in the first round and, after two goalless draws, made progress on the spin of a coin – the only time this has happened in the history of the Cup. Sheffield, formed in 1855, played an important practical and moral role in the settling of the game's rules and structure. The *Illustrated Sporting and Dramatic News* wrote of them in 1874: 'Football nowhere thrives more rapidly or is cultivated with more enthusiasm than in the town of keen blades, of armour plates, of monster factories and monster chimneys that belch forth never ceasing clouds of smoke.' Sheffield lost in round three to Clapham Rovers who were, in turn, beaten by the 1874 winners Oxford University. Sheffield have not reached the first round proper since 1887.

1874

14 March at Oval　　　　　　Att 2,000

Oxford University 2
(Mackarness, Patton)

Royal Engineers 0

Oxford University: Neapean, Mackarness, Birley, Green, Vidal, Ottaway, Benson, Patton, Rawson, Chappell-Maddison, Johnson.

Royal Engineers: Merriman, Marindin, Addison, Onslow, Oliver, Digby, Renny-Tailyour, Rawson, Blackman, Wood, von Donop.

Referee: A. Stair

Above The Royal Engineers from Chatham, who won the Cup in the first replayed final. The Sappers were runners-up in 1872 and 1874 and would be again in 1878, but in 1875 their discipline and innovative thinking proved too much for the Old Etonians over two games. The Engineers set standards in sportsmanship and organisation and, having arrived in good time for a two o'clock start to the replay, were not pleased when a below-strength Old Etonian side failed to arrive until shortly before three. The match record book of the Sappers noted: 'The RE team were determined to bring the operation to some conclusion or other... on the whole the ball was generally about

the neighbourhood of the Etonian goal.' It was the last final in which ends were exchanged after every goal.

The story goes that Francis Marindin – now known as 'the Major' – did not know how to resolve the dilemma of being a Royal Engineer and an Old Etonian. He decided to play for neither.

Royal Engineers: *Back row (left to right)* – Lieut H. I. Mulholland, Lieut G. P. Onslow, Lieut W. F. H. Stafford, Lieut H. E. Rawson, Lieut A. L. Mein, Lieut C. V. Wingfield-Stratford. *Middle row* – Lieut R. M. Ruck, Major W. Merriman (captain), Lieut H. W. Renny-Tailyour, Lieut P. G. von Donop. *Front row* – Lieut G. H. Sim, Lieut G. T. Jones.

1875

13 March at Oval   Att 3,000
Royal Engineers I (Renny-Tailyour)
Old Etonians I (Bonsor)   **aet**
Royal Engineers: Merriman, Sim, Onslow, Ruck, von Donop, Wood, Rawson, Stafford, Renny-Tailyour, Mein, Wingfield-Stratford.
Old Etonians: Thompson, Benson, E. Lubbock, Wilson, Kinnaird, Stronge, Patton, Farmer, Bonsor, Ottaway, Kenyon-Slaney.
Referee: C. W. Alcock
Replay: 16 March at Oval   Att 3,000
Royal Engineers 2 (Renny-Tailyour, Stafford)
Old Etonians 0
Royal Engineers: Merriman, Sim, Onslow, Ruck, von Donop, Wood, Rawson, Stafford, Renny-Tailyour, Mein, Wingfield-Stratford.
Old Etonians: Drummond-Moray, Farrer, E. Lubbock, Wilson, Kinnaird, Stronge, Patton, Farmer, Bonsor, A. Lubbock, Hammond.
Referee: C. W. Alcock

1876

11 March at Oval   Att 3,000

The Wanderers 1 (Edwards)

Old Etonians 1 (Bonsor)   **aet**

The Wanderers: Greig, Stratford, Lindsay, Chappell-Maddison, Birley, Wollaston, H. Heron, F. Heron, Edwards, Kenrick, Hughes.

Old Etonians: Hogg, Welldon, E. Lyttelton, Thompson, Kinnaird, Meysey, Kenyon-Slaney, A. Lyttelton, Sturgis, Bonsor, Allene.

Referee: W. S. Rawson

Replay: 18 March at Oval   Att 3,500

The Wanderers 3 (Wollaston, Hughes 2)

Old Etonians 0

The Wanderers: Greig, Stratford, Lindsay, Chappell-Maddison, Birley, Wollaston, H. Heron, F. Heron, Edwards, Kenrick, Hughes.

Old Etonians: Hogg, E. Lubbock, E. Lyttelton, Faner, Kinnaird, Stronge, Kenyon-Slaney, A. Lyttelton, Sturgis, Bonsor, Allene.

Referee: W. S. Rawson

Many brilliant and eminent men take their place in the history of the FA Cup. Among the Old Etonians who faced the Wanderers in 1876 were Quintin Hogg and two of the Lyttelton brothers as well as Arthur Kinnaird and William Kenyon-Slaney.

Below Quintin Hogg, founder of the London Polytechnic and grandfather of Lord Hailsham of St Marylebone, was a great philanthropist who devoted himself to the poor and suffering of Victorian London. Hogg's closest friend was Arthur Kinnaird (who had been his fag at Eton) and, to be near the scene of their social work, they rented a modest room near Charing Cross, often sleeping in hammocks because of rats. Hogg donated more than £100,000, then a massive sum, to his cause. He was also a very keen and able footballer, who played for Scotland in early unofficial internationals. He played, too, at the age of fifty-seven, so that he could claim to have played 'fifty years of footer'. Hogg started the 1876 final in goal but changed places with Kinnaird, who was injured.

Right The Lyttelton brothers, Alfred (pictured) and Edward, were members of a large, celebrated and immensely talented family. They played for the Old Etonians in both parts of the 1876 final and also for England a year or two later. Both were first-class cricketers, Alfred again playing for England and later becoming president of MCC. Alfred was also one of the finest real tennis players of his day, English champion for more than a decade, and excelled at fives and racquets. He was a barrister who became MP for Warwick and later for St George's, Hanover Square, and served as Colonial Secretary under Balfour.

In *Alfred Lyttelton, An Account of his Life* (1917), Edith Lyttelton, his second wife, wrote of his football: 'He was over six foot one, and his onrush was like a tornado... when things grew to be exciting his ardour waxed to a formidable heat, and he would come thundering down with the heavy knees far advanced and all the paraphernalia of a Homeric onset.'

Edward, who was two years older than Alfred, became head-master of Haileybury and then Eton.

Curiously, the Wanderers also fielded two brothers, Hubert Heron, who played in the 1876, 1877 and 1878 finals, and Frank Heron. Both played for England and both were wine merchants.

1877

24 March at Oval   Att 3,000

The Wanderers 2 (Kenrick, Lindsay)

Oxford University 1 (Kinnaird og)   **aet**

The Wanderers: Kinnaird, Lindsay, Stratford, Birley, Denton, Green, H. Heron, Hughes, Kenrick, Wace, Wollaston.

Oxford University: Allington, Bain, Dunnell, Savory, Todd, Waddington, Fernandez, Hills, Otter, Parry, Rawson.

Referee: S. H. Wright

The FA Cup came near to a final between the Universities of Cambridge and Oxford in 1877. Cambridge overcame Clapham Rovers and the Royal Engineers, among others, to reach their only semi-final – but were then beaten 1–0 at Kennington Oval by the all-conquering Wanderers, for whom Hubert Heron scored.

Above Oxford University, in turn, gave the Wanderers a spirited run in the final, the decisive goal by William Lindsay coming in extra-time – 'a hardly contested and well played match,' reported the *Oxford University Herald.* Six (*) of the players in the picture played in the sixth final of the Cup: *Back row (left to right)* – R. T. Thornton, H. S. Otter*, T. E. B. Guy, J. Bain*, C. H. T. Metcalfe, J. H. Savory*, P. H. Fernandez*. *Seated* – T. A. C. Hampson, W. S. Rawson*, E. H. Parry*. Edward Hagarty Parry, the Oxford captain and later an England international, played in the final again in 1881 – but this time, once more as captain, for the Old Carthusians.

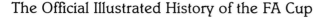

FOOTBALL ASSOCIATION CHALLENGE CUP.

WANDERERS v. ROYAL ENGINEERS.—The final tie in this competition was decided on Saturday last at Kennington Oval. The two clubs have taken such a prominent part in the contests for the Cup since its first institution, that their meeting in the last struggle was sure to be attractive; but on this occasion there was additional interest attached to the match from the fact that a victory to the Wanderers would entitle them to the permanent possession of the Cup, as they had held it for the two previous years. A glorious afternoon favoured the two elevens, and at twenty minutes to four o'clock, when the game commenced, there could not have been less than three thousand spectators present, amongst whom was a goodly proportion of ladies. Hedley, who had lost the toss, started the ball for the Engineers, who began with the sun in their faces, and the wind rather against them. The Wanderers were warm favourites, and within a very few minutes they were able to score, Kenrick securing the downfall of the Sappers' goal after a neat run by Wace. After the kick off the Engineers set to work with energy, and for a time their policy of hustling the opposite backs was effective. The ball was chiefly in Wanderers' territory for nearly a quarter of an hour, and at last, after a well-directed throw from touch by Morris, the ball was carried through the Wanderers' posts in a scrimmage. For a few minutes after the resumption, the Sappers had slightly the best of the play; but the Wanderers' forwards, who had the pace of their opponents, steadily succeeded in clearing their lines, some fine runs being made by Denton and Kenrick on the lower side of the ground. A free kick soon fell to Kinnaird, and, after a short scrimmage, a second goal was secured for the Wanderers. During the ten minutes that remained of the first half some spirited play was shown on both sides, but no further result was obtained. At the end of three-quarters of an hour ends were changed, and soon after this operation had been completed Hedley got the ball safely into the Wanderers' goal, though, as he was off side, the score was not allowed. The Wanderers now began to press rather heavily on their adversaries, and a miss-kick by Morris enabled Heron to get well away on the upper side, the result of a neat middle being another goal for the Wanderers from the foot of Kenrick. The Engineers played up hard to the last, but they certainly did not stay so well as their opponents and, though nothing more fell to either side, the Wanderers had the best of the game. The Engineers were thus defeated by three goals to one, and their defeat enabled the Wanderers to claim the cup as the property of their club. The victory was won by good play all round, and was thoroughly well deserved. Heron, during the second half, showed in quite his old form, and all the forwards worked hard, while Kinnaird and Lindsay did excellent service. Kirkpatrick fractured his left arm early in the game, but played on to the last.—Wanderers: Hon. A. F. Kinnaird (captain) F. J. Green (half backs), A. H. Stratford, W. Lindsay (backs), J. G. Wylie, H. Wace (centres), C. H. Wollaston Hubert Heron (right side) J. Kenrick, C. A. Denton (left side), J. Kirkpatrick (goal), C. Warner (Upton Park), umpire. Royal Engineers: Lieut R. S. Hedley (captain), C. E. Haynes (centres), M. Lindsay, H. H. Barnett (right side), F. G. Bond, O. E. Ruck (left side), F. Heath, C. B. Mayne (half backs), J. H. Cowan, W. G. Morris (backs), L. B. Friend (goal); B. G. Jarrett (Old Harrovians), umpire; S. R. Bastard (Upton Park), referee.

The result of the final ties since the institution of the Cup have been as follows:

1872. Wanderers beat Royal Engineers by one goal to none.
1873. Wanderers beat Oxford University by two goals to none.
1874. Oxford University beat Royal Engineers by two goals to none.
1875. Royal Engineers beat Oxford University by one goal to none.
1876. Wanderers beat Old Etonians by three goals to none.
1877. Wanderers beat Oxford University by two goals to none.
1878. Wanderers beat Royal Engineers by three goals to one.

1878

23 March at Oval   Att 4,500

The Wanderers 3 (Kenrick 2, Kinnaird)

Royal Engineers 1 (unknown)

The Wanderers: Kirkpatrick, Stratford, W. Lindsay, Kinnaird, Green, Wollaston, H. Heron, Wylie, Wace, Denton, Kenrick.

Royal Engineers: Friend, Cowan, Morris, Mayne, Heath, Haynes, M. Lindsay, Hedley, Bond, Barnet, Ruck.

Referee: S. R. Bastard

Above The Wanderers' third victory in a row meant that the Cup could have become their permanent property – but they gave it back to the Football Association on condition that no club in future should be allowed to win it outright. It was the Wanderers' fifth victory in five finals in seven years, a period in which they used only thirty-two players. Charles H. R. Wollaston, a Sussex man and an England international who was a dashing forward, played in all five of Wanderers' finals.

Yet this was the beginning of the end for the great Wanderers. They had always recruited their players from other clubs and began to find increasing difficulty in raising teams of quality. They were heavily beaten by the Old Etonians in the next two years and in 1881 even had to scratch from the tournament they had helped launch with such panache. They quietly disappeared, but 'the celebrated Wanderers', as Francis Marindin called them, have a very special place in the game's history.

Charles Alcock:

The Inventor of Modern Sport

Charles Alcock was 'the inventor of modern sport', a rhapsodic title to which he has an absolute claim. There are no serious rivals – not even Baron de Coubertin for his Olympic vision.

Consider Alcock's credentials. The FA Cup was his idea; and so was international football. The World Cup itself is an extension of his two priceless notions and, of course, his concept of a sudden-death knockout tournament is now used by most other sports. He captained the Wanderers to victory in the first Cup final and led England against Scotland in the first unofficial football international. Alcock also championed and proposed the acceptance of professionalism in football.

Alcock was secretary of the FA for twenty-five years (1870–95 but paid only from 1887) and secretary of Surrey County Cricket Club for thirty-five years (1872 until his death at the age of sixty-four in 1907), combining the posts for more than twenty years.

Kennington Oval, the Wembley of the time and the stage for the FA Cup final for all but one of its first twenty-one years, was

Above Charles William Alcock: born 2 December 1842 at 10 Norfolk Street, Sunderland. Died 26 February 1907 at 7 Arundel Street, Brighton. Left a widow, Eliza Caroline Alcock (1841–1937), and two daughters. Buried at West Norwood cemetery in a plot acquired for his son, Charles Ernest, who died at the age of five months in 1874.

Alcock's home from home. Here he instigated and organised cricket's first Test match in England in 1880, and he was the presiding official two years later when Australia beat England for the first time and the Ashes were born. He was also instrumental in giving shape and order to the County Cricket Championship.

Alcock was heavily involved, too, in organising the first Rugby Union international in England and provided the Varsity match with its first neutral home. Hockey, lacrosse and even baseball also took place at the Oval, which Alcock promoted with sharp business acumen.

He was, moreover, a prolific sports journalist, a pioneer in the field, who wrote the first history of football, edited its first annual as well as a highly acclaimed cricket annual, started several magazines and contributed regularly to *The Sportsman* (in whose offices the FA Cup was conceived) and *The Field*. He made history and then recorded it with insight and style.

Ebenezer Cobb Morley, the first secretary of the Football Association, must properly be regarded as the man who gave organised football its first push. It was his initiative which led to the formation of the parent body in 1863 and it was he who drafted their first set of playing laws. But it was Alcock who led the way in the development and promotion of team games during the last thirty years of the nineteenth century. It was the birth-time of modern sport and Alcock, with his vision and energy, was its father figure.

He was one of five sons of a wealthy Sunderland shipping man and left Harrow School in 1859 as a tall, straight figure, a talented footballer ('excellent dribbler and goal-getter, very hard to knock off the ball'), a useful cricketer who played for the Gentlemen of Essex, a willing organiser and a natural leader.

Alcock was not quite thirty years old and had been the FA secretary for little more than twelve months when he had his vision of a national knockout tournament in 1871. He remembered playing in an inter-house, sudden-death competition at Harrow, and recognised that the format could be employed on a national scale. Only fifteen clubs entered the first tournament, three scratched without playing a game and Alcock led the Wanderers (a club he helped form) to victory by 1–0 over the Royal Engineers in the final.

Alcock captained England to victory in an unofficial international against Scotland at the Oval in 1870 and, but for injury, would have led them in the first official one in Glasgow two years later – which he arranged 'to further the interests of the Association in Scotland'. He captained England against Scotland in 1875, however, and a week later he refereed the FA Cup final. He became the first president of the Referees' Association.

As an administrator Alcock was liberal, catholic, a perceptive judge of character, a calm man who used words tellingly but who could also be caustic and stubborn. William Pickford, an FA contemporary, described him as lovable and genial.

He also moved with the times and adjusted smoothly to the quickening tempo and broad-ening democracy of football. The balance of power in the game swung away from the universities and public schools of the South, with their doughty principles of amateurism, towards the clubs of the North, who saw nothing wrong in profit and success. Alcock said he objected to the argument that it is immoral to work for a living and, on his proposal, professionalism was legalised in 1885. He believed it would be better to control it than drive it underground.

Surrey County Cricket Club, with Alcock at the helm, became the country's most successful club. In nine seasons, 1887–95, they won the County Championship seven times and shared it once. By this time, too, Alcock had moved English cricket on to a new and higher plateau: the international game.

The second Australian team to visit England, in 1880, had a modest, rather messy fixture list. But Alcock somehow persuaded Sussex to call off their game with W. L. Murdoch's men at Hove and arranged, instead, the first Test between England and Australia. At the Oval, of course, W. G. Grace, a friend of Alcock's, duly scored the first Test century for England.

Alcock's Oval was also the scene of Australia's first triumph over England, in 1882, which led to the birth of the Ashes. N. L. 'Pa' Jackson, the founder of the celebrated Corinthians, remembered seeing the Surrey secretary in his office afterwards 'sitting down on a huge iron safe, burying his head in his hands, oblivious to everything'.

Alcock, though, had missed nothing, and wrote a luminous account of that turning point in history. 'Men who were noted for their coolness at critical moments were trembling like a leaf,' he wrote. 'Some were shivering with cold; some even fainted. At times there was an awful silence.'

Someone had to point sport in the right direction. It happened to be Alcock. An inspired contemporary wrote of him: 'When the flashing meteors have come and gone, when the league tables are full and complete, and when the present fades into the past, the name of C. W. Alcock will stand out all the more prominently like a rugged rock in a sea of bubbles.'

**J. Pardoe, F. E. Adams, R. Edmunds, C. Bigland, J. F. Alcock, C. W. Alcock,
C. D. Jackson, C. M. Tebbut, W. B. Standidge, A. M. Tebbut, A. L. Cutbill**

Above Forest Football Club in 1863, the year in which they changed their name to the Wanderers. Perhaps the most precious football picture of all and probably the earliest authentic photograph of a private football club. The Alcock brothers, James and Charles, stand fifth and sixth from the left – James, the elder, one of the most influential founder members of the Football Association and captain of the Forest team.

Charles Alcock wrote later (*The Association Game*, 1894): 'It was the winter of 1859–60 that really saw the first game of the great football revival. Great things, it is said, from trivial things spring. The trivial cause in this instance was the humble desire of a few Old Harrovians, who had just left school, to keep up the practice at all events of the game at which they had shown some considerable aptitude. From the primitive commencement of a mere kickabout under the shadow of the Merchant Seamen's Orphan Asylum at Snaresbrook sprang the Forest Football Club, the progenitor of all the now numerous clubs playing football of any kind throughout the Kingdom.' There followed, added Alcock, 'the transmutation of the Forest chrysalis into the resplendent butterfly – the Wanderers, a name to conjure with in the primeval days of the Association game'.

1879

29 March at Oval   Att 5,000

Old Etonians 1 (Clerke)

Clapham Rovers 0

Old Etonians: Hawtrey, Christian, Bury, Kinnaird, Lubbock, Clerke, Pares, Goodhart, Whitfield, Chevallier, Beaufoy.

Clapham Rovers: Birkett, Ogilvie, Field, Bailey, Prinsep, Rawson, Stanley, Scott, Bevington, Growse, Keith-Falconer.

Referee: C. W. Alcock

The Old Etonians won the Cup for the first time; but along the way they were hugely embarrassed by a team of millworkers from Darwen in Lancashire. Darwen's bravado established the democracy of the tournament and was an early warning of the rise of provincial football. They did not topple their giant; but they made the big fellow totter.

Below Darwen stretched the Old Etonians – Kinnaird and all – to three games in the fourth round, the quarter-final stage, at Kennington Oval. The first was drawn 5–5, with Darwen scoring four in the last quarter-hour and the Old Boys

refusing to play extra-time and 'finish it there and then'. The second was again drawn, 2–2 after extra-time, and it was only then, drained and dispirited by the travelling, that the Darruners were overcome by 6–2 in the third encounter.

Darwen had beaten the Remnants in London in the third round and when they were drawn to play there again, against the mighty Old Etonians, they considered scratching. Their first trip to London had cost them £31 1s. 2d. at a time when a man could sail to Australia for fourteen guineas or buy a grand country estate in the south for £800. But the people of Darwen, enthused

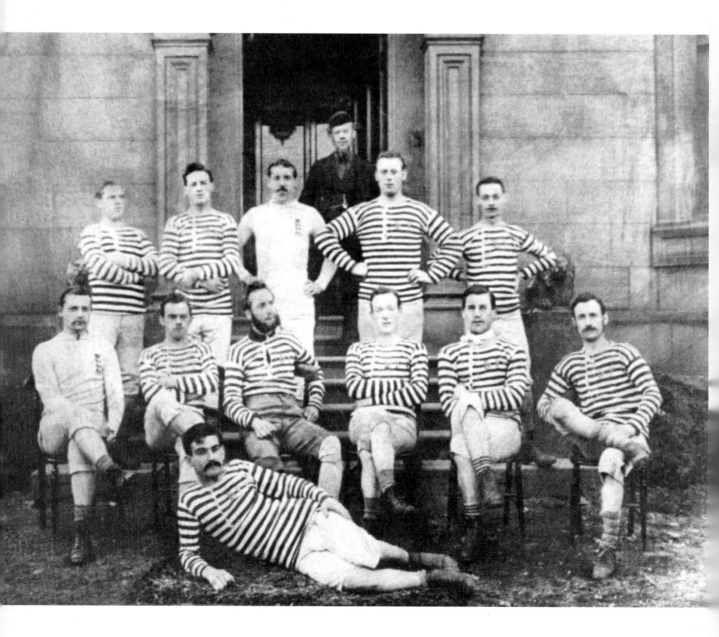

with pride, set up a 'London Fund', and the town was gripped fast in what was, perhaps, the first case of that grave derangement known as 'Cup fever'. It was grossly unfair, of course, that Darwen had to make so many trips to London and a year later, under pressure from the press, the FA changed the regulation which stipulated that the final three rounds of every tournament should be played at the Oval.

Darwen: *Back row (left to right)* – J. Duxbury, S. Fish, T. Brindle, L. Broughton, W. H. Moorhouse. *Middle row* – T. Marshall, T. Rostron, Dr J. Gledhill, Dr J. C. Holden, R. Kirkham, T. Bury. *Front* – Fergie Suter, who was one of the first professional imports from Scotland. Tom Brindle and Tom Marshall are wearing England shirts, won soon after Darwen's success.

Above Victorian Darwen with more than fifty mills of the 'dark, Satanic' variety. Its townspeople put their hands deep into their pockets to send their football team to London. Barley Bank, Darwen's ground, is centre picture.

1880

10 April at Oval   Att 6,000

Clapham Rovers 1 (Lloyd-Jones)

Oxford University 0

Clapham Rovers: Birkett, Ogilvie, Field, Weston, Bailey, Brougham, Stanley, Barry, Sparks, Lloyd-Jones, Ram.

Oxford University: Parr, Wilson, King, Phillips, Rogers, Heygate, Childs, Eyre, Crowdy, Hill, Lubbock.

Referee: Major Marindin

Above Reginald Halsey Birkett, Clapham Rovers' goalkeeper, centre, without cap, was the first man to represent England at both football and rugby union. He played for the Rovers in both their finals, 1879 and 1880, and his fine keeping was a key factor in their narrow victory over Oxford University. Birkett scored the first try in the first rugby international against Scotland and he was a member of the original Rugby Union committee. His brother, Louis, and son, John Guy, outstandingly, also played rugby for England.

Clapham Rovers, who played both football and rugby union, were the first club outside the big four (Wanderers, Royal Engineers, Oxford University and Old Etonians) to win the Cup. Nottingham Forest reached the semi-finals for the second year in succession and the early rounds of the tournament were regionalised. The Cup was slowly becoming a national affair.

The day of the amateur was passing. The 1881 final between Old Carthusians and Old Etonians was the last between amateurs; the Wanderers had played their last Cup game; and the Universities of Oxford and Cambridge were not among the sixty-three entrants.

Right and below This was the season in which Henry Cursham of Notts County made his first mark on the Cup: by the time he finished in 1887, he had scored forty-eight goals in the tournament – still a record. Cursham, who won eight England caps, scored twice in his first Cup tie against Derbyshire FC and, altogether, managed seven hat-tricks. Cursham, however, was convinced he had scored more. He is credited with scoring six in Notts County's 11–1 win over Wednesbury Strollers in the second round in December 1881 but, as his comment beside a contemporary report clearly shows, he believed he'd scored nine. The report did not give the name of any scorer and simply observed that 'goal after goal was quickly secured'.

1881

9 April at Oval   Att 4,500

Old Carthusians 3 (Todd, Wynyard, Parry)

Old Etonians 0

Old Carthusians: Gillett, Norris, Colvin, Prinsep, Vintcent, Hansell, Richards, Page, Wynyard, Parry, Todd.

Old Etonians: Rawlinson, Foley, French, Kinnaird, Farrer, Chevallier, Anderson, Goodhart, Macaulay, Whitfield, Novelli.

Referee: W. Pierce Dix

1882

25 March at Oval   Att 6,500

Old Etonians 1 (Anderson)

Blackburn Rovers 0

Old Etonians: Rawlinson, French, de
Paravicini, Kinnaird, Foley, Novelli,
Dunn, Macaulay, Goodhart,
Anderson, Chevallier.

Blackburn Rovers: Howarth,
McIntyre, Suter, Sharples, F. W.
Hargreaves, Duckworth, Douglas,
Strachan, Brown, Avery, J.
Hargreaves.

Referee: J. C. Clegg

Right The first ten finals of the FA
Cup involved only six clubs; but now
Blackburn Rovers, standard bearers
of the North, became the first
provincial club to intrude on the
big day at Kennington Oval. The
Rovers, unbeaten all season, scored
twenty-eight goals in six games on
the road to the final and they had
also recruited the experienced
Fergie Suter from Darwen.
Thousands were at Blackburn
railway station to cheer them south.

The Old Etonians, though, had
enough zest and expertise to make
one last defiant gesture before
custody of the Cup fell into professional hands. They won 1–0 and
Kinnaird celebrated his fifth winner's
medal by standing on his head in
front of the pavilion.

This stylised impression of the
game in the *Illustrated Sporting and
Dramatic News* was by Stephen T.
Dadd, who worked in south London
and contributed sporting, domestic
and animal scenes to many magazines. He faithfully shows the
bearded Kinnaird in his long white
trousers.

Chapter Two

Pay for Play

1883–1900

'Members of the Kennington Oval ground committee were in the habit of collecting half a crown from each person in the enclosure. Tom Gunning, of the London Association, and myself used to fill our pockets. There were others, and we all went into the pavilion and poured our treasure on the tables to those who were appointed to receive the money.'

**A Cup final memory from *Fifty Years of Football*
by Sir Frederick Wall, FA secretary 1895–1934.
He played for the long defunct London club Rangers FC
in their only Cup tie (beaten 6–0 by the Royal Engineers)
at the Oval in season 1880–81, and when he became FA
secretary his staff consisted of one junior clerk.**

The amateurs of English football, southern gentlemen all, hung on to their golden age as long as they dared, but the game could not be cramped forever by their cherished notions of playing for health and fun. The public schools, universities and officers' messes had refined a rowdy folk-game after picking it up off the streets of Victorian England but, in turn, it was joyously adopted by the working masses of the North and Midlands, who saw nothing shameful in paying a man for doing a job – even if that job was just kicking a football.

Professionalism was legalised in 1885 and the birth of the Football League three years later was a natural sequel. It was a period of accelerating progress and open conflict, in which the game and its organisation found a shape that would endure for more than a hundred years. Here was Eden with its tree of good and evil.

Football came of age as industrial boom and social revolution changed the face of England in just a few decades. The growth of towns, more leisure time and better public transport created challenging needs and opportunities and, as part of this interlocking progress, the game found an important role. It provided escape, as J. B. Priestley so memorably put it, from 'the clanking machinery of this lesser life'. It added an extra dimension to the national merry-go-round and was perfectly suited to the mutating shape and rhythms of urban life. It turned strangers into brothers and, for many, gave new point to every dawn.

The Cup was at the heart of it all. It gave the country its appetite for the game, accelerated the acceptance of professionalism after years of shady payments and divisive hypocrisy, and, without sacrificing any of its own popularity, emphasised the need for another kind of competition which would sustain the hungry clubs of the North and Midlands from week to week. The Football League, the idea of a bearded and ample Scot called William McGregor, an Aston Villa man, duly saw light in 1888, when it consisted of a dozen clubs – six from Lancashire and six more from central England.

Clubs were formed all over the country, popping up like mushrooms as the need for organised recreation grew. Churches, chapels and Sunday schools were the inspiration behind many teams, and so were schools, factories, railways, cricket clubs, warehouses and pubs. Newcastle have their roots in a humble club called Stanley, Arsenal's origins were in a munitions factory, Doncaster surfaced as a scratch team playing against the Yorkshire Institution for the Deaf, Leicester City trace themselves back to a casual meeting on the Roman Fosse Way and Millwall began life as a jam and marmalade maker's side.

The game itself also evolved. Crosstapes gave way to crossbars (1875); the first shrill of a referee's whistle was heard (1878); the two-handed throw was introduced

(1882); goal-nets arrived and so did penalty-kicks (1891). Caution found its way on to the pitch. The early formation of eight forwards, chasing the ball like children in a playground, was reduced to five. The manufacture of boots and balls became a highly profitable industry.

While just twelve clubs had played in the first FA Cup tournament, by the time the Cup was joined by the Football League it was a strapping adolescent with 149 entries and a firm hold on the affections of the public. But it, too, was changing.

In the beginning, the Football Association and its Cup were open to all the countries of the United Kingdom. Queen's Park and later Glasgow Rangers led the Scottish challenge and clubs from Wales and even Ireland took part. But a delicate situation arose when sides from north of the border were drawn together: there were arguments about jurisdiction and the FA of Scotland eventually forbade its clubs to compete for any national trophy other than its own. Glasgow Rangers reached the semi-finals in 1886–87 in a brave but last tilt at the FA Cup. The Irish FA followed suit, but the FA of Wales continued to allow its clubs to take part in the tournament; and, of course, they still do.

Disparity in strength among clubs was another problem which was gradually solved. Games between big and small were often very one sided – Preston North End 26 Hyde 0 in October 1887 for example. The FA's solution in 1888 was to split the country into ten divisions and the tournament into a qualifying competition and a competition proper. It worked well.

The Wanderers and the other celebrated amateur sides of the Cup's early years were now fading gently into the mists of history. The first concrete evidence of a shift in power was in 1882, when a provincial club managed, at last, to reach the final – the beginning of the tradition of 'coming up' (rather than 'going down') for the big day in London. Blackburn Rovers were the first invaders, but it wasn't their time yet – not quite – and they were beaten by the zestful Old Etonians at the Oval by 1–0, although as their local MP said at the post-match dinner: 'I wouldn't say the winning goal was a fluke, far from it, but it was a happy accident.' That, as it happened, was the end of an era. The tournament was never again won by an amateur club and another nineteen years would pass before it was won again by a London club.

It was now, emphatically, the turn of Blackburn and the North. Blackburn Olympic, a club founded only five years before by the merging of two minor sides, won the Cup in 1883; and then Blackburn Rovers kept the trophy in the same proud cotton town for the next three years to emulate the record of the Wanderers a decade before. There was more to come. Blackburn Rovers won the tournament again in 1890 and 1891, which meant the town of Blackburn had been involved in seven out of ten finals – winning six of them. Never since has the Cup been so dominated by one community.

The professionals of the game were now too well prepared and organised to be disturbed by the honest dash and resolution of the old boys. They took training breaks beside the sea, adapted their strategies according to need and began to cast their nets wide in search of talent. Money talked and inspired. Preston North End, above all, emphasised that a cheerful exercise had now become a business and something of a science. Well named the 'Invincibles', they won the first League Championship without losing a game in 1888–89 and, in that same season, they won the Cup without conceding a goal. They had a major role in legalising professionalism, being one of the first clubs to entice players from Scotland with offers of good jobs, and played their football with the same kind of initiative and calculation. Their superiority, according to one observer of the time, was 'great and transcendent'.

Preston were the first club to complete the League and Cup double but not the last before the turn of the century. Aston Villa soon took a grip of iron on the game, winning the League five times in seven seasons, the FA Cup twice and, in 1896–97, completing the double. Villa were brilliant and consistent, but were they better than Preston?

Perhaps one day, on a green Elysian field, the old heroes of Preston and Villa will be allowed to settle it. Perhaps, too, they will be allowed to play for the original 'little tin idol' which Villa, to their eternal embarrassment, managed to win and lose in one season. A few months after winning the Cup in 1895 (in the first final to be played at Crystal Palace) they allowed it to be exhibited in the shop window of a Birmingham football and boot manufacturer – from where, at dead of night, it was stolen and never seen again. The destiny of the Cup is always a mystery.

1883

31 March at Oval   Att 8,000

Blackburn Olympic 2 (Matthews, Costley)

Old Etonians 1 (Goodhart)   **aet**

Blackburn Olympic: Hacking, Ward, Warburton, Gibson, Astley, Hunter, Dewhurst, Matthews, Wilson, Costley, Yates.

Old Etonians: Rawlinson, French, de Paravicini, Kinnaird, Foley, Chevallier, Anderson, Macaulay, Goodhart, Dunn, Bainbridge.

Referee: C. Crump

Above Blackburn Olympic, the first northern club to win the FA Cup. Formed only five years before, by the merger of two minor teams, they were trained, coached and organised systematically, even going to Blackpool for a week to round off their preparations. Olympic's ability to switch the ball from wing to wing stretched the Old Etonians who lost a player, Arthur Dunn, an England international, because of injury. It was a long pass which enabled Jimmy Costley to close in from the left and score Olympic's winner in extra-time. Major Marindin, the FA's pres-ident, made the first public presentation of the trophy on the stand next to the pavilion.

Blackburn Olympic: *Back row (left to right)* – W. Bramham (secretary), G. Wilson (professional), T. Dewhurst (weaver), T. Hacking (dentist's assistant), J. T. Ward (cotton machine operator), A. Astley (treasurer). *Middle row* – J. Costley (spinner), J. Hunter (professional), J. Yates (weaver), W. Astley (weaver). *Front row* – T. Gibson (iron-moulder's dresser), S. Warburton (master plumber), A. Matthews (picture framer).

Below The 1883 final by way of the eye and pen of J. Dinsdale in the *Illustrated Sporting and Dramatic News*. He names the scorer of Olympic's winner as Crossley.

Above Blackburn Rovers and silverware, 1884. The FA Cup, which they had won for the first time, sits modestly between the towering splendour of the East Lancashire Charity Cup and the Lancashire FA Cup. But this was just the beginning. Blackburn Rovers won the Cup again in 1885 and 1886 and then twice more in 1890 and 1891. Thus, following the success of Blackburn Olympic, the cotton town was the home of the Cup for six years out of nine.

The first Cup final crowd of more than ten thousand watched this thirteenth final, and a writer in the *Pall Mall Gazette* observed: 'London witnessed an incursion of Northern barbarians, hot-blooded Lancastrians, sharp of tongue, rough and ready, of uncouth garb and speech. A tribe of Soudanese Arabs let loose in the Strand would not excite more amusement and curiosity. Strange oaths fell upon Southern ears.' These comments were deeply resented in the parish of Blackburn.

There was crowd trouble before the start, with supporters rushing the gates, and Blackburn were perplexed early in the game by the clever dribbling and close passing of Queen's Park. But Rovers' all-round strength and goals by Joe Sowerbutts and James Forrest earned them the trophy; and, back home, they toured the town in a 'gaily beflagged wagonette drawn by six spanking greys'.

Blackburn Rovers: *Standing* – J. M. Lofthouse, H. McIntyre, J. Beverley, H. Arthur, F. Suter, J. H. Forrest, R. Birtwistle (umpire). *Sitting* – J. Douglas, J. E. Sowerbutts, J. Brown, G. Avery, J. Hargreaves. The acceptance of professionalism was still a year away but Fergie Suter, Hugh McIntyre and Jimmy Douglas were undoubtedly paid – as Suter put it: 'We interviewed the treasurer as occasion arose.'

1884

29 March at Oval   Att 14,000

Blackburn Rovers 2 (Sowerbutts, Forrest)

Queen's Park 1 (Christie)

Blackburn Rovers: Arthur, Beverley, Suter, McIntyre, Hargreaves, Forrest, Lofthouse, Douglas, Sowerbutts, Inglis, Brown.

Queen's Park: Gillespie, Arnott, McDonald, Campbell, Gow, Anderson, Watt, Smith, Harrower, Allan, Christie.

Referee: Major Marindin

1885

4 April at Oval	Att 12,500

Blackburn Rovers 2 (Forrest, Brown)

Queen's Park 0

Blackburn Rovers: Arthur, Turner, Suter, McIntyre, Haworth, Forrest, Lofthouse, Douglas, Brown, Fecitt, Sowerbutts.

Queen's Park: Gillespie, Arnott, MacLeod, Campbell, McDonald, Hamilton, Anderson, Sellar, Gray, McWhannel, Allan.

Referee: Major Marindin

Above Charles Campbell, one of the great men of Scottish football and captain of the Queen's Park team which lost to Blackburn Rovers in the final for the second successive year. This meeting generated even more interest than the first and was widely recognised as a form of 'international' contest, for Rovers had the best side in England and Queen's Park, the mother club of Scottish football, fielded most of Scotland's finest players. Their defeat by two goals, one in each half, caused intense disappointment back home.

Campbell was a household name. He played for Queen's Park for thirteen years, captained his club and country (facing England ten times and losing only once) and became president of both Queen's Park and the Scottish FA. He was an outstanding half-back, though some claimed he was too fair: he always apologised after flooring an opponent. An eloquent speaker and persuasive committee man, he was also very nervous and could not bear to watch important games. He would stay below the stand, dashing upstairs only when cheers indicated his side had scored. At the end he would feign indifference, and after defeat he would always say: 'We must do better next time.' He was even-tempered, never extreme, and devoted much time to educating young footballers.

Queen's Park had joined the Football Association in their early days because they were the only governing body then in existence. Costs and distance prevented them making much of an impact on the first two FA Cup tournaments and they didn't compete again until the mid-1880s. The Scottish FA (formed 1873) later stopped its clubs taking part in the FA Cup.

1886

3 April at Oval   Att 15,000

Blackburn Rovers 0

West Bromwich Albion 0

Blackburn Rovers: Arthur, Turner, Suter, Douglas, Forrest, McIntyre, Heyes, Strachan, Brown, Fecitt, Sowerbutts.

West Bromwich Albion: Roberts, H. Green, H. Bell, Horton, Perry, Timmins, Woodhall, T. Green, Bayliss, Loach, G. Bell.

Referee: Major Marindin

Replay:

10 April at Baseball Ground   Att 12,000

Blackburn Rovers 2 (Sowerbutts, Brown)

West Bromwich Albion 0

Blackburn Rovers: Arthur, Turner, Suter, Douglas, Forrest, McIntyre, Walton, Strachan, Brown, Fecitt, Sowerbutts.

West Bromwich Albion: Roberts, H. Green, H. Bell, Horton, Perry, Timmins, Woodhall, T. Green, Bayliss, Loach, G. Bell.

Referee: Major Marindin

Above The famous silver shield presented to Blackburn Rovers by the Football Association 'in commemoration of their winning The Challenge Cup three years in succession 1884–1885–1886'. The Wanderers, before them, had won three in a row, but no club has managed it since.

West Bromwich Albion held the Rovers to a poor goalless draw in the 1886 final, which may have been due to the fact that the Cup-holders watched the Boat Race in chill conditions in the morning, gulped down their lunch and arrived at Kennington Oval with barely enough time to change. However, they were at their best for the replay at Derby, again scoring a goal in each half, and Francis Marindin promised that they would get 'some distinctive trophy to commemorate their performance'.

Blackburn Rovers played twenty-two Cup games during the three triumphant seasons, scoring eighty-seven goals, conceding ten, and they were taken to a replay only in the third final. This was the first time the Cup had been won outside London.

Charles Francis, in his *History of the Blackburn Rovers Football Club* (1925), wrote: 'The prowess of the early "Blue and Whites" is still the subject of conversation in sporting circles all over the world. In the back blocks of the Antipodes, on the Canadian prairies, and in far-away China and Japan their stirring deeds on the football field are discussed as eagerly as in factories, shops and offices in the homeland.'

Below Aston Villa 1887, winners of the first all-Birmingham final. Although West Bromwich Albion were the favourites, they lost, for the second year running, to a controversial goal by Dennis Hodgetts and, in the last minute, to another by Archie Hunter, a revered figure in Villa's history. Hunter collided with Albion's goalkeeper Bob Roberts, and fell to the ground, but still managed to hook the ball over the line.

Aston Villa (players only): *Back row (left to right)* – F. Coulton, F. Dawson, J. Warner, R. Davis, J. Burton.

Middle row – D. Hodgetts, H. Vaughton, A. Hunter (captain), J. Simmonds. *Front row* – H. Yates, A. Brown. On the left of the middle row, bearded, is William McGregor who founded the Football League in 1888.

This was the last season in which Scottish clubs took part in the FA Cup. They signed off in style. Renton beat the mighty Blackburn Rovers 2–0 in a second-round replay – an honest-to-goodness sensation – and Glasgow Rangers reached the semi-finals.

1887

2 April at Oval   Att 15,500

Aston Villa 2 (Hodgetts, Hunter)

West Bromwich Albion 0

Aston Villa: Warner, Coulton, Simmonds, Yates, Dawson, Burton, Davis, Brown, Hunter, Vaughton, Hodgetts.

West Bromwich Albion: Roberts, H. Green, Aldridge, Horton, Perry, Timmins, Woodhall, T. Green, Bayliss, Paddock, Pearson.

Referee: Major Marindin

Below Sir C. Aubrey Smith, Hollywood film star, Sussex and England Test cricketer – and FA Cup footballer. He was a left-winger in the Old Carthusians side, which gave Preston North End a fright in the 1887 quarter-finals before losing 2–1, with Aubrey Smith going close to scoring late in the game. This was the last real fling of an amateur side after the legalisation of professionalism (1885).

Aubrey Smith is shown with Marion Davies in *Bachelor Father*, 'A Metro-Goldwyn-Mayer All-Talking Picture'. His Hollywood career was distinguished and prodigious, stretching from 1911 until shortly before his death in 1948. He appeared in seventy-six films, including *Tarzan the Ape Man*, *Lives of a Bengal Lancer*, *Prisoner of Zenda* and *Sixty Glorious Years*. He also introduced Hollywood to cricket.

Above Preston North End in mufti 1888 – a team ahead of its time. They were preparing at Southport for their fifth-round tie against Aston Villa at Perry Barr, which they won 3–1 in front of a record crowd of 27,000. This gate raised £544 in sixpences alone. Their defeat of Hyde by 26–0 in the first round that season is still a record. Eight of the Preston side scored, yet the story goes that after the game they all asked the Hyde goalkeeper for his autograph – because he had played so well. Preston led the way in legalising professionalism and enticing players with offers of good jobs, and turned a vigorous exercise into something of a science.

Back row (left to right) – J. Concannon (trainer), J. Gordon, J. Ross, N. J. Ross, A. S. Robertson, J. Graham, R. Holmes, R. Howarth, J. Ferguson, D. Russell. *Middle row* – J. Addison, J. Goodall, S. Thomson, T. A. Livesey. *Front row* – G. Drummond, F. Dewhurst.

1888

24 March at Oval   Att 19,000

West Bromwich Albion 2
  (Bayliss, Woodhall)
Preston North End 1
  (Dewhurst)

West Bromwich Albion: Roberts, Aldridge, Green, Horton, Perry, Timmins, Bassett, Woodhall, Bayliss, Wilson, Pearson.

Preston North End: Mills-Roberts, Howarth, N. J. Ross, Holmes, Russell, Graham, Gordon, J. Ross, Goodall, Dewhurst, Drummond.

Referee: Major Marindin

Right William Isaiah 'Billy' Bassett, 5ft 5½in star right-winger of the West Bromwich Albion side which won the Cup at last in 1888 – the first all-English side to win the trophy. Bassett's part in the defeat of Preston North End's professionals was so outstanding that he was immediately selected for the first of his sixteen England caps. He was fast, tricky as a fox and a man who relished the big occasion. He served Albion for fifty years as player, director and chairman. One of the great figures of Black Country football.

1889

30 March at Oval   Att 22,000

Preston North End 3 (Dewhurst, Ross, Thompson)

Wolverhampton Wanderers 0

Preston North End: Mills-Roberts, Howarth, Holmes, Drummond, Russell, Graham, Gordon, Ross, Goodall, Dewhurst, Thomson.

Wolverhampton Wanderers: Baynton, Baugh, Mason, Fletcher, Allen, Lowder, Hunter, Wykes, Brodie, Wood, Knight.

Referee: Major Marindin

Below The 'Invincibles' of Preston North End complete the first double at Kennington Oval. They won the first Football League Championship without losing a match and the Cup without conceding a goal. League record: Played 22 Won 18 Drawn 4 Goals 74–15 Points 40. Aston Villa were runners-up with 29 points and Wolves third with 28. FA Cup: Bootle (3–0 away), Grimsby (2–0 away), Birmingham St Georges (2–0 home), West Bromwich (1–0 Bramall Lane), Wolverhampton Wanderers (3–0 Oval).

Preston were the creation of their chairman and manager, Major William Sudell, perhaps the first outstanding member of this precarious profession, whose ambition from the start was to build 'the finest team in the country'. His method was definitive: he acquired many of the best players in the game, including the great centre-forward Johnny Goodall (known as 'Johnny Allgood') and then shrewdly made the most of them.

Entrants for the FA Cup had now risen to 149 and the tournament was split into two sections, qualifying (ten divisions) and proper.

S.T. DADD.

Below One of the most precious of all programmes. The players are set out in classic 2–3–5 formation.

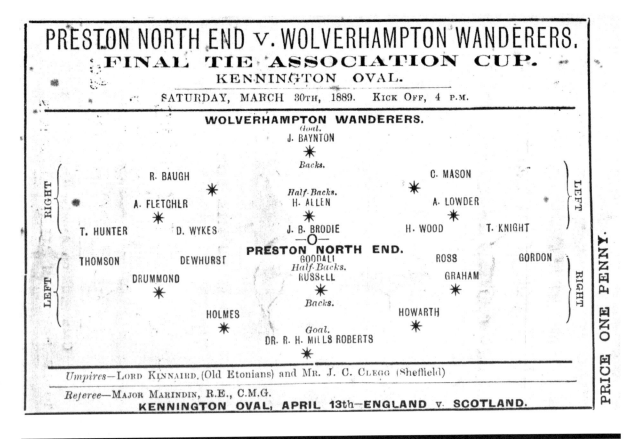

PRESTON NORTH END v. WOLVERHAMPTON WANDERERS.

FINAL TIE ASSOCIATION CUP.

KENNINGTON OVAL.

SATURDAY, MARCH 30TH, 1889. KICK OFF, 4 P.M.

WOLVERHAMPTON WANDERERS.

Goal.
J. BAYNTON

Backs.
R. BAUGH   C. MASON

Half-Backs.
A. FLETCHLR   H. ALLEN   A. LOWDER

T. HUNTER   D. WYKES   J. B. BRODIE   H. WOOD   T. KNIGHT

PRESTON NORTH END.

GOODALL   ROSS   GORDON
Half-Backs.
THOMSON   DEWHURST   RUSSELL   GRAHAM

DRUMMOND   GRAHAM

Backs.
HOLMES   HOWARTH

Goal.
DR. R. H. MILLS ROBERTS

RIGHT / LEFT / LEFT / RIGHT

Umpires—LORD KINNAIRD. (Old Etonians) and Mr. J. C. CLEGG (Sheffield)

Referee—MAJOR MARINDIN, R.E., C.M.G.

KENNINGTON OVAL, APRIL 13th—ENGLAND v. SCOTLAND.

PRICE ONE PENNY.

1890

29 March at Oval   Att 20,000

Blackburn Rovers 6 (Townley 3, Walton, Southworth (John), Lofthouse)

Sheffield Wednesday 1 (Bennett)

Blackburn Rovers: Horne, Southworth (James), Forbes, Barton, Dewar, Forrest, Lofthouse, Campbell, Southworth (John), Walton, Townley.

Sheffield Wednesday: Smith, Brayshaw, Morley, Dungworth, Betts, Waller, Ingram, Woodhouse, Bennett, Mumford, Cawley.

Referee: Major Marindin

Blackburn Rovers again. They overwhelmed Sheffield Wednesday in the first 'Roses' final, with William Townley, one of their nine internationals, scoring the first hat-trick in a final. But, commented the *Lancashire Evening Express,* 'A trifle less off-side tactics would be better.'

Right Francis Marindin, now a distinguished figure, refereed his eighth and last final (plus a replay) in 1890. It was also his sixteenth and last year as president of the FA. He was one of the founders of the FA Cup, founder of the Royal Engineers football club, twice a finalist, Old Etonian, full-back or goalkeeper, captain, referee and administrator. He was Officer of Railways at the Board of Trade, making several important reforms, and was knighted in 1897. An FA president of conscience, he disguised his misgivings about the coming of professionalism and, once it was clear the age of the amateur had gone, he stepped down gracefully.

1891

25 March at Oval   Att 23,000

Blackburn Rovers 3 (Dewar, Southworth, Townley)

Notts County 1 (Oswald)

Blackburn Rovers: Pennington, Brandon, Forbes, Barton, Dewar, Forrest, Lofthouse, Walton, Southworth (John), Hall, Townley.

Notts County: Thraves, Ferguson, Hendry, Osborne, Calderhead, Shelton, McGregor, McInnes, Oswald, Locker, Daft.

Referee: C. J. Hughes

Below Blackburn Rovers equalled the record of the Wanderers when they won the Cup for the fifth time with a comfortable victory over Notts County. Yet only a week before, Notts County had beaten the Cup-holders, who were under-strength, by 7–1 in a League game at Blackburn.

Rovers Cup-winners: *Back row (left to right)* – R. Birtwistle (umpire), T. Brandon, R. Pennington, J. Barton, John Southworth, G. Dewar, J. Forrest, F. Murray (trainer). *Front row* – J. Lofthouse, N. Walton, J. Forbes (captain), C. Hall, W. Townley.

James Forrest played in all five of Blackburn Rovers' finals. Only two others, both before him, have won five winner's medals – Arthur Kinnaird (Wanderers and Old Etonians) and Charles Wollaston (Wanderers). Forrest, left-half, centre-half or left-back, was the first professional to play for England. A tape-sizer by profession, but later became land-lord of the Darwen and County Arms and a Blackburn director.

The twenty-first final was the last at Kennington Oval where the authorities, including Charles Alcock, had become worried about the size of crowds at football's big event. It was also the first final in which goal-nets were used.

West Bromwich Albion's triumph was hugely deserved, for they had to beat Old Westminsters, Blackburn Rovers (thus denying them a second hat-trick of wins), Sheffield Wednesday and Nottingham Forest (in a second replay in a blizzard) to reach their fourth final in seven seasons. They then made amends for their defeat by Aston Villa five years before with an admirably disciplined performance. Quicksilver runs by Billy Bassett led to their first two goals and John Reynolds scored a late third from more than thirty yards.

HE INVENTED FOOTBALL GOAL NETS

Above John Alexander Brodie, inventor of the goal-net first used in a Cup final in 1892. He became chief engineer of the Mersey tunnel.

1892

19 March at Oval   Att 25,000

West Bromwich Albion 3
  (Geddes, Nicholls, Reynolds)
Aston Villa 0

West Bromwich Albion: Reader, Nicholson, McCulloch, Reynolds, Perry, Groves, Bassett, McLeod, Nicholls, Pearson, Geddes.

Aston Villa: Warner, Evans, Cox, H. Devey, Cowan, Baird, Athersmith, J. Devey, Dickson, Campbell, Hodgetts.

Referee: J. C. Clegg

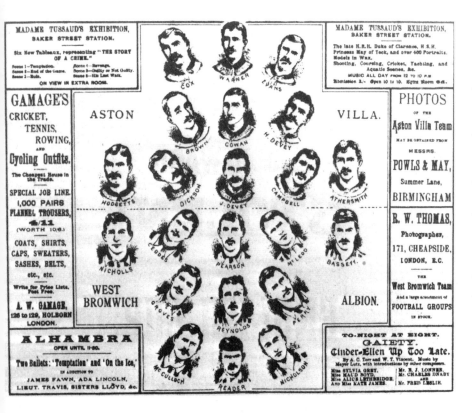

Right John Reynolds, 5ft 5in tall, a brilliant half-back, played for two countries and in Cup finals for two clubs. He represented Ireland on five occasions (twice against England) before it was established he belonged to England, for whom he then won eight caps. Reynolds' performance in the 1892 final attracted Villa's attention and he was accused by Albion's directors of 'playing for a transfer'. They threatened to fine him £1 a week until his form improved. But he got his own back after joining Villa: he helped them beat Albion in the 1895 final.

Left Cup final programmes were now becoming more ambitious. Two music halls, Alhambra and Gaiety, join the advertisers.

1893

26 March at Fallowfield   Att 45,000

Wolverhampton Wanderers 1
   (Allen)

Everton 0

Wolverhampton Wanderers: Rose, Baugh, Swift, Malpass, Allen, Kinsey, Topham, Wykes, Butcher, Wood, Griffin.

Everton: Williams, Howarth, Kelso, Stewart, Holt, Boyle, Latta, Gordon, Maxwell, Chadwick, Milward.

Referee: C. J. Hughes

London was unable to provide a ground big enough for the 1893 final, after the Oval had decided to keep itself for cricket, so the FA turned to the Manchester Athletic Ground at Fallowfield. A crowd of 45,000, yet another record, hemmed the pitch so chaotically that Everton protested. But this was only after their elegant side had been beaten. Wolverhampton Wanderers won the Cup for the first time with conviction and a goal in the sixtieth minute by their redoubtable centre-half Harry Allen. Pressmen complained bitterly that they could not see the game from the pavilion.

Above Wolves: *Back row (left to right)* – R. Baugh, A. Hollingsworth (chairman), J. Lewis (trainer), A. Blackham, H. Allen (captain). *Middle row* – R. Topham, W. Malpass, W. Rose, G. Swift, G. Kinsey, J. Addenbrooke (secretary). *Front row* – D. Wykes, J. Butcher, H. Wood, A. Griffin.

Opposite Fallowfield Terrace, Wolverhampton. An enterprising local builder quickly marked Wolves' success by naming a new row of houses after the scene of their triumph – and adorning it with a stone image of the Cup.

Below Football funeral cards were all the rage. They were usually printed before a game, with alternative verses covering all possibilities, and sold as crowds came out.

In Memoriam of
❧ Everton Football Team ❧

Who departed from the Cup Competition through a severe attack of Wolves,

And whose hopes were interred at the Football Cemetery, the same day.

They came in all their glory,
From that noted Toffy Town,
To fight the famous 'Wolves'
A team of English renown

The 'Toffy's' came on boldly,
'Their victory for to seek ;
But now they go home gravely
O'er their troubles for to weep,

Farewell, farewell dear old Everton,
No more for the Pot you will dribble ;
You have lost it to-day through difficult play
And we'll shout farewell for ever and ever.

1894

31 March at Goodison Park   Att 37,000

Notts County 4 (Watson, Logan 3)

Bolton Wanderers 1 (Cassidy)

Notts County: Toone, Harper, Hendry, Bramley, Calderhead, Shelton, Watson, Donnelly, Logan, Bruce, Daft.

Bolton Wanderers: Sutcliffe, Somerville, Jones, Gardiner, Paton, Hughes, Dickenson, Wilson, Tannahill, Bentley, Cassidy.

Referee: C. J. Hughes

Notts County were the first club from the Second Division (introduced in 1892) to win the Cup. Although they are the oldest League club (formed 1862), their masterly triumph over Bolton at Goodison Park, Liverpool, in 1894 remains their only major success.

Right Harry Butler Daft, Notts County's outside-left in their Cup-winning side, was one of the celebrated Corinthians who kept alight the spirit of amateurism. He scored County's semi-final winner against Blackburn Rovers at Bramall Lane, the last of his eighteen Cup goals for the East Midlands club, and had an outstanding game in the final – along with Jimmy Logan who scored a hat-trick. Daft won five caps for England and also played county cricket for

Nottinghamshire, just as his father and uncle had done before him.

1895

20 April at Crystal Palace   Att 42,560

Aston Villa 1 (Chatt)

West Bromwich Albion 0

Aston Villa: Wilkes, Spencer, Welford, Reynolds, Cowan, Russell, Athersmith, Chatt, Devey, Hodgetts, Smith.

West Bromwich Albion: Reader, Williams, Horton, Taggart, Higgins, Perry, Bassett, McLeod, Richards, Hutchinson, Banks.

Referee: J. Lewis

Aston Villa won the Cup, with panache, in the spring of 1895; and then, embarrassingly, lost it five months later. The story is the FA Cup's most durable whodunit, a first-class mystery.

The opening part of the tale is straightforward. Villa beat their old adversaries, West Bromwich Albion, with a goal in the first minute of the first final at Crystal Palace. Later that year they allowed the trophy to be exhibited in the shop window of a local boot and shoe maker, William Shillcock, a business friend of William McGregor, the

founder of the Football League.

Then, on the night of 11 September 1895, the 'little tin idol' was stolen from 73 Newtown Row and never seen again. The thieves left a hole, eighteen inches by twelve inches, in the low roof above the window – and a set of size five footprints. Curious crowds gathered. Newspapers had their indignant say ('little short of a national disaster,' said one). Shillcock himself wrote later: 'I pictured myself a ruined man, a hated individual.' A £10 reward was offered with no success. It was assumed the Cup had been melted down to make counterfeit coins.

But who pinched the pot? In 1958, the *Sunday Pictorial* carried a front-page confession by eighty-two-year-old Harry Burge, an old rascal living in a welfare hostel who had spent half his life in prison. 'Sensational confession ends Soccer's biggest riddle,' claimed the paper. But there were discrepancies in Burge's story and he may have been simply squeezing a few bob from a tabloid. In 1975, moreover, the *Birmingham Mail* carried a story which pointed a finger at a certain Joseph Piecewright, who had certainly been gaoled for counterfeiting coins. The 'informant' was his grandson, Edwin Tranter, from Acocks Green.

Most convincing of all, however, were the findings of *Claret and Blue*, the official magazine of Aston Villa, whose painstaking investigation revealed that four men may have been involved, and that when they took the melted-down Cup to a receiver, they were told, 'Ten bob, take it or leave it.' The receiver claimed the Cup was not made of pure silver but an alloy.

No names had surfaced at that point, but then BBC Radio WM followed up with a programme about the theft, which was heard by eighty-year-old Mrs Violet Stait. She remembered her husband Jack saying, before they were married, that 'Our dad pinched that Cup out of Shillcock's window' and, behind a row of back-to-backs near the boot-maker's shop, that 'this is the yard where our dad helped to melt the Cup down'.

Bernard Gallagher, editor of *Claret and Blue*, and his team decided this new line was worth serious inquiry. They spent months verifying facts and, in the end, everything seemed to confirm that Violet's father-in-law was one of the thieves. He was John 'Stosher' Stait. But were Burge and Piecewright two of his accomplices? The story is not complete yet.

£10 REWARD.

STOLEN!

From the Shop Window of W. Shillcock, Football Outfitter, Newtown Row, Birmingham, between the hour of 9-30 p.m. on Wednesday, the 11th September, and 7-30 a.m., on Thursday, the 12th inst., the

ENGLISH CUP,

the property of Aston Villa F.C. The premises were broken into between the hours named, and the Cup, together with cash in drawer, stolen.

The above Reward will be paid for the recovery of the Cup, or for information as may lead to the conviction of the thieves.

Information to be given to the Chief of Police, or to Mr. W. Shillcock, 73, Newtown Row.

Above Is this the man who stole the Cup? John Stait – known as 'Stosher' because of his luxuriant moustache.

1896

18 April at Crystal Palace   Att 48,836

Sheffield Wednesday 2
(Spiksley 2)

Wolverhampton Wanderers 1
(Black)

Sheffield Wednesday: Massey, Earp, Langley, Brandon, Crawshaw, Petrie, Brash, Brady, Bell, Davis, Spiksley.

Wolverhampton Wanderers: Tennant, Baugh, Dunn, Owen, Malpass, Griffiths, Tonks, Henderson, Beats, Wood, Black.

Referee: Captain W. Simpson

The second FA Cup, an honest replica, cost £25, which was exactly the sum Aston Villa were fined for losing the old trophy. It found a new home immediately, Sheffield Wednesday taking it back to Yorkshire for the first time after Fred Spiksley, their dynamic England winger, had scored twice against Wolverhampton Wanderers. The shot which gave him his second was so hard, the ball springing straight out of the net, that the Wolves goal-keeper didn't realise he'd been beaten. 'When's the replay?' he asked Wednesday's captain, Jack Earp, at the end. 'There's no replay,' came the reply. 'We won 2–1 as you'll see when we take the medals.'

Right Tommy Crawshaw, a Wednesday legend, indomitable centre-half and pillar of the Yorkshire club's side during their finest era. He made nearly five hundred League and Cup appearances in fourteen years, played in two Cup finals eleven years apart (1896 and 1907) and in two Championship sides (1903 and 1904). He won ten caps for England and his advice was always: 'Up with the play and get among the goals.' He loved gardening and was especially fond of chrysanthemums.

Below Souvenir mug marking Sheffield Wednesday's first Cup triumph in 1896.

Aston Villa became the second club to complete the League and Cup double in a decade of towering achievement. Between 1892 and 1900 they won five League Championships, two FA Cups and were losing finalists once – with their finest hours in 1896–97 when they won the Championship by eleven points and beat Everton 3–2 in a brilliant final. All five goals came in the space of twenty-five minutes before half-time, with Everton proving clever and spirited opponents. Villa were a side without a weakness, but at the heart of their success were John Devey, an inspiring captain and centre-forward, and the skill and bravado of the half-back line of John Reynolds, James Cowan and James Crabtree. William McGregor, the League's founder, wrote of them with understandable partiality: 'For brilliancy and, at the same time, for consistency of achievement, for activity in philanthropic enterprise, for astuteness of management and for general alertness, the superiors of Aston Villa cannot be found.'

Below Albert Evans, left-back in Villa's double side, pictured with his wife in 1965 at the age of nearly ninety – the last surviving member of that great team. Evans broke a leg three times during his playing career and was unlucky not to be capped. He travelled all over the world, trying many jobs, and even took part in the Canadian gold rush. He eventually became a Villa talent scout.

Behind Evans is a picture of his 1897 team-mates: **Players only:** *Back row (left to right)* – H. Spencer, J. Whitehouse, A. Evans, J. Crabtree. *Front row* – James Cowan, C. Athersmith, J. Campbell, J. Devey, G. Wheldon, John Cowan, J. Reynolds (hidden).

1897

10 April at Crystal Palace   Att 65,891

Aston Villa 3 (Campbell, Wheldon, Crabtree)

Everton 2 (Bell, Boyle)

Aston Villa: Whitehouse, Spencer, Evans, Reynolds, Cowan (James), Crabtree, Athersmith, Devey, Campbell, Wheldon, Cowan (John).

Everton: Menham, Meecham, Storrier, Boyle, Holt, Stewart, Taylor, Bell, Hartley, Chadwick, Milward.

Referee: J. Lewis

Above Nottingham Forest 1898, surprise winners of the first East Midlands final. Derby County had beaten both the previous season's finalists, Aston Villa and Everton, in earlier rounds and overwhelmed Forest 5–0 in a League game at the Baseball Ground only the Monday before the final. Derby's forward line included two of the giants of the game, John Goodall (the former Preston 'Invincible', then thirty-five years old) and the peerless Steve Bloomer (twenty-four), who scored nearly three hundred goals for Derby. On the day, though, Forest were manifestly the better side: 'With nothing to lose and every-

thing to win,' commented *The Graphic*, 'they played as many an inferior club has done with far more dash and vigour than their more talented opponents.' There was also a busy black market. Many tickets, revealed another paper, were sold at 'considerably enhanced prices'.

Nottingham Forest: *Back row (left to right)* – H. Hallam (secretary), T. McInnes, Mr T. W. Hancock, A. Ritchie, D. Allsop, Mr B. W. Winter, A. Scott, Mr H. S. Radford, A. Spouncer, G. Bee (trainer). *Seated* – C. Richards, Frank Forman, J. McPherson, W. Wragg, A. Capes. *Front* – L. Benbow.

1898

16 April at Crystal Palace   Att 62,017
Nottingham Forest 3 (Capes 2, McPherson)
Derby County 1 (Bloomer)
Nottingham Forest: Allsop, Ritchie, Scott, Forman, McPherson, Wragg, McInnes, Richards, Benbow, Capes, Spouncer.
Derby County: Fryer, Methven, Leiper, Cox, A. Goodall, Turner, J. Goodall, Bloomer, Boag, Stevenson, McQueen.
Referee: J. Lewis

Right The famous Druids of Ruabon, 1897–98, the oldest club in Wales and the first Welsh club to compete in the FA Cup. Formed in 1869, they entered the Cup for the first time in 1877 and reached the fifth round in 1883, beating Bolton in a second replay before falling to Blackburn Olympic, the eventual winners. They won the Welsh FA Cup in 1898 but didn't do so well in the FA Cup, being beaten 3–2 by Rock Ferry in the second qualifying round.

Players only: *Back row (left to right)* – C. Thomas, Woodward, A. Hughes. *Middle row* – G. Richards, J. Price, T. Davies. *Front row* – J. Vaughan, B. Butler, T. Owen, J. Davies, R. Jones.

Left A comical illustration by *The Graphic* of Nottingham Forest's second goal. Jack Fryer, Derby's goalkeeper, palms the ball to the feet of Arthur Capes.

1899

15 April at Crystal Palace   Att 73,833
Sheffield United 4 (Bennett, Beers, Almond, Priest)
Derby County 1 (Boag)
Sheffield United: Foulke, Thickett, Boyle, Johnson, Morren, Needham, Bennett, Beers, Hedley, Almond, Priest.
Derby County: Fryer, Methven, Staley, Cox, Paterson, May, Arkesden, Bloomer, Boag, McDonald, Allen.
Referee: A. Scragg

Above Sheffield United won the Cup the hard way. They were drawn away in every round, were involved in five replays (three against Liverpool in the semi-finals, one of which was abandoned because of crowd trouble and darkness) and were a goal down to Derby County at half-time in their first final. But they were a dauntless side, League champions the season before, who were led with wonderful verve by Ernie 'Nudger' Needham, 5ft 5in tall, an England regular, an audacious dribbler and unflinching tackler. Sheffield United came back brilliantly in the second half of a memorable final to score four goals.

Sheffield United: *Back row (left to right)* – G. Hedley, W. Beers, H. Thickett, W. Foulke, J. Almond, P. Boyle. *Seated* – N. Bennett, W. Johnson, E. Needham (captain), T. Morren, A. Priest. The mighty Bill Foulke, their goalkeeper, was soon to put on even more weight; by the time United reached their next final in 1901, he weighed twenty-two stone.

Right A portly Shaker. John Plant of England played for Bury for sixteen seasons, in two phases. He was a rotund left-winger, noted for his powerful shooting – his goal in the 1900 final, Bury's fourth, coming from 'a lightning shot', according to *Sporting Sketches*. Southampton, the first southern club for seventeen years to reach the final, had no answer to a dashing and intelligent Bury side. Earlier that year Lord Derby opened a bazaar in Bury 'to relieve the club from debt and thereby ensure its continuation as an organisation of the first class'. It was a success.

1900

21 April at Crystal Palace   Att 68,945
Bury 4 (McLuckie 2, Wood, Plant)
Southampton 0
Bury: Thompson, Darroch, Davidson, Pray, Leeming, Ross, Richards, Wood, McLuckie, Sagar, Plant.
Southampton: Robinson, Meehan, Durber, Meston, Chadwick, Petrie, Turner, Yates, Farrell, Wood, Milward.
Referee: A. G. Kingscott

Chapter Three

New Dawn
1901–1910

'The Crystal Palace era was more than the venue of a football match; it took on the character of a picnic. Long before the game happy parties sat in groups, under the trees, munching sandwiches, and generations of football folk met there to renew acquaintance. But though the turnstiles registered six figures, by no means all could see all the play. But there was room to move about, and even if late comers only heard the cheers and saw the ball when it was in the air, there was little grumbling and to "rush" the strong iron railings was not practicable. Yes, they were great days, and as "Dan" Woolfall, the hon. treasurer, received the "box office" reports his face beamed. All the leading officials wore top hats, but by the time one had been in a packed railway carriage later on such headgear was rather more troublesome than useful.'

William Pickford (FA Council member 1888–1937,
FA president 1937–39) in *A Few Recollections of Sport (1939).*

Football, happily in accord with the world about it, moved into the twentieth century with a stout heart and jaunty step. Edwardian man was to witness a remarkable decade of progress and adventure.

The Boer War was tidied up in South Africa, Germany began its arms race with Britain and there were the first rumblings of revolution in Russia. Machines that were heavier than air left the ground. Henry Ford produced cheap motor cars, wireless telegraph skipped messages across the seven seas and Scott of the Antarctic made his mark on history. The Labour Party was born, Mrs Pankhurst rallied her suffragettes and the old-age pension was introduced – five shillings a week for the over-seventies under certain conditions. The Boy Scouts were formed and the Royal Navy's first submarine was launched.

The British Empire was still growing; and so, too, was the empire of football as servicemen, settlers, teachers, businessmen and travellers continued to carry the word, like missionaries, to every corner of the globe. The formation of FIFA in 1904 pointed football towards a new future and eventually, of course, the World Cup.

It cost sixpence to watch the professionals of the Football League, whose maximum weekly wage of £4 was double that of the average skilled man. Middlesbrough paid the first £1,000 transfer fee for the Sunderland and England inside-forward Alf Common in 1905 ('Flesh and blood for sale,' thundered one correspondent) and the rapid development of organised labour led to the Football Association giving its approval to a young Players' Union.

The FA Cup, for its part, was sharing out success and goodwill with admirable impartiality. Ten different clubs won the Cup in the first ten full seasons of the century. Manchester United (a new force in the land) and Manchester City held the trophy aloft; so did Sheffield United and Sheffield Wednesday; and Aston Villa and Wolverhampton Wanderers did their bit for the Midlands. Bury, moreover, having beaten Southampton 4–0 in the final of 1900, did even better three years later when they scored six against Derby County – still a record – and matched Preston North End's famous achievement of not conceding a goal in the tournament. Ten goals in two finals! They are the only finals Bury have played in and they join the Wanderers, Old Carthusians, Blackburn Olympic and, from later days, Bradford City, Coventry City, Ipswich Town and Wimbledon as the Cup's only unbeaten finalists.

However, the most significant Cup triumph of the decade was Tottenham Hotspur's in 1901. They were the first southern club to win the tournament since the aristocratic Old Etonians eighteen years before, and they remain the only non-League club to have won it since the formation of the Football League in 1888.

Spurs' timing was inspired, because football had split the country neatly into two. The playing standards of the South had fallen so far behind the sleeves-up professionals of the North and Midlands that many feared the gap would never be bridged. A Southern League (won by Spurs in 1900) had been formed in 1894 as a rival to the Football League, but it was always a junior partner, and the big northern clubs, in particular, regarded the first faltering steps towards professionalism in the South with amusement and even some contempt. Arsenal, alone, carried the flag for the South in the Football League which by 1901, its thirteenth season, consisted of two divisions of eighteen clubs.

'Jack and his master' was how one observer referred to the final between Sheffield United and Spurs – 'the master' undoubtedly being Sheffield United, who boasted nine full internationals. Yet Spurs were undaunted and, by way of a 2–2 draw at Crystal Palace and a 3–1 victory in the replay at Bolton, they made an indelible mark on the history of the Cup.

North versus South! There was a huge sense of occasion about their meeting in south London, which was watched by 110,820 spectators, the first six-figure crowd to witness a final and a world record which stood until 1913, when 120,081 watched Aston Villa and Sunderland. Tottenham's celebrations lasted three days, once they had triumphed in the replay, and included a night out in Luton where the hotel manager asked the team to honour 'Women and Wine'. 'The Ladies,' according to the *Tottenham Weekly Herald*, 'were evidently desirous of smiling their appreciation of the merry Spurs. In this department the whole team scored heavily.'

The South, at last, was on the march; but the outstanding club of the Edwardian era belonged to the top right corner of the country. Newcastle United won the League Championship three times in five seasons (1905, 1907 and 1909) and reached the Cup final five times in seven seasons – although they won the trophy only once, and then by way of a poor replay against Barnsley of the Second Division at Goodison Park. Not once, in five attempts, did this side of rich ability and character manage to win a final at the second great home of the Cup. The turf at Crystal Palace, according to one theory, was much thicker than at St James' Park and did not suit their smooth passing game.

There was still solid opposition to professionalism in die-hard pockets of the South, and some religious conventions saw football itself as a pursuit of the ungodly. But of the 12,000 clubs and 300,000 players in England, 400 clubs and 6,000 players were now professional. The FA Cup was a salient part of the nation's calendar, and its ties were watched by crowds half as big again as League gates.

Tottenham Hotspur, famously, became the first and only non-League club to win the Cup since the formation of the Football League in 1888. They were in the Southern League and did not join Division Two of the League until 1908, when they immediately won promotion.

This confrontation between North and South went to a replay but, first, the biggest crowd to have watched a football match – 110,820 – gathered at Crystal Palace. Forty thousand supporters came down from Sheffield and the scene in that corner of south London was chaotic. White handkerchiefs were placed on heads and hats and bonnets pulled low as protection against the sun. The *Tottenham Weekly Herald* said the crowd looked like 'a forest of trees covered with pink and white blossom'.

Sheffield United, strong favourites with nine internationals, were lucky to survive. Their equaliser, to make the score 2–2, was hugely controversial. George Clawley, Spurs' goalkeeper, dropped the ball after saving a shot from Bert Lipsham and, when challenged by Walter Bennett, quickly pushed the ball outside a post, whereupon the linesman signalled a corner. Referee Arthur Kingscott then arrived on the scene. He

appeared to wave aside his linesman's decision and Clawley, relieved, placed the ball for a goal-kick. But, suddenly, Kingscott pointed to the centre-spot, having decided that the ball had crossed the line when Clawley dropped it. A rumble of disbelief was followed by a roar of southern anger. Every shot that followed was accompanied by derisive shouts of 'Goal', and the controversy raged for weeks.

United thus managed a replay but, the following Saturday, Spurs took the Cup with a 3–1 win at Bolton – a curious choice after both clubs had suggested Villa Park. With the railways refusing to issue cheap excursion tickets, only 20,470 turned up, the lowest crowd for a final this century. On the field, however, there were no arguments about the outcome. Ernie Needham was again outstanding for Sheffield United but Tottenham, 3–1 winners, were the better team.

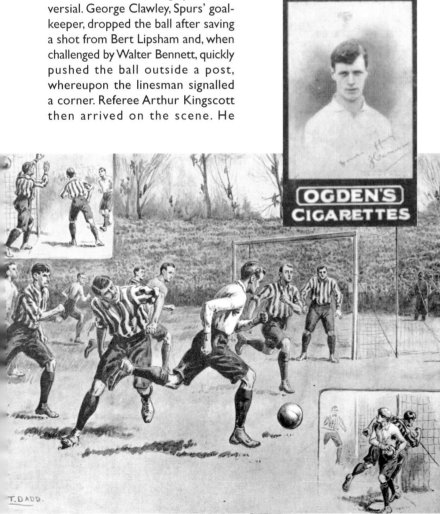

T. DADD.

1901

20 April at Crystal Palace   Att 110,820
Tottenham Hotspur 2 (Brown 2)
Sheffield United 2 (Priest, Bennett)
Tottenham Hotspur: Clawley, Erentz, Tait, Morris, Hughes, Jones, Smith, Cameron, Brown, Copeland, Kirwan.
Sheffield United: Foulke, Thickett, Boyle, Johnson, Morren, Needham, Bennett, Field, Hedley, Priest, Lipsham.
Referee: A. G. Kingscott
Replay:
27 April at Burnden Park   Att 20,470
Tottenham Hotspur 3 (Cameron, Smith, Brown)
Sheffield United 1 (Priest)
Tottenham Hotspur: Clawley, Erentz, Tait, Morris, Hughes, Jones, Smith, Cameron, Brown, Copeland, Kirwan.
Sheffield United: Foulke, Thickett, Boyle, Johnson, Morren, Needham, Bennett, Field, Hedley, Priest, Lipsham.
Referee: A. G. Kingscott

Inset left John Cameron, Tottenham's player-manager-secretary and the father, perhaps, of the north London club's tradition for elegance and style. He was an engaging but precise man who picked his players with great care. He believed a good player 'must have exceptional qualities of a personal character... education makes all the difference'. He was a cool and intelligent inside-forward, who had played for Queen's Park and Everton, and was the first secretary of the Professional Football Players' Union.

Left *Centre:* A powerful run by Spurs' outside-right Tom Smith, a former sprint champion, in the first game at Crystal Palace. *Top left:* Alexander 'Sandy' Brown puts Spurs into the lead, off the underside of the bar, which meant he had scored in every round. *Bottom right:* George Clawley, Spurs' goalkeeper, dodges United's Walter Bennett.

Above Usual result after a collision in the replay with Billy 'Fatty' Foulke, Sheffield United's 6ft 2½in goalkeeper, who now weighed twenty-two stone. He once swung on his crossbar and snapped it and, more than once, dangled an irritating opponent by his ankles. Described as 'one of the curiosities of football… a wonder to everyone who visits the classic grounds of the game', Foulke responded: 'I don't mind what you call me as long as you don't call me late for lunch.' His technique was good, he was remarkably nimble and he played for England.

Below Sandy Brown (hidden) about to score Tottenham's third goal in the replay with a glancing header from a corner by John Cameron. It took Brown's total for the tournament to fifteen which is still a record.

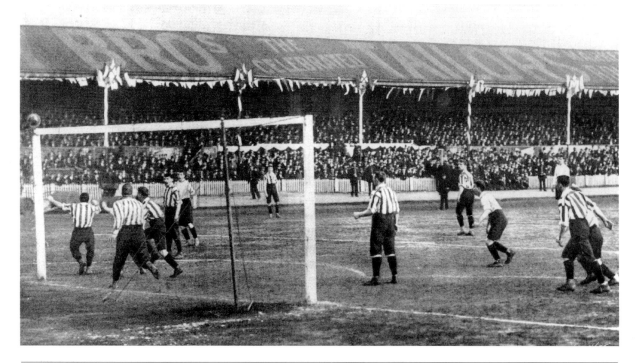

Above Frank Gillett's witty view of Sheffield United's 2–1 victory over Southampton in the 1902 replay at Crystal Palace. The experience of Sheffield United (Needham, Foulke and all) was decisive and, afterwards, Sheffield MP Howard Vincent sent greetings '…especially to our giant goalkeeper, Foulke, with his tremendous smite and prodigious kick, the best goalkeeper football has ever seen. May he live a thousand years.' Crowds were smaller, but earlier in that same month twenty-six people had been killed when wooden terracing collapsed at Ibrox during an international between Scotland and England. Even so, nearly 110,000 people saw the two games.

1902

19 April at Crystal Palace   Att 76,914

Sheffield United 1 (Common)
Southampton 1 (Wood)

Sheffield United: Foulke, Thickett, Boyle, Needham, Wilkinson, Johnson, Bennett, Common, Hedley, Priest, Lipsham.

Southampton: Robinson, Fry, Molyneux, Meston, Bowman, Lee, A. Turner, Wood, Brown, Chadwick, J. Turner.

Referee: T. Kirkham

Replay:

26 April at Crystal Palace   Att 33,068

Sheffield United 2 (Hedley, Barnes)
Southampton 1 (Brown)

Sheffield United: Foulke, Thickett, Boyle, Needham, Wilkinson, Johnson, Barnes, Common, Hedley, Priest, Lipsham.

Southampton: Robinson, Fry, Molyneux, Meston, Bowman, Lee, A. Turner, Wood, Brown, Chadwick, J. Turner.

Referee: T. Kirkham

Right Charles Burgess Fry, Southampton's right-back and a Sporting Olympian: England cricketer (ninety-four first-class centuries) and footballer, world long-jump record holder, rugby union wing threequarter for Oxford University and Surrey, classical scholar, author, editor, journalist, schoolmaster, Parliamentary candidate, sailor and dedicated grandee.

Above Bury, 1903, whose 6–0 victory over Derby County has never been matched. They beat Wolverhampton Wanderers, Sheffield United, Notts County and Aston Villa on the way to the final – and did not concede a goal. Thus, in their only two finals (1900 and 1903) Bury scored ten without reply.

Bury: *Back row (left to right) –* W. Johnstone, J. Lindsay, F. Thorpe, H. Monteith, G. Ross (captain), J. McEwen. *Seated –* W. Richards, W. Wood, C. Sagar, J. Leeming, J. Plant.

Poor Derby. In eight years they had played in three finals and three semi-finals (and they reached the semi-finals again in 1904) but always finished second best. Derby were without Steve Bloomer, injured, in 1903, and goalkeeper Jack Fryer began the game with groin trouble which forced his withdrawal after sixty-five minutes, when Bury were leading 5–0. The *Daily Chronicle* described the final as 'a fiasco'.

1903

18 April at Crystal Palace　　Att 63,102

Bury 6 (Ross, Sagar, Leeming 2, Wood, Plant)

Derby County 0

Bury: Monteith, Lindsay, McEwen, Johnstone, Thorpe, Ross, Richards, Wood, Sagar, Leeming, Plant.

Derby County: Fryer, Methven, Morris, Warren, Goodall, May, Warrington, York, Boag, Richards, Davis.

Referee: J. Adams

1904

23 April at Crystal Palace   Att 61,374

Manchester City 1 (Meredith)

Bolton Wanderers 0

Manchester City: Hillman, McMahon, Burgess, Frost, Hynds, Ashworth, Meredith, Livingstone, Gillespie, Turnbull, Booth.

Bolton Wanderers: Davies, Brown, Struthers, Clifford, Greenhalgh, Freebairn, Stokes, Marsh, Yenson, White, Taylor

Referee: A. J. Barker

Above and right Billy Meredith of Manchester City scoring the goal which won the first all-Lancashire final. The photograph and the drawing (by Ralph Cleaver in the *Illustrated Sporting and Dramatic News*) capture the moment from different angles, but they are in accord.

Meredith is one of the game's immortals: the 'Welsh wizard', the 'Lloyd George of Welsh football', a right-winger of genius and, in many ways, the Stanley Matthews of his time. Meredith's career spanned thirty-one years (1893–1924), but the number of games he played for Northwich Victoria, Manchester City, Manchester United (with whom he would win the Cup again in 1909), Manchester City once more and Wales may never be settled beyond argument. He took a great interest in records and claimed to have played 1,568 games and scored 470 goals, which may be right if benefit games

and friendlies are included. He played in forty-eight official internationals for Wales – all in the Home Championship – the last when he was forty-five. He also played in an FA Cup semi-final (for Manchester City against Newcastle United, 0–2, 1924) when he was four months short of his fiftieth birthday. He was a spare, angular man with a pale face, cropped hair and bandy legs, which increasingly carried evidence of the frustration he invoked in opposing defences. In his mouth, invariably, there was a toothpick.

Meredith also had a mind of his own: he was an outspoken reformer and rebel, a champion of players' rights and a driving force in the establishment of the Players' Union. His career was blighted by accusations of bribery and match-fixing which led to suspension, although his popularity ensured his survival.

Left 'On such a glorious afternoon there was only one possible way of reaching Sydenham in anything like comfort, and that was by walking,' declared a Birmingham newspaper. Part of the crowd of 101,117 approaching the ground through the ornate gardens of the Crystal Palace.

1905

15 April at Crystal Palace   Att 101,117
Aston Villa 2 (Hampton 2)
Newcastle United 0
Aston Villa: George, Spencer, Miles, Pearson, Leake, Windmill, Brawn, Garratty, Hampton, Bache, Hall.
Newcastle United: Lawrence, McCombie, Carr, Gardner, Aitken, McWilliam, Rutherford, Howie, Appleyard, Veitch, Gosnell.
Referee: P. R. Harrower

Left Harry Hampton of Aston Villa, who had just celebrated his twentieth birthday, scoring the first of his two goals against Newcastle United. Newcastle, League champions and beginning the most successful time in their history, were thus deprived of the double. "Appy 'Arry' was a powerful dreadnought, who would give the ball to one of his wingers and then look to ram in the return with foot, head or any other handy part of his anatomy. Villa's supporters loved him. Opposing goalkeepers were not so keen. Newcastle, playing in their first final, were undone by the pace of Aston Villa, who won the Cup for the fourth time.

Below A contortionist provides entertainment before Aston Villa beat Fulham by 5–0 (Hampton two) in the third round at Villa Park.

Above Two of Lancashire's most celebrated sportsmen helped Everton win the Cup for the first time. They were Jack Sharp and Harry Makepeace, two of that small and precious breed of men (only twelve) who have played both football and cricket at full international level for England.

Sharp, right-winger, was the outstanding player in the 1906 final, and Makepeace, right-half, was always a model of consistency and exemplary behaviour. Between them, for Lancashire, they scored nearly eighty hundreds. Makepeace, indeed, is the only man to have won a Cup-winner's medal, a League Championship medal (1915), a County Cricket Championship medal (four) and played for England at both football and cricket. Sharp provided the centre from which Sandy Young scored the Everton goal, fifteen minutes from the end of the 1906 final, which meant defeat at the Crystal Palace for Newcastle United for the second year running.

Everton: *Standing (left to right)* – Mr A. R. Wade, H. Makepeace, Mr W. C. Cuff, A. Young, Mr J. Davies, Mr E. A. Bainbridge, J. Taylor (captain) (leaning on draped stand with the Cup), Mr G. Mahon, W. Scott, Mr B. Kelly, W. Balmer, Mr H. Wright, J. Elliott. *Sitting* – Mr W. R. Clayton, Dr J. C. Baxter, J. Sharp, H. Bolton, W. Abbott, J. Settle, J. Crelley, H. Hardman, Dr W. Whitford, Mr D. Kirkwood.

1906

21 April at Crystal Palace   Att 75,609

Everton I (Young)

Newcastle United 0

Everton: Scott, Balmer, Crelley, Makepeace, Taylor, Abbott, Sharp, Bolton, Young, Settle, Hardman.

Newcastle United: Lawrence, McCombie, Carr, Gardner, Aitken, McWilliam, Rutherford, Howie, Veitch, Orr, Gosnell.

Referee: F. Kirkham

1907

20 April at Crystal Palace   Att 84,584

Sheffield Wednesday 2 (Stewart, Simpson)

Everton 1 (Sharp)

Sheffield Wednesday: Lyall, Layton, Burton, Brittleton, Crawshaw, Bartlett, Chapman, Bradshaw, Wilson, Stewart, Simpson.

Everton: Scott, W. Balmer, R. Balmer, Makepeace, Taylor, Abbott, Sharp, Bolton, Young, Settle, Hardman.

Referee: N. Whittaker

Above Only four minutes left and George Simpson, Sheffield Wednesday's 5ft 6in left-winger, scores a simple goal to win the 1907 final. Among Wednesday's rewards was a stage appearance with George Robey at Sheffield's music hall. When Wednesday won the Cup in 1896, Southampton St Mary's, Sunderland, Everton and Wolverhampton Wanderers were among their opponents; in 1907, they faced Southampton, Sunderland, Wolves and Everton.

Above Jack Sharp, half hidden, pops in Everton's goal from six yards. However, for a side lauded for their 'brilliance, style, polish, shooting ability and superior speed', the holders (with ten of their previous year's team) were disappointing.

1908

25 April at Crystal Palace   Att 74,967

Wolverhampton Wanderers 3
  (Hunt, Hedley, Harrison)

Newcastle United 1 (Howie)

Wolverhampton Wanderers: Lunn, Jones, Collins, Hunt, Wooldridge, Bishop, Harrison, Shelton, Hedley, Radford, Pedley.

Newcastle United: Lawrence, McCracken, Pudan, Gardner, Veitch, McWilliam, Rutherford, Howie, Appleyard, Speedie, Wilson.

Referee: T. P. Campbell

Wolverhampton Wanderers' triumph in 1908 was one of the most extraordinary Cup final upsets of all. Wolves were a middle-of-the-road Second Division side, strong but ordinary, while Newcastle United were the most popular and successful side of the Edwardian era. They were League champions in 1905, 1907 and 1909, their names known in every household from Camborne to Carlisle, a team of footballing aristocrats who filled grounds wherever they played. They had been beaten in two finals (1905 and 1906) but now, surely, the Cup was theirs for the taking. Yet they were devoured by the Wolves, who scored twice in five minutes just before half-time. Newcastle had ninety per cent of the play, but it was Wolves who took the Cup.

There was Newcastle talk of a 'Crystal Palace hoodoo'; the grass, it was said, was too lush for their style of short-passing. And Tyneside was still nursing the mighty indignity of being beaten at home, in the first round the previous season, by a lowly Southern League side. That side was Crystal Palace.

WOLVES' GLORIOUS CUP-FINAL VICTORY
Speed and Determination overcome Skill and Science
HARE AND TORTOISE:
A NEW VERSION OF AN OLD PROVERB
How Pretty Football Failed To Win The Cup

PLAY UP WOLVES!

WOLVERHAMPTON WANDERERS.
English Cup Team, 1908.

LUNN (GOAL)
JONES   COLLINS (BACKS)
HUNT WOOLDRIDGE BISHOP (HALF BACKS)
HARRISON SHELTON HEDLEY RADFORD PEDLEY
(FORWARDS)

Left Wolves' Cup-winners, 1908. The Rev. Kenneth Hunt, their Corinthian right-half and scorer of the first goal, attributed the Black Country club's success to 'dash, quick tackling and direct methods'.

Right Edwardian mascots showed great originality. Here is a 'wolf' (with flat cap) jubilantly entertaining the Crystal Palace crowd at half-time – with the Wolves two goals up.

Twenty clubs had won the Cup, and they were now joined by Manchester United who had not even reached a semi-final before. United's time had come. They won the League Championship for the first time in 1908 and, the following season, the gods were with them all the way to Crystal Palace. They were drawn at home in the first three rounds, and in the fourth, against Burnley at Turf Moor, they had the great British weather on their side. They were a goal down with only eighteen minutes left when a storm of sleet and snow forced the tie to be abandoned. United won the replay 3–2. Even on the big day Bristol City, playing in the only final in their history, were undermined by injuries. It was a poor final which United won with a goal in the twenty-first minute by Alex 'Sandy' Turnbull, who played with a painful knee injury. A year later United moved from Clayton to a handsome new home which they called Old Trafford.

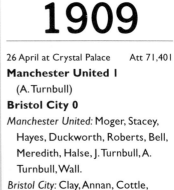

1909

26 April at Crystal Palace   Att 71,401

Manchester United 1
  (A. Turnbull)
Bristol City 0

Manchester United: Moger, Stacey, Hayes, Duckworth, Roberts, Bell, Meredith, Halse, J. Turnbull, A. Turnbull, Wall.

Bristol City: Clay, Annan, Cottle, Hanlin, Wedlock, Spear, Staniforth, Hardy, Gilligan, Burton, Hilton.

Referee: J. Mason

Above Manchester United are a split second away from their winning goal. A shot from Harold Halse (second from right) has rebounded off the bar and Sandy Turnbull (not in picture) is about to return the ball into the net. Turnbull was killed in action at Arras on 3 May 1917. Billy Meredith is on the left of the picture.

Above Manchester United 1909, with bowlers, boaters, ball and Cup. *Standing (left to right)* – E. Mangnall (secretary/manager), F. Bacon, J. Picken, H. Edmonds, Mr Murray (director), H. Moger, Mr J. H. Davies (chairman), T. Homer, Mr G. H. Lawton (director), A. Bell, Mr W. Deakin (director). *Sitting* – W. Meredith, R. Duckworth, C. Roberts (captain), A. Turnbull, E. West, G. Stacey. *Front* – A. Whalley, L. Hofton, H. Halse, G. Wall. John Henry Davies, managing director of Manchester Breweries, and Ernest Mangnall were the men who put Manchester United on the map. United's captain and centre-half Charlie Roberts, together with Billy Meredith, was instrumental in the controversial establishment of the Players' Union.

Newcastle United's Cup at the fourth time of asking! A victory at Crystal Palace still eluded them, though. They managed only a rugged 1–1 draw (after being a goal down for forty-six minutes) against Barnsley of the Second Division in south London – and then, deservedly, won the replay at Goodison Park with two second-half goals (one a penalty) by centre-forward Albert Shepherd. Newcastle's triumph, however, was flawed. They were fined for playing a below-strength side in an earlier round, censured for their handling of Cup final tickets and, during the replay, invoked cries of 'Dirty Newcastle' for their win-at-all-costs toughness. Back home, of course, they were lauded as heroes and, led by a pipe band, the team moved through the streets of Newcastle in eight landaus. It was the last time this Cup, the second edition of the 'little tin idol', was on parade. Unofficial duplicates had been made in Manchester and the FA decided to present it to Lord Kinnaird to mark his twenty-one years as president.

1910

23 April at Crystal Palace   Att 77,747
Newcastle United 1 (Rutherford)
Barnsley 1 (Tufnell)
Newcastle United: Lawrence, McCracken, Whitson, Veitch, Low, McWilliam, Rutherford, Howie, Shepherd, Higgins, Wilson.
Barnsley: Mearns, Downs, Ness, Glendinning, Boyle, Utley, Bartrop, Gadsby, Lillycrop, Tufnell, Forman.
Referee: J. T. Ibbotson
Replay:
28 April at Goodison Park   Att 69,000
Newcastle United 2 (Shepherd 2 (1 pen))
Barnsley 0
Newcastle United: Lawrence, McCracken, Carr, Veitch, Low, McWilliam, Rutherford, Howie, Shepherd, Higgins, Wilson.
Barnsley: Mearns, Downs, Ness, Glendinning, Boyle, Utley, Bartrop, Gadsby, Lillycrop, Tufnell, Forman.
Referee: J. T. Ibbotson

Above and left Confirmation received by Miss Theobald of somewhere in Norfolk that a cigar-smoking Magpie had acquired 'ye beggar' at last. The front of the postcard showed what the 'beggar' was – the Cup.

Far left Newcastle were skilful and intelligent and led with style by Colin Campbell McKechnie Veitch, an educated and personable man as well as a supremely accomplished player who, over the years, figured in most positions on the field. He later became a journalist.

Right Not even 'Amos' the donkey could stymie Newcastle, although many believed he had a major hoof in getting Barnsley as far as a final replay. The Edwardian era was the golden age of postcards which showed, often brilliantly, that football can be a game of humour as well as blood and sweat.

Chapter Four

All Change
1911–1922

'A treasured recollection is one of those fine exhibitions of sportsmanship that really mark the great man. It occurred in the replayed Cup final on the Manchester United ground at Old Trafford between Bradford City and Newcastle United in 1911. Colin Veitch, the Newcastle captain, had collided heavily with Thompson, the little Irishman of Bradford City, who was knocked out. Veitch himself was not much the worse, and his side was in grave danger and needed his help, but he made the great sacrifice of assisting his smaller opponent while Bradford City were actually scoring the winning goal, and when the end came he slipped quietly across to Speirs, the City captain, to be the first to congratulate him. I wrote at the time: "Those of us who observed saw the sportsman rising superior to the mere man, the spirit of camaraderie shining brightly at a time when another might have been wrangling with the referee."'

V. A. S. Beanland in *Great Games and Great Players* (1945).

The pyramid shape of the FA Cup tournament, from monumental base in late summer to starry pinnacle in early May, is one of the reasons why it has such a hold on the affections of this sporting nation. It is a perilous climb, full of hazards and secrets, and is no more to be taken for granted than an ascent of Everest. Its shape has evolved down the years, in a slow and continuous process of development, but there have been times when it might have lost its way and much of its charm and democracy.

There was a bold move by Football League clubs after the 1914–18 war to change the whole nature of the tournament. They wanted to kill the qualifying competition and restrict the first round proper to Football League clubs, the First Division of the Southern League (soon to become the Third Division of the Football League) and four others – a total of 64 clubs. The guardians of the Cup were not impressed. They took the view, wisely, that a restricted tournament would be a poorer thing and would 'seriously infringe the rights' of hundreds of its smaller clubs.

The Football League quickly expanded to eighty-six clubs, a Third Division from the South and then the North being added to its portfolio, and the Cup accommodated these changes comfortably. But then more clubs felt they should not have to play in the early stages and, in 1922, the high and low lands of the tournament were squarely balanced with six qualifying rounds and six more (including the final) in the competition proper.

Still searching for a formula that would satisfy everyone, the FA suggested that all Football League clubs should go into the draw for the first round proper. The First and Second Division clubs, not surprisingly, were implacably opposed to the idea, which would have put them on the same starting line as their Third Division colleagues. Their temper was not improved when it was disclosed that the idea had come from the Third Division clubs themselves and the proposal was still-born. However, for the 1925–26 season, the Cup adopted the basic shape which works so well today. Two qualifying rounds were lost and two added to the competition proper, making eight including semi-finals and final. The new balance allowed the tournament to develop its pace and drama more evenly until, with loud fanfare, the First and Second Division clubs entered the lists in the third round proper.

The seasons which sandwiched World War One – five before and three after – were restless but interesting. Seven out of the eight finals finished 1–0; Yorkshire clubs won the tournament four times; the final moved from its home at Crystal Palace to Old Trafford, briefly, and then Stamford Bridge; three successive drawn finals led to the introduction of 30 minutes extra-time; and the trophy was changed yet again.

The Cup was replaced in 1910 simply because several copies of it had surfaced in Manchester. The FA had no copyright on the design so they decided to commission something finer, properly registered, and to present the second edition of the 'little tin idol' to Lord Kinnaird, the grand old man of the game, to mark his twenty-one years as president of the FA.

The FA set aside fifty guineas for the new pot, invited the best silversmiths in the land to submit a design which placed more emphasis on pattern and workmanship, and were happily surprised by the large number of models and ideas they received. They chose the work of Messrs Fattorini & Sons, a Bradford firm founded by a travelling pedlar at the time of the Napoleonic Wars, and their handsome urn was to be the star of every Cup final. It was an inspired choice. Its first winners in 1911, by way of a replay, were Bradford City on the one and only occasion they have reached the final. Made in Bradford... won by Bradford.

Crystal Palace was now nearing the end of its twenty years as the second great home of the Cup final, but it still had time to stage one of the tournament's mightiest climaxes. The Cup was filled to its brim again in 1913, when the finalists were Sunderland and Aston Villa – first and second in Division One and both hell-bent on completing the first League and Cup double of the twentieth century. Sunderland, who were appearing in their first final, had one of the best sides in their history; Aston Villa, who had won three of their games on the way to the final by 5–0, were the most admired team in the country.

Villa had the one and only Sam Hardy in goal, Charlie Wallace who was to give fifty years service to the club as player, scout and back-room boy, the legendary Harry Hampton at centre-forward and Clem Stephenson, their stocky inspiration, who would later help Huddersfield win three Championships in a row. Sunderland had Charlie Buchan, who later joined Arsenal but always regarded the 1912–13 season as 'the most successful and thrilling' of his career, and such indomitables as Frank Cuggy and Jack Mordue – the trio forming the famous 'Sunderland triangle'.

The match attracted more than 120,000, then the biggest crowd to have watched a game of football, although many claimed they were unable to see much of a turbulent battle which Aston Villa won with a late, headed goal by their right-half Tommy Barber for their fifth Cup triumph. Sunderland, by way of compensation, drew a League game at Villa Park the following Wednesday and went on to pip the Birmingham club for the title.

King George V, the first monarch to attend a final, sported a red rose for the all-Lancashire confrontation between Burnley and Liverpool in 1914 – the last final to be played at Crystal Palace with its little 'flower pot' stands and open acres of grass, on which supporters had paraded and laid out their picnics for two decades. It had served the game well.

Three months later, war was declared and Lord Kitchener of Khartoum, the Secretary of State for War, pointed his finger at the nation's young men and urged them to volunteer for a more important contest. The Cup and League were to have one more season, however, despite muddled claims that football was somehow undermining enlistment and therefore contributing to a German victory. In fact, the FA had taken advice from the War Office and it was considered that football, as well as being a useful antidote to the poison of war, provided a valuable platform for recruitment.

Crystal Palace became a war depot and so the 1915 final, football's last big scene for five years, was played at Old Trafford. The five-year-old stadium was the pride of Manchester but the game between Sheffield United and Chelsea matched the greyness of the day and the gloom of the period. It has become known as the 'Khaki final', because so many uniformed soldiers were present, and is remembered more for the Earl of Derby's parting words than for its football. There are several versions of what he said, but the most stirring is: 'You have played with one another and against one another for the Cup. It is now the duty of everyone to join with each other and play a sterner game for England.'

A new home had to be found for the final after the war and, with Stamford Bridge, Chelsea's home in south-west London, chosen for three years, the character of the event changed again. Finals at Crystal Palace had been social as well as sporting occasions, but Stamford Bridge was a football ground, nothing much more, and its big banks enabled everyone to follow every kick. Minimum charge was three shillings and, for that, supporters were offered a final with no trimmings.

The game once more provided pleasure and diversion for a country that would soon know depression. Aston Villa won the Cup for a record sixth time in 1920, Tottenham followed with their first triumph for twenty years, and in 1922 Huddersfield Town lifted the trophy for the first time. Only a few seasons before, the Yorkshire club had been on the point of financial collapse, but the townspeople rallied to their cause and, almost overnight, Huddersfield entered the most successful period in their history. The Cup, too, was about to begin a new era.

1911

22 April at Crystal Palace   Att 69,098

Bradford City 0
Newcastle United 0

Bradford City: Mellors, Campbell, Taylor, Robinson, Gildea, McDonald, Logan, Speirs, O'Rourke, Devine, Thompson.

Newcastle United: Lawrence, McCracken, Whitson, Veitch, Low, Willis, Rutherford, Jobey, Stewart, Higgins, Wilson.

Referee: J. H. Pearson

Replay:

26 April at Old Trafford   Att 58,000

Bradford City 1 (Speirs)
Newcastle United 0

Bradford City: Mellors, Campbell, Taylor, Robinson, Torrance, McDonald, Logan, Speirs, O'Rourke, Devine, Thompson.

Newcastle United: Lawrence, McCracken, Whitson, Veitch, Low, Willis, Rutherford, Jobey, Stewart, Higgins, Wilson.

Referee: J. H. Pearson

Left Crystal Palace during the 1911 final between Bradford City and Newcastle United (0–0). 'It seemed as if every vehicle in London might have been pressed into service to take the people to Sydenham,' observed the *Daily Mirror*. The ground's three stands were all on the north side, two with decorated gables and a smaller pavilion between them. Most of the crowd were on grassy banks, many more than fifty yards from the pitch and able to catch only glimpses of play. The National Recreation Centre is now on the site.

Above Bradford City's winning goal in the replay at Old Trafford, a soft affair scored by captain J. H. Speirs after fifteen minutes. Speirs, an international and one of eight Scots in Bradford's side, was killed in World War One. Newcastle United, runners-up yet again, had thus taken part in five finals in seven years — and won only one.

Below Made in Bradford, won by Bradford. A glittering new FA Cup, the tournament's third trophy, waits to be presented by Charles Crump (hatless, left of Cup), vice-president of the FA. **Players** (*left to right*) – D. Taylor, F. Thompson, G. Robinson, A. Devine, R. Torrance, P. Logan, J. Speirs. The season was the finest in Bradford's history: Cup winners for the one and only time and fifth position (their best) in Division One. The new trophy, made by Messrs Fattorini & Sons of Bradford, served until 1991.

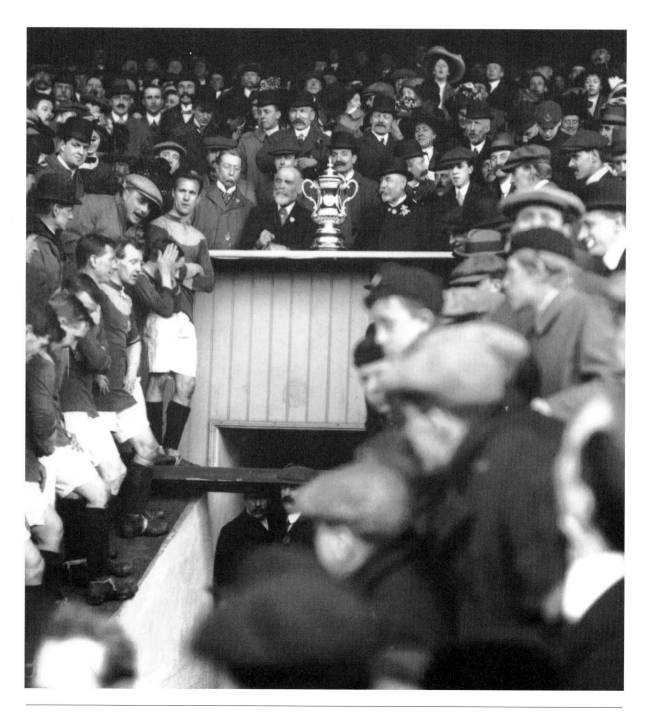

1912

20 April at Crystal Palace   Att 54,556

Barnsley 0

West Bromwich Albion 0

Barnsley: Cooper, Downs, Taylor, Glendinning, Bratley, Utley, Bartrop, Tufnell, Lillycrop, Travers, Moore.

West Bromwich Albion: Pearson, Cook, Pennington, Baddeley, Buck, McNeal, Jephcott, Wright, Pailor, Bowser, Shearman.

Referee: J. R. Schumacher

Replay: 24 April at Bramall Lane   Att 38,555

Barnsley 1 (Tufnell)

West Bromwich Albion 0   aet

Barnsley: Cooper, Downs, Taylor, Glendinning, Bratley, Utley, Bartrop, Tufnell, Lillycrop, Travers, Moore.

West Bromwich Albion: Pearson, Cook, Pennington, Baddeley, Buck, McNeal, Jephcott, Wright, Pailor, Bowser, Shearman.

Referee: J. R. Schumacher

'Battling' Barnsley conceded only three goals in twelve Cup ties (including four games against the holders Bradford City) to become the third Second Division club to win the Cup. For the third season running, the final went to a replay, which Barnsley won with a runaway goal by inside-right Harry Tufnell two minutes from the end of extra-time. But would they have won if Jesse Pennington had been less of a gentleman? The Albion captain was the last defender in front of Tufnell and could have brought him down – but that wasn't his way. And Tufnell won the Cup.

Above and left Backyard background for two backs. Archie Taylor, (left) captain of Barnsley, the 1912 Cup winners, and Jesse Pennington, West Bromwich Albion's skipper, both left-backs. Pennington was a classic defender for Albion (nearly five hundred games) and England (twenty-five caps), a sportsman and one of the game's outstanding figures who won almost everything worth winning. But, unlike the vested Taylor (5ft 9in, 13½ stone), he never managed a Cup-winner's medal.

Below A record crowd watched Aston Villa face Sunderland, two clubs bent on the first League and Cup double of the century. The attendance was given first as 121,919 but later amended to 120,081. Many inside saw very little of the game. Many outside, perched precariously in trees, saw everything.

It was Sunderland's first final and many believed that their side, built around the famous 'triangle' of Charlie Buchan, Frank Cuggy and Jackie Mordue, was the best in the club's history. But they lost to a seventy-fifth-minute goal by right-half Tommy Barber, who headed in a corner by Charlie Wallace to give Villa their fifth Cup triumph. Sunderland, though, finished as League champions.

Opposite The full ground, Barber's winning goal and presentation by the Earl of Plymouth were pictured in the *Illustrated London News*, which commented: 'It has been suggested of late that a good many British workmen spend too much time watching football matches, and it has even been asserted that the fact that three large steamers are now being built in France for a British shipping firm is due to the refusal of shipbuilding hands in this country to work full time: in support of this it is said that the men's officials acknowledge that 18.8 per cent of the possible working time is lost – chiefly by the craze for attending such matches.'

1913

19 April at Crystal Palace   Att 120,081
Aston Villa 1 (Barber)
Sunderland 0
Aston Villa: Hardy, Lyons, Weston, Barber, Harrop, Leach, Wallace, Halse, Hampton, Stephenson, Bache.
Sunderland: Butler, Gladwin, Ness, Cuggy, Thomson, Low, Mordue, Buchan, Richardson, Holley, Martin.
Referee: A. Adams

Below Tommy Boyle of Burnley was the first captain to receive the Cup from a reigning monarch – the last formal act of the last and twentieth final to be played at Crystal Palace. King George V sported a red rose, for an all-Lancashire occasion and, according to the *Daily Mirror*, 'there was no mistaking the heartiness of the greeting football gave His Majesty'. The game itself was not much of a dish to set before a king, but Burnley were honest winners of the Cup for the first time with a goal by their England centre-forward Bertie Freeman thirteen minutes after half-time. The entry for the tournament was a record 476. Just three months later, war was declared.

1914

25 April at Crystal Palace   Att 72,778
Burnley 1 (Freeman)
Liverpool 0
Burnley: Sewell, Bamford, Taylor, Halley, Boyle, Watson, Nesbitt, Lindley, Freeman, Hodgson, Mosscrop.
Liverpool: Campbell, Longworth, Pursell, Fairfoul, Ferguson, McKinlay, Sheldon, Metcalfe, Miller, Lacey, Nicholl.
Referee: H. S. Bamlett

THE ILLUSTRATED LONDON NEWS, MAY 2, 1914.–718

THE KING'S FIRST CUP FINAL: THE GREAT ASSOCIATION EVENT

DISCIPLES OF ST. SIMEON STYLITES: LIVING "STATUES" WATCHING THE FOOTBALL ASSOCIATION CUP FINAL.

SEEING MORE OF THE CROWD THAN OF THE GAME: SOLDIERS SEATED ON POSTS.

WINNERS OF THE CHIEF TROPHY OF ASSOCIATION FOOTBALL FOR THE FIRST TIME: THE BURNLEY TEAM.

SOME OF THE 120,000 SPECTATORS: A SECTION OF THE VAST CROWD AT THE CRYSTAL PALACE.

THE DECISIVE MOMENT: FREEMAN, THE BURNLEY CENTRE FORWARD SCORES THE ONLY GOAL OF THE MATCH.

WEARING THE RED ROSE OF LANCASTER IN HIS BUTTON-HOLE: THE KING AT THE CUP FINAL.

PUNCH, OR THE LONDON CHARIVARI.—October 21, 1914.

THE GREATER GAME.

Mr. Punch (*to Professional Association Player*). "NO DOUBT YOU CAN MAKE MONEY IN THIS FIELD, MY FRIEND, BUT THERE'S ONLY ONE FIELD TO-DAY WHERE YOU CAN GET HONOUR."

1915

24 April at Old Trafford   Att 49,557
Sheffield United 3 (Simmons, Masterman, Kitchen)
Chelsea 0
Sheffield United: Gough, Cook, English, Sturgess, Brelsford, Utley, Simmons, Fazackerley, Kitchen, Masterman, Evans.
Chelsea: Molyneux, Bettridge, Harrow, Taylor, Logan, Walker, Ford, Halse, Thomson, Croal, McNeil.
Referee: H. H. Taylor

Left A tart comment by *Punch* on the FA's decision to let the FA Cup run its course in the first winter after the outbreak of the Great War – 'just as if the country did not need the services of all its athletes for the serious business of war'. *Punch* was apparently unaware that the FA had taken advice from the War Office and football, it had been agreed, would help national morale.

Left The 1915 final is remembered as the 'Khaki final' because of the number of servicemen (many of them wounded) who were present. Progress of the game was also wired to ships at sea. It was held at Old Trafford because the Crystal Palace had become a war depot – but, in keeping with the weather and the mood of the nation, it was a grey and joyless occasion. It was also the last big match in England for four years.

Aston Villa won the Cup for a record sixth time, at Stamford Bridge, the home of the final for three years after World War One. Although Stamford Bridge was not as big or as much fun as Crystal Palace, its lofty terraces enabled everyone to see the game. Minimum charge: three shillings.

Aston Villa also solved an embarrassing dilemma for the Football Association. Chelsea reached the semi-finals and, arrangements being too far advanced to switch to a neutral venue, the possibility of Chelsea playing in a Cup final on their own ground loomed large. Villa, however, beat them 3–1 in their semi-final at Bramall Lane with Billy Walker scoring twice.

Above Eight Huddersfield Town players are in the picture as they defend against Aston Villa. They held out until extra-time and the hundredth minute, when Villa's Billy Kirton and Tom Wilson, Huddersfield's centre-half, jumped together for a corner and the ball seemed to go into the net off Kirton's head – a fact confirmed by referee Jack 'Jimmy' Howcroft. Sixty-one years later, at the hundredth final, Jack Swann, another of Huddersfield's team, insisted it was an own goal by Wilson. But Howcroft, the strongest and most respected referee of his day, was rarely wrong.

Huddersfield's season was remarkable. At its start they were near to liquidation for financial reasons, but the townspeople rallied generously, players were sold – and they finished it by winning promotion from the Second Division and reaching the FA Cup final.

1920

24 April at Stamford Bridge   Att 50,018

Aston Villa 1 (Kirton)

Huddersfield Town 0   aet

Aston Villa: Hardy, Smart, Weston, Ducat, Barson, Moss, Wallace, Kirton, Walker, Stephenson, Dorrell.

Huddersfield Town: Mutch, Wood, Bullock, Slade, Wilson, Watson, Richardson, Mann, Taylor, Swann, Islip.

Referee: J. T. Howcroft

Above The Invincibles of Preston North End who completed the first double, winning the League without losing a game and the Cup without conceding a goal, in season 1888–89. *Back row (left to right)* – G. Drummond, R. Howarth, Right Hon. R. W. Hanbury MP, Sir W. E. M. Tomlinson MP, D. Russell, R. Holmes, W. Sudell (manager), J. Graham, Dr Mills-Roberts. *Front row* – J. Gordon, J. Ross, J. Goodall, F. Dewhurst, S. Thomson.

Left Nineteenth-century Staffordshire mug. The match depicted is a matter of debate. Some believe it is an early Cup final. Others think it shows the Old Etonians in action.

THE FOOTBALL ASSOCIATION.

1881

President.

Major F. A. Marindin, R.E. (Old Etonians.)

Hon. Treasurer.	Hon. Secretary.
Hon. A. F. Kinnaird. (Old Etonians)	C. W. Alcock. (Wanderers.)

COMMITTEE.

J. H. Clark (Maidenhead)	N. L. Jackson (Finchley)	R. A. Ogilvie (Clapham Rovers)	S. R. Bastard (Upton Park)
R. de C. Welch (Old Harrovians)	C. E. Hart (Pilgrims)	E. H. Bambridge (Swifts)	E. D. Ellis (Nottingham)
E. J. Wild (Cambridge University)	H. H. Massey (Royal Engineers)	J. H. Evans (Grisham)	Hart Buck (Hendon)
C. H. R. Wollaston (Wanderers)	F. G. Guy (Oxford University)	F. Ted (Queens Park Glasgow)	E. J. Sparks (Clapham Rovers)

At a Meeting of the Committee, held on Wednesday, February 9th 1881, Major F. A. Marindin, R.E. President of the Football Association, in the Chair. the following Resolution, proposed by the Honble A. F. Kinnaird, and Seconded by Mr R. A. Ogilvie,

Was Carried by Acclamation:—

THAT the Committee of the Football Association, acting on behalf of the Subscribers to the 'Alcock Testimonial Fund.' Present to

Mr Charles W. Alcock,

Honorary Secretary of the Football Association, a Silver Inkstand & Candlesticks, with a Purse of Three Hundred Guineas, in recognition of all that he has done, during the past eighteen years, to establish and further the Association Game: and that the Committee, in their name and in the name of all players scattered throughout the Kingdom, tender to Mr Alcock the expression of their sincere thanks for the zeal and energy with which, since its foundation in 1863, he has discharged his duties as Honorary Secretary to the Association: and further record their unanimous conviction that the success which has attended the Association in all its undertakings and the established position the Game now occupies among Winter Sports, are due, in no ordinary degree, to the loyal and untiring devotion with which he has ever sought to promote its interests and prosperity.

On the Motion of Mr J. H. Clark, Seconded by Mr R. de C. Welch.

It was Unanimously Resolved; **That** the above Resolution, suitably engrossed, be presented to Mr Alcock as a lasting memento of his long connection with the Football Association.

President of the Football Association.

Left The Charles Alcock scroll, presented by the FA to the 'father' of the Cup in 1881 'in recognition of all that he has done during the past eighteen years to establish and further the Association game'. The scroll was accompanied by a silver inkstand and candlesticks and a purse of 300 guineas – then a very handsome sum.

Above A remarkable illustration from *Boy's Own Paper*, 1881. It shows many of the leading players in the first decade of the FA Cup.

Back row (left to right) – Charles Campbell (captain of Queen's Park and Scotland, FA Cup finalist 1884 and 1885), Charles Caborn (played in Nottingham Forest's first Cup tie, against Notts County, 16 November 1878), Tom Marshall (Darwen, Blackburn Olympic and England), Harry Swepstone (Pilgrims and England, founder member of Corinthians), John Hunter (Wednesday, FA Cup winner with Blackburn Olympic 1883, Blackburn Rovers and England), Sam Weller Widdowson (Nottingham Forest and England, inventor of shinguards), Edwin Luntley (Nottingham Forest, member of their first Cup side, and England), James Frederick McLeod Prinsep (youngest Cup finalist, 17 years 245 days, for Clapham Rovers in 1879, Cup winner with Old Carthusians in 1881, and England), Harry McNeil (Queen's Park and Scotland), William Lindsay (Cup winner with Wanderers 1876, 1877 and 1878, and England), John Sands (England goalkeeper and another of Forest's first Cup team), Tom Brindle (Darwen, Blackburn Olympic and England), William Mosforth (Sheffield Wednesday, Sheffield United and England). *Seated (on right)* – Francis Sparks (Cup winner with Clapham Rovers 1880, and England). *Front row* – Herbert Whitfield (Cup winner with Old Etonians in 1879, finalist 1881, and England), Norman Bailey (Old Westminsters, Cup finalist Clapham Rovers 1879, Cup winner 1880, Corinthians, Wanderers and England), Edward Bambridge (Upton Park, Clapham Rovers, Swifts and England, later secretary of Corinthians) and F. W. Earp (who also played in Forest's first Cup tie in 1878).

Above Kennington Oval: first home of the FA Cup final (1872, 1874–92).

Below Sheffield Wednesday Cup winner's medal 1907 (left), won by Andrew Wilson of Scotland, one of the finest centre-forwards Wednesday ever had. Blackpool runners-up medal 1948 (right), received by inside-right Alex Munro, also of Scotland, after one of Wembley's best finals. His partner on the right wing was Stanley Matthews.

STADIUM FROM THE LAKE.

Tower Entrance
Stadium, Wembley.

Visions of splendour. Artistic
impressions of Wembley for the
British Empire Exhibition in 1924.

TRAVEL BY 'METRO'
TO THE CUP FINAL
SATURDAY 28TH APRIL 1923
BOLTON WANDERERS v WEST HAM

SPECIAL RETURN
FARE FROM THIS
STATION TO
WEMBLEY PARK

1s 0d

'METRO' STATION
ACTUALLY ADJOINS
BRITISH EMPIRE
EXHIBITION GROUNDS

QUICKEST, MOST DIRECT
AND CONVENIENT ROUTE

BAKER STREET STATION. LONDON, N.W.I.

R.H. SELBIE, General Manager.

Left An advertisement which might have worked too well. More than 200,000 turned up for the first FA Cup final at Wembley in 1923.

Below The Rev. Henry Francis Lyte of All Saints Church, Brixham, Devon – and the hymn he wrote shortly before his death in 1847.

Below left Options open. A postcard sold before the 1903–4 season featuring the names and colours of thirty-two possible winners. Woolwich and Stockton are among them – but this was Manchester City's year.

Right The programme for the 1930 final between Arsenal and Huddersfield Town, Herbert Chapman's new club versus his old. Charlie Buchan, Chapman's first signing as Arsenal manager in 1925, had now retired and was a much publicised football correspondent – a job he did until 1956.

ABIDE WITH ME
(HENRY FRANCIS LYTE)

Abide with me; fast falls the eventide;
The darkness deepens; Lord, with me abide!
When other helpers fail, and comforts flee,
Help of the helpless, O abide with me.

I need Thy presence every passing hour;
What but Thy grace can foil the tempter's power?
Who like Thyself my guide and stay can be?
Through cloud and sunshine, Lord, abide with me

Hold Thou Thy Cross before my closing eyes;
Shine through the gloom, and point me to the skies;
Heav'n's morning breaks, and earth's vain shadows flee;
In life, in death. O Lord, abide with me.

Swift to its close ebbs out life's little day;
Earth's joys grow dim, it's glories pass away;
Change and decay in all around I see;
O Thou, who changest not, abide with me.

I fear no foe, with Thee at hand to bless;
Ills have no weight, and tears no bitterness;
Where is death's sting? where, grave, thy victory?
I triumph still, if Thou abide with me.

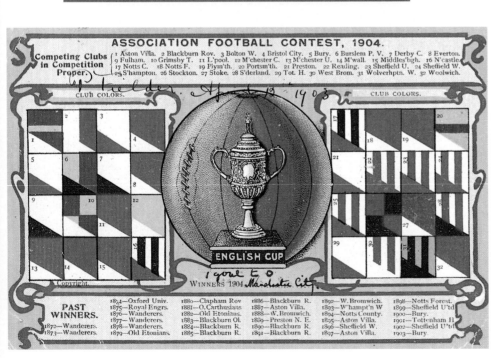

ASSOCIATION FOOTBALL CONTEST, 1904.

Competing Clubs in Competition Proper.

1 Aston Villa. 2 Blackburn Rov. 3 Bolton W. 4 Bristol City. 5 Bury. 6 Burslem P. V. 7 Derby C. 8 Everton. 9 Fulham. 10 Grimsby T. 11 L'pool. 12 M'chester C. 13 M'chester U. 14 M'wall. 15 Middles'bgh. 16 N'castle. 17 Notts C. 18 Notts F. 19 Plym'th. 20 Portsm'th. 21 Preston. 22 Reading. 23 Sheffield U. 24 Sheffield W. 25 S'hampton. 26 Stockton. 27 Stoke. 28 S'derland. 29 Tot. H. 30 West Brom. 31 Wolverh'ptn. W. 32 Woolwich.

CLUB COLORS. CLUB COLORS.

ENGLISH CUP

WINNERS 1904 Manchester City

PAST WINNERS.				
	1874—Oxford Univ.	1880—Clapham Rov	1886—Blackburn R.	1892—W. Bromwich.	1898—Notts Forest.
	1875—Royal Engrs.	1881—O. Carthusians	1887—Aston Villa.	1893—W'hampt'n W	1899—Sheffield U'td
	1876—Wanderers.	1882—Old Etonians.	1888—W. Bromwich.	1894—Notts County.	1900—Bury.
	1877—Wanderers.	1883—Blackburn Ol.	1889—Preston N. E.	1895—Aston Villa.	1901—Tottenham H
1872—Wanderers.	1878—Wanderers.	1884—Blackburn R.	1890—Blackburn R.	1896—Sheffield W.	1902—Sheffield U'td
1873—Wanderers.	1879—Old Etonians.	1885—Blackburn R.	1891—Blackburn R.	1897—Aston Villa.	1903—Bury.

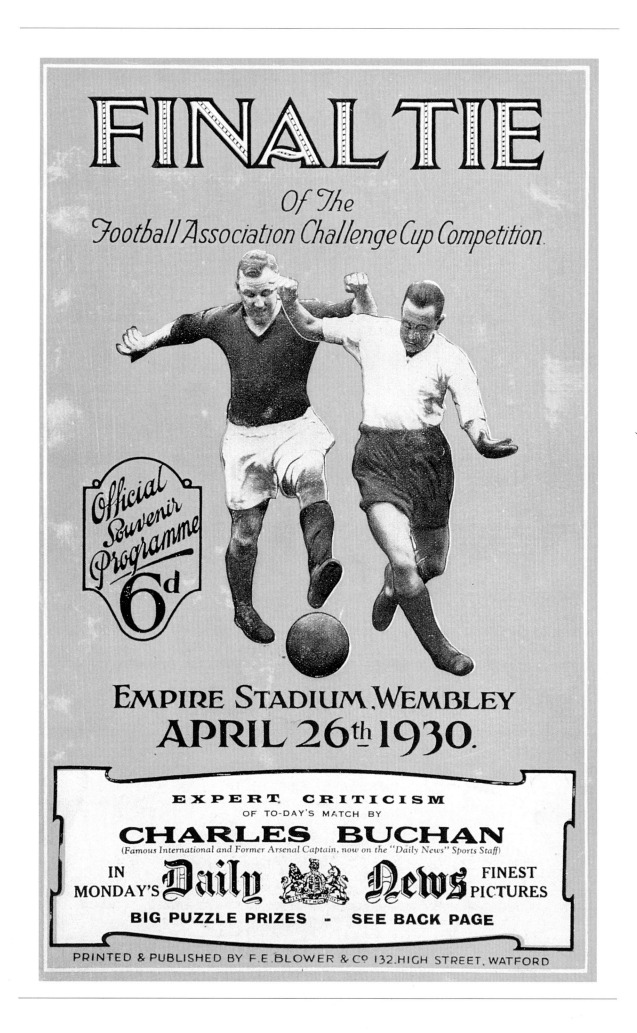

FINAL TIE

Of The
Football Association Challenge Cup Competition.

Official Souvenir Programme 6d

EMPIRE STADIUM, WEMBLEY
APRIL 26th 1930.

EXPERT CRITICISM
OF TO-DAY'S MATCH BY

CHARLES BUCHAN

(Famous International and Former Arsenal Captain, now on the "Daily News" Sports Staff)

IN MONDAY'S *Daily News* FINEST PICTURES

BIG PUZZLE PRIZES — SEE BACK PAGE

PRINTED & PUBLISHED BY F.E. BLOWER & Cº 132, HIGH STREET, WATFORD

Left The subtle humour of football.

Below Two 1925 biscuit tins, in the manner of the FA Cup, by Huntley and Palmer. They were sold at a Christie's auction in 1996 for more than £1,000.

Below Billy Walker, a cardinal figure in Aston Villa's success in 1920 and a man who would win the Cup twice more, as a manager with different clubs – Sheffield Wednesday (1935) and Nottingham Forest (1959). Walker, the son of a Wolverhampton Wanderers full-back, George Walker, played his first game (scoring twice) for Villa in the first round of their 1920 Cup run and went on to 531 League and Cup games (244 goals) and eighteen caps for England (1921–33). An inspiring inside-forward with a stunning swerve, he was the most popular Villa player since "Appy 'Arry" Hampton. His career as a player and manager spanned forty years.

Left Jimmy Dimmock (white shirt above photographers to right of goal) scores Tottenham Hotspur's winner against Second Division Wolverhampton Wanderers in the 1921 final at Stamford Bridge. Dimmock, not yet twenty-one and a brilliant outside-left soon to be picked for England, finds the bottom right corner of Wolves' net in the fifty-third minute – and the Cup is won by a London club for the first time since Spurs' own triumph in 1901. The pitch was a quagmire after morning rain, sunshine and then a violent thunderstorm just before kick-off. The photographer who took this picture said later: 'I was without a permit so I climbed up a gigantic advertising display board. The picture earned me a ten guinea bonus.'

1921

23 April at Stamford Bridge   Att 72,805

Tottenham Hotspur 1
(Dimmock)

Wolverhampton Wanderers 0

Tottenham Hotspur: Hunter, Clay, McDonald, Smith, Walters, Grimsdell, Banks, Seed, Cantrell, Bliss, Dimmock.

Wolverhampton Wanderers: George, Woodward, Marshall, Gregory, Hodnett, Riley, Lea, Burrill, Edmonds, Potts, Brooks.

Referee: J. Davies

Above Spurs begin their journey home from Stamford Bridge to White Hart Lane with the Cup, decorated by the original blue and white ribbons, lovingly preserved, from their 1901 victory. There are twenty-five people in the charabanc which, for the final part of its journey through crowded streets, was led by the Tottenham Town Band. A *Daily News* reporter wrote: 'The Cup returns to the South, like a wanderer from strange lands, beaming on London with its silver arms akimbo and still wondering why it is that only one Southern professional club has ever given it hospitality.'

Below Huddersfield Town on the threshold of greatness. Herbert Chapman was their manager, the mercurial Clem Stephenson (a Cup winner in 1913 and 1920) had joined them from Aston Villa and Sam Wadsworth of England, an impeccable left-back, was the cornerstone of a resolute defence. The Cup in 1922 was their first major success and they went on to win the League Championship three seasons in a row (1924, 1925 and 1926).

Huddersfield Town: *Back row (left to right)* – H. Chapman (manager), J. Wood, C. McKay, C. Slade, A. Mutch, T. Wilson (captain), W. Watson, S. Wadsworth, J. Chaplin. *Seated* – G. Richardson, F. Mann, G. Brown, E. Islip, W. Johnstone, C. Stephenson, W. Smith.

The 1922 final was identified as a candidate for 'the worst final of all time' – cautious, mistake-ridden and remembered mostly for Huddersfield's controversial winner, the first penalty-kick to decide a final. Most reporters were convinced that Billy Smith of England was outside the area when he was brought down in the sixty-seventh minute – an opinion confirmed by news film – with Smith himself then converting the kick.

James Frederick Mitchell (inset), Preston's amateur goalkeeper who wore glasses and a bandeau, danced about on his line, waving his arms, in a vain attempt to distract Smith. The outcome was a new rule forbidding goalkeepers to move before a penalty is taken.

1922

29 April at Stamford Bridge   Att 53,000
Huddersfield Town 1
  (Smith (pen))
Preston North End 0
Huddersfield Town: Mutch, Wood, Wadsworth, Slade, Wilson, Watson, Richardson, Mann, Islip, Stephenson, Smith.
Preston North End: Mitchell, Hamilton, Doolan, Duxbury, McCall, Williamson, Rawlings, Jefferis, Roberts, Woodhouse, Quinn.
Referee: J. W. D. Fowler

Chapter Five

Horse and Hymn
1923–1930

'Bolton Wanderers, by winning the FA Cup a third time in seven years, earned a new nickname. They are now likely to be known as the "3–6–9's" instead of the "Trotters". They won the Cup in 1923, 1926 and 1929 and gave an improved display in each match. One thing was proved beyond question in 1929 and that was that the old style of football with the forwards all in a line can still be exploited successfully, for after Bolton had failed to score with the exaggerated "W" formation in the first-half they resorted to the old style and won. What was still more pleasing to Englishmen was that their team included no fewer than eight English-born players.'

Daily Express Football Annual **(1929–30).**

The FA Cup began a new and ardent romance in 1923. Wembley Stadium appeared, handsomely, on the north London skyline and it was love at first sight. They are still together.

Wembley timed its grand entrance perfectly, because the Football Association were looking urgently for a new home for the final of their big annual shindig. Stamford Bridge was too small and the FA were even considering a return to Crystal Palace, despite the daunting costs involved. But the FA were then told that the centre-piece of the British Empire Exhibition, a spectacle designed to bring the dominions and colonies closer together by way of business, education and a bit of fun, would be 'a great national sports ground'. Were they interested? They were indeed!

Wembley was then a green and pleasant suburb, six crow-miles to the north-west of central London, with a golf course and a metropolitan railway station. Many considered it too far out of town and even the idea of an Empire exhibition raised little enthusiasm or money. But, when it was revealed that a new home for football was part of the plan, attitudes suddenly changed. Funds and guarantees flowed in. Glasgow alone raised £105,000 in two months.

The FA signed an agreement in 1921 to stage the final at Wembley for twenty-one years, an act of faith and courage which had enormous significance. It made the building of the stadium possible, ensured that the British Empire Exhibition would take place and changed forever the character of the suburb of Wembley. Shortage of time meant the exhibition had to be put back a year, but this did not affect the plan to hold the 1923 Cup final on its new stage.

The Duke of York (later King George VI) cut the first piece of turf on 10 January 1922 and, almost at once, the stadium began to rise dramatically. It took just three hundred working days to build, from first sod to last lick of white paint, a marvel in reinforced concrete, the mightiest stadium on earth. It was 890 feet long, 650 feet wide, 76 feet high and built with 25,000 tons of concrete, 2,000 tons of steel and 500,000 rivets. Its two domed towers soared up to 126 feet, grand symbols of pride and confidence. Its capacity was estimated at 127,000 (and perhaps a few more). Total cost was £750,000 and it was completed just four days before the meeting of Bolton Wanderers and West Ham United in the forty-eighth Cup final. Regulated admission by ticket was not even considered. There was room for all.

Saturday 28 April 1923 dawned brightly: the FA and Wembley waited confidently. And the people came … enough to fill two Wembley stadiums. By one o'clock the ground was full, and by 1.45, when the gates were eventually closed, nearly 200,000 were inside, with tens of thousands more besieging the stadium's 104 turnstiles. Gates were broken down and walls scaled. One newspaper reported that police, officials and stewards were 'whirled away like twigs in a Severn spate'. The only escape from the crush on the terraces was on to the pitch, which was soon black with people; yet, somewhere in the middle of all this chaos, the bands of the Grenadier and Irish Guards played light and lilting music. King George V arrived at 2.45 to be told by Frederick Wall, the secretary of the FA: 'I fear, sir, that the match may not be played. The crowd has broken in and the ground is covered with people.'

But the game did start, forty-five minutes late, and there were several reasons for this considerable miracle. The crowd, above all, remained largely good-tempered, a testimony to British character, and it responded to both the presence of the King and firm and patient control by the police – with a thirteen-year-old white horse called Billy, ridden by Constable George Scorey, at the heart of it all. Wembley's first final is thus remembered as the White Horse final.

The pitch, when the game eventually began, had a human wall pressing in on the touchlines and goal-lines, so that the ball and even players disappeared regularly into the crowd. The final was completed with difficulty, but without serious mishap, and Bolton became the first club to win the Cup at Wembley. They beat West Ham 2–0 and the great David Jack became the first player to score a goal there.

Although this dramatic day is remembered with affection and wonder, it must also be seen as a near disaster. The Government immediately inquired into the management of crowds on big occasions – the first significant effort to face the problem – and its proposals embraced policing, crush barriers, pens, channelled approaches, licences for grounds and, reasonably, advance booking. Every Cup final since has been all-ticket.

Wembley's authorities carried the can for the 1923 fiasco, but the FA were not blameless. Experienced observers estimated the attendance at around 250,000, while the FA's official figure was 126,047. Nearly £3,000 was returned to ticket-holders who had been unable to claim their seats. A famous day, yes, but also one of many salutary lessons for football.

The challenge of the South was growing and four London clubs as well as Southampton reached the last eight in 1923. But Bolton Wanderers, one of the founder members of the Football League, sturdily and wholesomely Lancastrian, were the outstanding Cup side of the decade. They won the Cup again in 1926 and 1929, and in three finals they used only seventeen players. Newcastle United, Sheffield United and Blackburn Rovers were other northern warriors who quickly enjoyed the ritual of victory at the game's new Mecca. Two fresh names, however, were soon to be inscribed on the Cup: Cardiff City and Arsenal. They met in the 1927 final, a game with an international flavour, and Cardiff's 1–0 victory meant the Cup left England for the only time in its history. It was also the first final to be broadcast by BBC Radio.

Cardiff have never matched their Cup success of the 1920s, when they reached at least the quarter-finals five times in seven seasons, but Arsenal's arrival as a power in the land was much more significant. The reason was an ample Yorkshireman called Herbert Chapman.

Chapman's influence on his clubs and the game was remarkable: he made history from raw putty. Huddersfield Town, when he joined them in 1920, had crippling debts, modest resources and frustratingly poor crowds in a town devoted to Rugby League. Arsenal, when he moved to north London in 1925, had only just avoided relegation and were run on eccentric lines. They refused to sign players who were under 5ft 8in or 11st; the top transfer fee they would pay was £1,000 (the record fee at the time was £5,500); and, abandoning their scouting system, they aimed to sign only local players.

Yet Chapman built a side for each club that was good enough to win the League Championship in three successive seasons (Huddersfield 1924–26, Arsenal 1933–35) as well as becoming regular visitors to Wembley. Arsenal and Huddersfield even met in the 1930 final, symbolically, with his new club beating his old by 2–0 in a game of high skill and breathless action. Another power also cast its shadow over Wembley that day – the German airship Graf Zeppelin.

Chapman redefined the job of the football manager. He demanded power, loyalty and obedience and, in return, he was scrupulously true to his word. He was a strategist, motivator, businessman, gambler and publicist, a man with a natural nose for talent and a rare ability to make the most of it. He was also an innovator. He advocated white balls, all-weather pitches and floodlights; he experimented with numbered shirts, independent time-keepers and goal-judges; he introduced the stopper centre-half when the off-side law was changed in 1925; and he even had the name of Highbury's local underground station changed from Gillespie Road to Arsenal. He was years ahead of his time.

The Cup final, meanwhile, was still acquiring new traditions, and in 1927, the year in which organised community singing began at Wembley, it added a hymn to its list. It was 'Abide With Me', the favourite hymn of King George and Queen Mary who asked for its inclusion on the song sheet. It is a melancholy oblation, a dirge, a hymn about approaching death which was written by a Devon vicar in 1847, but it does not matter because the Cup has more to do with emotion than logic. 'Abide With Me' has become part of the Wembley ritual, its deep, stirring sound knitting together different loyalties and backgrounds and providing a moment of unity before the battle to come.

Wembley's grand opening. A crowd of more than 200,000 turned up to launch 'the mightiest stadium on earth' and a thirteen-year-old white horse called Billy nosed his way into history as he helped control the huge but good-natured crowd.

This, always, will be 'the White Horse final'. The official attendance was given as 126,047 with gross receipts of £27,776, but these figures reveal nothing of a chaotic occasion which stopped only just short of disaster.

Above The scene which met King George V when he arrived at 2.45 p.m. FA secretary Frederick Wall told him: 'I fear, sir, that the match may not be played.'

Left and right Same aim, different approach. Some found an easy way into Wembley. One took the scenic route.

1923

28 April at Wembley   Att 126,047

Bolton Wanderers 2 (Jack,
    J. R. Smith)

West Ham United 0

Bolton Wanderers: Pym, Haworth,
    Finney, Nuttall, Seddon, Jennings,
    Butler, Jack, J. R. Smith, J. Smith,
    Vizard.

West Ham United: Hufton,
    Henderson, Young, Bishop, Kay,
    Tresadern, Richards, Brown,
    Watson, Moore, Ruffell.

Referee: D. H. Asson

Right Billy, the White Horse of
Wembley, ridden by Constable
George Scorey. 'He dominated the
crowd by the sheer force of his
personality,' wrote one observer.
Other horses also did a splendid
job, but only one was white. Scorey,
a former Scots Greys trumpet major
who was not keen on football, said
later: 'We were given orders to clear
the pitch. Clear the pitch indeed!
You couldn't see it. I felt like giving it
up as hopeless. Anyway, Billy knew
what to do. He pushed forward
quietly but firmly and the crowd
made way for him. They seemed to
respect him. I told them to link
hands and push back and I remember telling one chap with one leg
to get in the goal and stay there.'
And the band played on.

Above The final is under way, forty-five minutes late, and the pitch is surrounded by a human wall. Ball and players disappeared into it at regular intervals. David Jack of Bolton scored Wembley's first Cup final goal in the third minute and, after the players had remained on the field at half-time, John Smith added a controversial second – with West Ham United protesting that a Bolton Wanderers fan had kicked the ball back into play before Ted Vizard centred. West Ham then asked for the game to be abandoned. It was too late for that.

Opposite top An admirably restrained headline on the morning after.

Right One of the 35,527 tickets issued for the 1923 final. All finals since have been all-ticket.

SUNDAY PICTORIAL, April 29, 1923.

Only 5 Weeks to Win Film Prizes

SUNDAY·PICTORIAL
THE GREAT SUNDAY PICTURE NEWSPAPER

Three whole columns of fun—

—for boys and girls on page 21.

BOLTON WIN THE CUP AGAINST A KEEN DEFENCE UNDER DIFFICULT CONDITIONS

The referee, players, Red Cross men and others intermingled when play was interrupted.

The Football Association
Challenge
Cup Competition.

FINAL TIE

TO BE PLAYED AT

The Empire Stadium, Wembley,
SATURDAY, 28th APRIL, 1923.
KICK-OFF 3 P.M.

Admit to
Council Seats
North Stand
BLOCK H
Row 1
No. 2
To be
RETAINED.

Secretary.

BRITISH EMPIRE
EXHIBITION
(1924)

PROGRAMME
& SOUVENIR
FINAL TIE
OF
THE FOOTBALL ASSOCIATION'S
ENGLISH CUP COMPETITION
To be played at
THE EMPIRE STADIUM
WEMBLEY
April 28th 1923
BOLTON WANDERERS
V
WEST HAM UNITED

PRICE THREEPENCE

1924

26 April at Wembley   Att 91,695

Newcastle United 2 (Harris, Seymour)

Aston Villa 0

Newcastle United: Bradley, Hampson, Hudspeth, Mooney, Spencer, Gibson, Low, Cowan, Harris, McDonald, Seymour.

Aston Villa: Jackson, Smart, Mort, Moss, Milne, Blackburn, York, Kirton, Capewell, Walker, Dorrell.

Referee: W. E. Russell

Above Geordie fans before Newcastle's semi-final with Manchester City at St Andrews in 1924. 'It is the glories of the past which they remember and the glories which they regard as a proper state of affairs. They want to be proud of their teams.' (*Hotbed of Soccer*, Arthur Appleton.)

Left It was an outstanding final, on a heavy pitch, which Newcastle won with two late goals in four minutes by Neil Harris and Stan Seymour. Seymour, a match-winning left-winger, served Newcastle for more than fifty years as player, manager, director, chairman and vice-president. And when he led Newcastle to victory in the 1951 final, he became the first man to win the Cup at Wembley as both player and manager with the same club.

Above Billy Hampson, Hudspeth's full-back partner, who played in the 1924 final at the age of forty-one years and eight months, is believed to be the oldest player to take part in a Cup final.

Opposite Frank Hudspeth, Newcastle United's captain, with Cup and cop. Hudspeth made around 500 League and Cup appearances for Newcastle (1910–1929) and just one for England (1926), at the age of thirty-five.

1925

25 April at Wembley   Att 91,763

Sheffield United 1 (Tunstall)

Cardiff City 0

Sheffield United: Sutcliffe, Cook, Milton, Pantling, King, Green, Mercer, Boyle, Johnson, Gillespie, Tunstall.

Cardiff City: Farquharson, Nelson, Blair, Wake, Keenor, Hardy, Davies, Gill, Nicholson, Beadles, Evans.

Referee: G. N. Watson

Above Five Cardiff City defenders and, in the background, five policemen take note of a bold example of poaching by Sheffield United in the 1925 final – an occasion with an international ring. Telegrams, cables and letters wishing the Bluebirds good luck arrived from all over the world.

One error often settles a Cup final and Cardiff made theirs after half an hour. Cardiff right-half Harry Wake hesitated and Fred Tunstall, Sheffield United's England left-winger, got behind the Welsh defence to win the Cup for United for the fourth time. Memorable headline in the *South Wales Echo*: 'Wake not Awake.'

Cardiff became a League club in 1920 and made an outstanding start: promotion from Division Two in 1921, Division One runners-up in 1924 (goal average 0.024 behind Huddersfield Town) and, in the Cup, quarter-finalists twice and semi-finalists once before reaching the 1925 final. And Cardiff's finest hour and a half was still to come.

1926

24 April at Wembley   Att 91,447
Bolton Wanderers 1 (Jack)
Manchester City 0
Bolton Wanderers: Pym, Haworth,
   Greenhalgh, Nuttall, Seddon,
   Jennings, Butler, Jack, J. R. Smith,
   J. Smith, Vizard.
Manchester City: Goodchild,
   Cookson, McCloy, Pringle,
   Cowan, McMullan, Austin,
   Browell, Roberts, Johnson, Hicks.
Referee: I. Baker

Left Bolton Wanderers – and David Jack – again. Jack (a foot in class above Manchester City's defence) scored the late goal which gave the Burnden Park club the Cup for the second time in three years.

Poor City's consolation was an undesirable double as they became the first club to reach the Cup final and to be relegated from Division One in the same season. Yet on the way to Wembley they scored thirty-one goals in six ties, beating the champions of Huddersfield Town 4–0 and Manchester United, in the semi-finals, by 3–0.

This was the first season under the new off-side rule (two players instead of three to keep a player on-side) and the immediate result was more pace and many more goals. The number of League goals scored in the last season under the old law was 4,700; the first season under the new produced 6,373. Arsenal were one of the first clubs to face the challenge by introducing the 'stopper' centre-half, but in the quarter-finals of the Cup in 1926 they were still beaten 2–1 by Swansea Town, who had won promotion from Division Three (South) to Division Two only a year before. Swansea lost their semi-final with Bolton by 3–0.

Above Nattily dressed Bolton pose beside a north London signpost before the 1926 final. 'Danger' lurks behind them, but they were never far from Wembley in the 1920s.

SOUTH WALES FOOTBALL ECHO. SATURDAY. APRIL 23. 1927.

CITY BRING THE ENGLISH CUP TO WALES.

WELSH PLAYER'S COSTLY MISTAKE
GIVES THE BLUEBIRDS VICTORY.

Opposite top Cardiff City became the first and only club to take the FA Cup out of England; and, charitably, Arsenal became the first and only club to let England's most celebrated sporting trophy be spirited away to another country. Hugh Ferguson, Cardiff's centre-forward, raises his arms in triumph as his soft ground shot finds the net – and Arsenal's goalkeeper Dan Lewis (a Welsh international) buries his face in his hands. Lewis was perfectly positioned to save comfortably in the seventy-third minute but, as he went down on one knee, the ball slipped out of his grasp, slid below his chest, passed under an arm and rolled towards the net. Lewis made a desperate attempt to clutch it a second time, but he could do no more than make contact with his elbow – and the ball trickled over the line. It was the only goal of a game largely dominated by Arsenal and the abundant talent of Charles Buchan, then thirty-five, who had played for Sunderland in the final fourteen years before. It was Arsenal's first Cup final and the beginning of their great years under Herbert Chapman. But now the Cup, famously, belonged to Cardiff. Contemporary estimates put the number of people who welcomed them home as a quarter of a million.

Right The Lions in their Den – with caps. An attentive corner of the Millwall crowd watching their Third Division (South) side hold Southampton to a 0–0 draw in the quarter-finals (Southampton won the replay 2–0) in 1927.

Above Fred Keenor, Cardiff City's Cup-winning captain, a hard-tackling, strong-running, big-voiced, chain-smoking wing-half, who was with the club for nearly twenty years. Nobody took liberties with him, but he was a popular man.

1927

23 April at Wembley   Att 91,206

Cardiff City 1 (Ferguson)

Arsenal 0

Cardiff City: Farquharson, Nelson, Watson, Keenor, Sloan, Hardy, Curtis, Irving, Ferguson, Davies, McLachlan.

Arsenal: Lewis, Parker, Kennedy, Baker, Butler, John, Hulme, Buchan, Brain, Blyth, Hoar.

Referee: W. F. Bunnell

Right Community singing, introduced at the Cup final in 1927, produced one of the biggest organised choirs of all. There was doubt whether the crowd would join in, but the response was so enthusiastic that it immediately became part of the event's ritual.

Left The first conductor was T. P. Ratcliff, who became famous as 'The Man in White'. He was followed after World War Two by Arthur Caiger, a London headmaster, and Frank Rea, who continued until the early 1970s when taste and emphasis changed. Now supporters tend to bellow their own songs of war and peace – but the tradition of singing 'Abide With Me', the hymn written by a Devon vicar in 1847, still endures.

Daily Express

NATIONAL COMMUNITY SINGING MOVEMENT

SONG SHEET

THE FOOTBALL ASSOCIATION CHALLENGE CUP

FINAL TIE.

THE STADIUM, WEMBLEY, APRIL 23rd, 1927.

The Community Singing will be conducted by Mr. Thomas P. Ratcliff, and accompanied by the Band of H.M. Grenadier Guards (by special permission of Colonel Sergison-Brooke, C.M.G., D.S.O.) under the Director of Music, Lieutenant George Miller.

1.

PACK UP YOUR TROUBLES

Pack up your troubles in your old
    kit bag
  And smile, smile, smile !
While you've a lucifer to light your
    fag,
  Smile, boys, that's the style ;
What's the use of worrying ?
  It never was worth while,
So, pack up your troubles in your old
    kit bag
  And smile, smile, smile !

*(Reproduced by permission of
Messrs. Francis, Day & Hunter.)*

2.

TIPPERARY

It's a long way to Tipperary,
  It's a long way to go ;
It's a long way to Tipperary,
  To the sweetest girl I know.
Good-bye, Piccadilly,
  Farewell, Leicester Square,
It's a long, long way to Tipperary,
  But my heart's right there.

*(Reproduced by permission of
Messrs. B. Feldman & Co.)*

3.

ALL THROUGH THE NIGHT

Deep the silence 'round us spreading,
  All through the night ;
Dark the path that we are treading,
  All through the night.
Still the coming day discerning,
  By the hope within us burning,
To the dawn our footsteps turning,
  All through the night.
Star of Faith the dark adorning
  All through the night ;
Leads us fearless t'wards the morning,
  All through the night.
Though our hearts be wrapt in sorrow,
  From the hope of dawn we borrow,
Promise of a glad to-morrow,
  All through the night.

4.

DRINK TO ME ONLY

Drink to me only with thine eyes,
  And I will pledge with mine,
Or leave a kiss within the cup
  And I'll not look for wine.
The thirst that from the soul doth rise
  Doth ask a drink divine ;
But might I of Jove's nectar sip,
  I would not change for thine.
I sent thee late a rosy wreath,
  Not so much hon'ring thee,
As giving it a hope, that there
  It could not wither'd be ;
But thou thereon didst only breathe
  And sent'st it back to me ;
Since when it grows and smells, I swear,
  Not of itself, but thee !

1928

21 April at Wembley   Att 92,041

Blackburn Rovers 3 (Roscamp 2, McLean)

Huddersfield Town 1 (Jackson)

Blackburn Rovers: Crawford, Hutton, Jones, Healless, Rankin, Campbell, Thornewell, Puddefoot, Roscamp, McLean, Rigby.

Huddersfield Town: Mercer, Goodall, Barkas, Redfern, Wilson, Steele, Jackson, Kelly, Brown, Stephenson, Smith.

Referee: T. G. Bryan

This, remarkably, was the first Cup final since 1910 in which both sides scored. It also provided yet another major surprise because Blackburn Rovers narrowly avoided relegation and Huddersfield Town were one of the nation's outstanding sides (champions in 1924, 1925 and 1926, runners-up in 1927 and 1928) with the dynamic Alex Jackson, one of Scotland's 'Wembley wizards', now added to their renowned attack. Yet Blackburn scored through James Roscamp in the first minute, added two more through Tommy McLean and Roscamp again, and controlled the game with their strong and direct play – a surprise which the *Illustrated Sporting and Dramatic News* attributed to 'the complexities of human nature'.

Right Tommy McLean (dark shirt beside the penalty spot) scores Blackburn's second goal – the best of the final, 'a beautiful drive' according to one report – which put the game beyond Huddersfield's reach.

Below and bottom right Crowd safety and control was not a pressing matter in 1928. Two scenes from Filbert Street as Tottenham Hotspur beat Leicester City 3–0 in the fifth round.

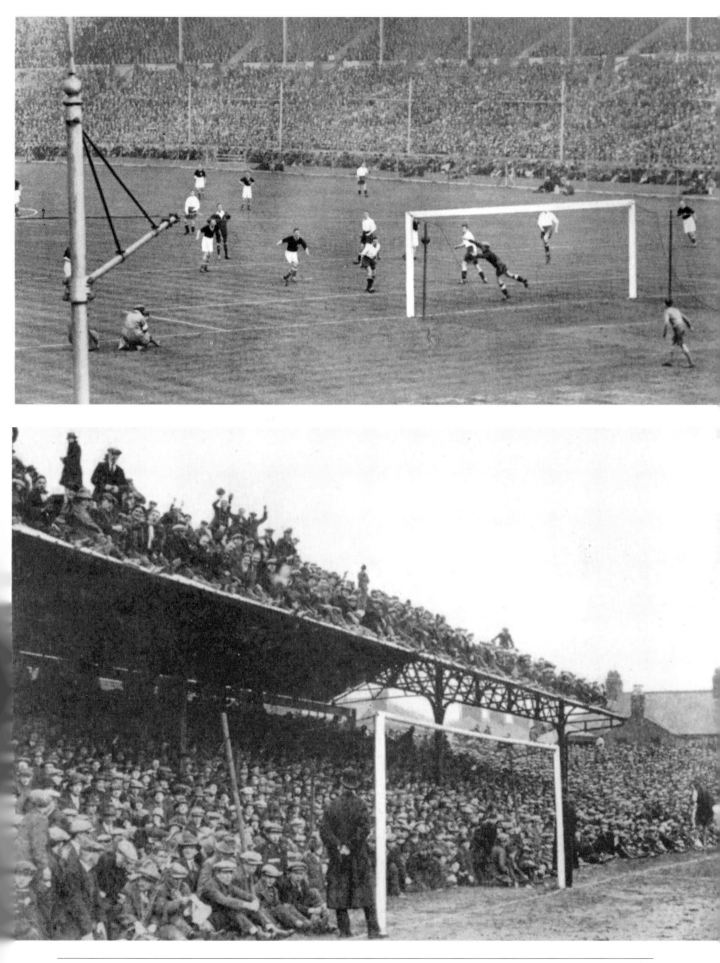

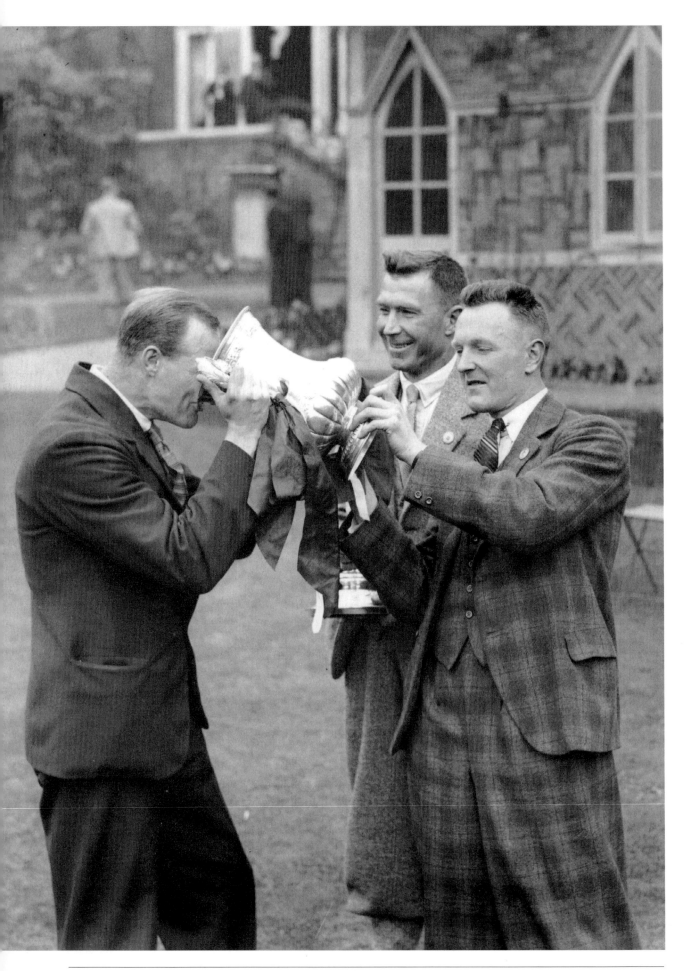

1929

27 April at Wembley   Att 92,576

Bolton Wanderers 2 (Butler, Blackmore)

Portsmouth 0

Bolton Wanderers: Pym, Haworth, Finney, Kean, Seddon, Nuttall, Butler, McClelland, Blackmore, Gibson, W. Cook.

Portsmouth: Gilfillan, Mackie, Bell, Nichol, McIlwaine, Thackeray, Forward, Smith, Weddle, Watson, F. Cook.

Referee: A. Josephs

Opposite Cup that cheers. Jimmy Seddon, Bolton Wanderers' captain, Dick Pym, goalkeeper, and Harry Blackmore, leading scorer, at a Harrow hotel the day after winning an old friend for the third time in six years. Seddon and Pym were two of five men who played in all three of Bolton's Cup triumphs in the 1920s, in which only seventeen players were used in all. The 1929 final was a cautious affair until Bolton won it with a late flourish. Billy Butler, who also played in the three finals, scored a spectacular goal eleven minutes from the end and then, in the last seconds, set up Blackmore for his seventh goal of the tournament. Pym, a fisherman from Devon, did not concede a goal in the three finals. He died in 1988, aged ninety-five.

Above A Portsmouth fan arrives in London for his club's first Cup final. He has his own ribboned Cup.

Left Herbert Chapman's final: a meeting of the two clubs he fashioned and inspired to greatness – Huddersfield Town, who won the League Championship three years in a row in the 1920s, versus Arsenal who would do the same in the 1930s.

The two sides took the field together, for the first time in a final, and produced a match of high and absorbing quality, observed by the silver German airship Graf Zeppelin. The deafening roar of its engines, according to some reports, disconcerted players and spectators alike. A few cheered, others booed. The giant craft, symbol of a rising Germany, dipped its nose in salute to King George V and slowly passed on.

Arsenal won their first major trophy with a goal in each half, the first impishly created and taken by Alex James, the second the product of a long, lone run by Jack Lambert. Huddersfield were worthy opponents but their day had really passed; they have never since won a major trophy. For Arsenal it was the beginning.

Below Arsenal, curiously, pose at one end of Wembley in front of terraces covered with rubbish. Herbert Chapman is on the far left, David Jack (who had joined Arsenal from Bolton Wanderers for £10,890) has his hands in the pockets of his light-coloured plus-fours, captain Tom Parker has the Cup and Alex James, as always a man apart, is on the far right.

Opposite bottom Arsenal parade

1930

26 April at Wembley   Att 92,488
Arsenal 2 (James, Lambert)
Huddersfield Town 0
Arsenal: Preedy, Parker, Hapgood, Baker, Seddon, John, Hulme, Jack, Lambert, James, Bastin.
Huddersfield Town: Turner, Goodall, Spence, Naylor, Wilson, Campbell, Jackson, Kelly, Davies, Raw, Smith.
Referee: T. Crew

the FA Cup and the London Combination Cup (won by their reserves) before a League match against Sunderland at Highbury on the Monday after the final.

Chapter Six

Beside a Laundry Wall
1931–1939

'At my first Cup final as FA secretary in 1935 I had a nervous day wondering if all would go according to plan – because as far as I could see there was no plan. Who was responsible for the guests, the officials, the balls? From past experience in refereeing a Cup final I knew that some arrangements were haphazard. No one had met my linesmen or me or told us where to find the dressing-rooms. We found we had to change in an office, and at the game's end there was no bath for us so we begged one off the winning team.

'All went right on that Cup final day, but immediately afterwards I sat down to write a comprehensive guide for future years. This covered all the timings and responsibilities of this complex operation and at Lancaster Gate it became known as "From Ball Boys to the King". It became a standard part of the tradition of the day.'

Sir Stanley Rous, Cup final referee 1934, FA secretary 1934–61
and then president of FIFA for 13 years. From *Football Worlds* (1978).

The FA Cup cast its favours among the strong and the eminent during the 1930s. West Bromwich Albion, the old 'Invincibles' of Preston North End, Manchester City, Portsmouth and the overlords of Arsenal all reached the final twice in this time of depression and political fever. It was a period, too, blessed with many players whose names would be remembered with reverence: Dixie Dean, Alex James, Warney Cresswell, Harry Hibbs, Ted Drake, Raich Carter and Stan Cullis among them. All members of the family of fame.

Yet if one triumph more than another lit up the uneasy decade before World War Two, it was that of a humble Black Country club with a laundry wall behind one of its goals and a ragbag team of foot-soldiers brought together at an all-in cost of £69. History beckoned to Walsall of the Third Division North on 14 January 1933. Walsall 2 Arsenal 0. It was, arguably, the most stunning giant-killing act of all. Here, on a grey day and soft pitch eight miles to the north-west of Birmingham, was an upset which mocked logic and perfectly symbolised the magic of the Cup.

Walsall's third-round victory was impossible: until it happened. They were a scratch mixture of lightweight saints and burly sinners whose careers were on the way up or down or rooted firmly to the ground. The papers pictured them eating oysters before the game but their preference, it was slyly reported, was for fish and chips and a few pints of beer. The week before they met Arsenal they had drawn 1–1 at home to Barnsley and the week after they lost 2–0 at Hartlepool.

Herbert Chapman's Arsenal, on the other hand, were in the process of winning the second of their five Championships in the thirties and the first of their three titles in successive seasons. They were the imperial power of English football, standard bearers for the prosperity and privileges of London, openly envied and cordially hated by all but their own. Arsenal bristled with household names: among them the elegant David Jack, for whom Chapman had paid the first five-figure transfer fee (£10,890 in 1928); Alex James, a genius with baggy shorts and buttoned-down sleeves; Cliff 'Boy' Bastin, an elusive prodigy from the rolling acres of Devon; and, behind them, Herbie Roberts, the red-haired central pillar of their defence, a stopper pure and simple and one of the most talked about men of his day.

Injuries and flu weakened Arsenal, but they still sent out a side which included seven full internationals, and for much of the game their superior skill was evident. However, Walsall, in the words of Bastin, were 'more like steamrollers than footballers'. Arsenal were awarded ten free-kicks in as many minutes, Roberts sustained a cut above an eye the first time he went for the ball and a less lenient referee than Mr A. Taylor from

Wigan might have sent off one or two Walsall players and changed the course of history. The Fellows Park crowd began to find its voice. Walsall's confidence grew and Arsenal discovered, painfully, that rank is not worth a handful of mist when it comes to the Cup.

Arsenal missed their chances: Walsall did not. The Black Country club went into the lead after an hour through centre-forward Gilbert Alsop, with a headed goal which instantly made him a folk hero, and then took the match with a penalty by Bill Sheppard. A nearby factory chimney chose that moment to throw huge clouds of grey-black smoke into the air and, for a few minutes, the pitch was a thing of hazy unreality. So, for Arsenal, was the match.

Back at Highbury the score was greeted with hoots of laughter. They thought it was a leg-pull. The voice of a BBC newsreader, it is said, trembled with surprise as he relayed the result to the nation. 'Is it true?' asked the *Walsall Times* reporter. 'Is it not a dream that I shall awake and smile at?' Down through the years, constant re-polishing of the facts has given Walsall's triumph a lovely patina. Only the Cup could have manufactured such a story.

Year by year during the 1930s, the Cup injected new life into winter, its democracy unruffled, its traditions inviolate, its charm irresistible, its climax still the game's day of days. West Bromwich Albion, uniquely, won the Cup and gained promotion from the Second Division in 1931. Newcastle beat Arsenal a year later with the help of an 'over the line' goal: was the ball out when Jimmy Richardson hooked it over for Jack Allen to score? Everton won the Second Division Championship in 1931, the League Championship in 1932 and the Cup in 1933 – the first final in which players' shirts were numbered.

Manchester City (1933 and 1934) and Preston (1937 and 1938) reached the final two seasons in succession, each losing the first and winning the second. Preston's win came with a penalty by George Mutch only sixty seconds from the end of extra-time against Huddersfield in the first game covered live by BBC Television cameras. Raich Carter's Sunderland took the trophy home for the first time in the Coronation year of 1937; and the last word before the war, before the country put on its gas-masks and headed for the air-raid shelters, belonged to Portsmouth. Jack Tinn (with his famous white spats) led them to victory – another 'impossible' result – over the universally fancied Wolves in 1939. And the Cup stayed with Portsmouth for six dark years.

May to May

The FA Cup fills the year. The actual playing of matches occupies a little over eight months, but the work done in the other four is essential to its smooth running.

The first priority is fixing dates. This is done more than a year in advance and is never easy, because mid-week replays must not clash with European tournaments, internationals and League Cup ties. Entry forms are sent out from January onwards, going automatically to those who have already competed, while first-time entrants must apply. Completed forms with the entry fee of £75 must be returned by 1 April.

No clubs, not even the aristocrats of the Premier League, are accepted without submitting a form. Entries are scrutinised by the Challenge Cup committee, with facilities, gates, results and so on being considered, to ensure that standards are not lowered. A small number, inevitably, have to be rejected.

Exemptions for some non-League clubs from the perils of the earliest rounds have to be agreed on – a complicated and sometimes controversial matter based on achievement and consistency. The draw for the first four rounds then takes place in early July, giving clubs plenty of time to plot their first steps on the long road to Wembley. Organising match officials is a major business, and life is further complicated by safety and crowd control factors; applications for changes of venue, particularly where matches are in close proximity; television requirements; and the need to re-arrange postponed games. The only thing which can never be organised is the weather.

Adrian Titcombe

FA Head of Competitions and Regulations

Above West Bromwich Albion became the first club to win the FA Cup and promotion from the Second Division in the same season. Their spirit and togetherness are apparent at Paddington Station as they prepare to return to the Black Country. Captain Tom Glidden holds the Cup, chairman Billy Bassett (an Albion Cup-winner in 1888 and 1892 at the Oval) has his newspaper, gloves and umbrella, and a refreshment boy, bottom left, takes a peek over the arm of the law.

Right W. G. Richardson scores the second of his two goals to win a Midlands dogfight in heavy rain – 'one of the hardest games in the history of modern football,' declared the *Daily Express*. Richardson's goal came straight from the restart after a Birmingham equaliser by Joe Bradford.

Right Billy Richardson, known as
'W. G.' to distinguish him from the
club's other Billy Richardson, their
stalwart centre-half. The G, added
to his initials by the club, stood for
'Ginger'. W. G. scored four in five
minutes in a League game at West
Ham in 1931 and is regarded as
Albion's finest centre-forward, with
228 League and Cup goals in 443
first-team games.

W. G. RICHARDSON

1931

25 April at Wembley   Att 92,406
West Bromwich Albion 2
 (W. G. Richardson 2)
Birmingham 1 (Bradford)
West Bromwich Albion: Pearson,
 Shaw, Trentham, Magee, W.
 Richardson, Edwards, Glidden,
 Carter, W. G. Richardson,
 Sandford, Wood.
Birmingham: Hibbs, Liddell, Barkas,
 Cringan, Morrall, Leslie, Briggs,
 Crosbie, Bradford, Gregg, Curtis.
Referee: A. H. Kingscott

Below Perhaps the most famous disputed goal in the history of the FA Cup: the 'over-the-line' goal which helped Newcastle United beat Arsenal at their zenith. Arsenal (without an injured Alex James) were leading 1–0 in the thirty-eighth minute when Newcastle's Jimmy Richardson chased a long pass on the right. The ball appeared to cross the line, but the Newcastle inside-right still hooked it inside to Jack Allen, who found the net easily. Referee W. P. Harper gave a goal and, despite uproar on nearby terraces, stuck to his decision. Allen then scored again in the seventy-second minute to win the Cup for Newcastle. While Arsenal's reaction was admirably restrained, the media sank its teeth into the controversy. Film and photographs indicated that the ball had crossed the line, among them this *British Movietone News* picture which also shows how far referee Harper and his linesmen were from the incident. 'Cup final goal was not a goal,' insisted the *Daily Herald* on its front page, alongside a story about the success of Hitler's Nazis in the German elections. But, of course, it was a goal, and Arsenal claimed another distinction. They were the first club to score first in a Wembley final and lose.

Opposite Johnny Goodall, one of the most illustrious of the old Preston 'Invincibles', pictured in 1932 at the age of nearly seventy. He ran a little business in Watford, was a bird fancier and was very proud of a fox he had tamed.

1932

23 April at Wembley   Att 92,298

Newcastle United 2 (Allen 2)

Arsenal 1 (John)

Newcastle United: McInroy, Nelson, Fairhurst, McKenzie, Davidson, Weaver, Boyd, Richardson, Allen, McMenemy, Lang.

Arsenal: Moss, Parker, Hapgood, Jones, Roberts, Male, Hulme, Jack, Lambert, Bastin, John.

Referee: W. P. Harper

SENSATIONAL GAME.

COMPLETE FAILURE OF MIGHTY ARSENAL.

Deplorable Penalty Incident.

ALSOP AND SHEPPARD SECURE VITAL GOALS.

WALSALL'S WINNING WAY.

How the Arsenal Machinery was Dislocated.

WHERE KEENNESS TRIUMPHED.

By "THE SWIFT."

Is it true? Is it not really a dream that I shall awake and smile at? No! Even now I cannot quite grasp that my little Walsall—the team I gaze upon so anxiously every week—has had the cheek, the impudence, to wipe the great and mighty Arsenal out of the English Cup, and send them back to the Metropolis bewailing a whipping at the hands of an insignificant club in the Northern Section of the Third Division!

And yet—it must be true, for I saw them with my own eyes—watched Alsop and Sheppard do the things that made their names famous throughout the football world—heard the mighty roars that followed these actions. Indeed, did I not so far forget my complete impartiality as to give vocal praise as the Saddlers left the field—triumphant! Oh, yes, it was a marvellous achievement.

1933

29 April at Wembley   Att 92,950

Everton 3 (Stein, Dean, Dunn)

Manchester City 0

Everton: Sagar, Cook, Cresswell, Britton, White, Thomson, Geldard, Dunn, Dean, Johnson, Stein.

Manchester City: Langford, Cann, Dale, Busby, Cowan, Bray, Toseland, Marshall, Herd, McMullan, Brook.

Referee: E. Wood

Right Walsall's heroes: *Back row (left to right)* – S. Bird, J. Reed, J. Bennett, H. Wait (trainer), J. Cunningham, J. Wilson (assistant secretary), G. Leslie, H. Salt, W. Sheppard (scorer of second goal, a penalty). *Middle row* – W. Slade (secretary-manager), E. Jackson (director), H. Fellows (chairman), Mrs W. Dean (mayoress), W. Dean (mayor), H. Lake and A. Eyre (directors). *Front row* – W. Coward, C. Ball, G. Alsop (scorer of first goal), F. Lee.

The two scorers, Bill Sheppard and particularly Gilbert Alsop, have acquired legendary status. Alsop (pictured with the match ball, already decorated with an inscribed silver medallion) had a stand named after him when Walsall moved to a new stadium nearly sixty years later.

Walsall lost 2–0 to Manchester City in the fourth round and City (with a young Matt Busby at right-half) duly reached the final. But their opponents at Wembley (right) were Everton, who were at one of the highest points in their history: Second Division champions in 1931, League champions in 1932 and now, by 3–0, FA Cup winners. Everton's armoury was too strong, with Warney Cresswell, ageless and unflappable in defence, the intuitive

Above A third-round game in 1933 is one of the most fabled of all the 50,000 and more ties manufactured by the FA Cup. Walsall's 2–0 defeat of Arsenal is regarded as the tournament's top shock and is a story which gets better with every telling. Herbert Chapman's omnipotent Gunners, on their way to winning the first of three successive League Championships, were bullied to defeat by a little Black Country club from the shadowy mid-region of the Third Division (North). The *Times and South Staffordshire Advertiser* was properly intoxicated.

Cliff Britton at right-half, Ted Sagar, forever 'The Boss' in goal, and, towering above all, the great William Ralph 'Dixie' Dean, arguably the greatest centre-forward of them all. Dean, a gladiator on the ground, a demon in the air, scored 473 goals (including thirty-seven hat-tricks) in 502 games in a career which stretched from 1923 to 1939. In one royal season, 1927–28, aged twenty-one, he scored sixty League goals, a record beyond reach. The picture shows him scoring Everton's second goal in the 1933 final – the first in which players were numbered: Everton one to eleven, Manchester City twelve to twenty-two.

1934

28 April at Wembley   Att 93,258

Manchester City 2 (Tilson 2)

Portsmouth 1 (Rutherford)

Manchester City: Swift, Barnett, Dale, Busby, Cowan, Bray, Toseland, Marshall, Tilson, Herd, Brook.

Portsmouth: Gilfillan, Mackie, W. Smith, Nichol, Allen, Thackeray, Worrall, J. Smith, Weddle, Easson, Rutherford.

Referee: S. F. Rous

Left The King presents Sam Cowan, Manchester City's captain, with the Cup, which was won with two late goals to the accompaniment of thunder and lightning. Portsmouth took an early lead but, after a second-half injury to their centre-half, Jimmy Allen, City scored twice through Fred Tilson – the winner only four minutes from time.

Frank Swift, City's goalkeeper, just nineteen and in his first season, fainted at the end as he bent to pick up his cap and gloves at the back of the net. The reason, he explained, was the mounting tension as a helpful photographer counted away time. 'Only fifty seconds, you're nearly there lad,' … 'forty seconds, you've done 'em now,' … 'thirty seconds, it's your Cup, son.'

Still feeling groggy, Swift, arrowed in the picture, was asked a few seconds later by the King: 'How are you feeling now, my boy?' 'Fine, sir,' said Swift. 'That's good. You played well. Here is your medal and good luck.' Swift became an automatic choice for England. He died in the Munich air crash.

Above Sir Frederick Wall, seventy-five, secretary of the FA, demonstrating the art of kicking at Wembley. He had played in the FA Cup against the Royal Engineers more than fifty years before.

Left Stanley Rous, the 1934 Cup final referee, who succeeded Sir Frederick Wall as FA secretary that same year. Rous, knighted in 1949, became president of FIFA twenty-seven years later.

Above The other team of 1934. Eleven members of the Wembley groundstaff (each with a dining fork) versus all dandelions, daisies and dockweeds.

Left All for tuppence. The numbered squares on the cover of the 1935 FA Cup final edition of the *Radio Times* were an aid to listeners: numbers were called out during radio commentary to indicate the position of the ball during play. An article inside quoted letters from listeners in Kenya Colony, the Naga Hills in Assam (who claimed to have heard one commentary while surrounded by head-hunters) and Mount Lawley, Australia. The *Radio Times* commented: 'It is not too much to say that the Cup final commentary plays its part in welding the Empire together.' The first final broadcast publicly on radio was Arsenal v Cardiff City in 1927. The first final shown live and in full on television was Preston North End v Huddersfield Town in 1938.

A FOOTBALL RECORD RECALLED

By Death of Well-Known Surgeon.

The death of a former Association football goalkeeper, a Welsh international, who did not concede a single goal in matches which gave his club the English Cup, is announced to-day. He was Lieut.-Colonel Robert Herbert Mills-Roberts, of Festiniog, North Wales. He died in a Bournemouth nursing home, aged 73.

The club which achieved this remarkable record was Preston North End, and the season was 1888-9. In that same season the club were champions of the Football League—without losing a match.

Colonel Mills-Roberts was a surgeon, and saw much war service. In the South African War he served with the Welsh hospital, and was mentioned in despatches. He was again mentioned in despatches during the Great War, when he was commanding officer of a stationary hospital.

He was a member of the British Medical Association, and a Fellow of the Royal Society of Medicine.

Above For the record. A cameraman filming a dramatic final in which the score, with only three minutes left, was 2–2. But then Ellis Rimmer, Sheffield Wednesday's lanky England winger, scored twice in little more than sixty seconds to give an evenly contested game a lop-sided result. Rimmer, a noted ballroom dancer, thus scored in every round.

Left The passing of another 'Invincible'. November 1935.

1935

27 April at Wembley	Att 93,204

Sheffield Wednesday 4
(Palethorpe, Hooper, Rimmer 2)
West Bromwich Albion 2
(Boyes, Sandford)

Sheffield Wednesday: Brown, Nibloe, Catlin, Sharp, Millership, Burrows, Hooper, Surtees, Palethorpe, Starling, Rimmer.

West Bromwich Albion: Pearson, Shaw, Trentham, Murphy, W. Richardson, Edwards, Glidden, Carter, W. G. Richardson, Sandford, Boyes.

Referee: A. E. Fogg

Below Arsenal, having won the League Championship three seasons in a row, now added the Cup to their collection again. Herbert Chapman had died, suddenly, two years before and David Jack had hung up his boots. George Allison, BBC Radio's first football commentator, was now manager, and the attack was led by Ted Drake, a formidable warrior, who earlier in the season had scored seven in a League game against Aston Villa. He only managed one, sixteen minutes from the end, in the final – but it was enough to beat a spirited Sheffield United from the Second Division.

It was Arsenal's sixth success in League or Cup in seven seasons, but their triumph didn't get the coverage it deserved. A dispute over terms between Wembley and the newsreel companies led to a ban on film cameramen inside the stadium. The companies therefore took to the air and, shortly before kick-off, a whirl of auto-giros rose above Wembley. But as the picture confirms, they scrupulously refrained from flying over the pitch. The only film of the match taken inside the ground was an 'official' one.

1936

25 April at Wembley   Att 93,384

Arsenal 1 (Drake)
Sheffield United 0

Arsenal: Wilson, Male, Hapgood, Crayston, Roberts, Copping, Hulme, Bowden, Drake, James, Bastin.

Sheffield United: Smith, Hooper, Wilkinson, Jackson, Johnson, McPherson, Barton, Barclay, Dodds, Pickering, Williams.

Referee: H. Nattrass

A little less noise, please.

1937

I May at Wembley   Att 93,495

Sunderland 3 (Gurney, Carter, Burbanks)

Preston North End 1 (F. O'Donnell)

Sunderland: Mapson, Gorman, Hall, Thomson, Johnson, McNab, Duns, Carter, Gurney, Gallacher, Burbanks.

Preston North End: Burns, Gallimore, Beattie, Shankly, Tremelling, Milne, Dougal, Beresford, F. O'Donnell, Fagan, H. O'Donnell.

Referee: R. G. Rudd

Below Horatio Stratton Carter married his Rosie on the last Monday of April in 1937, saw her for just a few hours during the next five days, captained and scored for Sunderland in their first FA Cup triumph and then received the trophy from the Queen in Coronation year. Raich Carter did things with style.

Sunderland had won the League title the season before, so now Carter had a League-winner's medal, a Cup-winner's medal, a home-town team with a household name, a place in the national side, a place in history – and a lovely wife. He was twenty-three years old.

Carter was an inside-forward of measured calmness, natural authority and expert technique. He made goals, with all known varieties of pass, but he also scored them – regularly and spectacularly. Tommy Lawton said Carter shot as if he hated both ball and goalkeeper.

Sunderland were a goal down to Preston North End at half-time in the 1937 final; but under Carter's leadership they were transformed afterwards and scored three through Bob Gurney, Carter himself (on ground, behind goalkeeper) and Eddie Burbanks.

Right Raich Carter receives the Cup from the Queen. 'That is a nice wedding present for you,' she said.

cently, Manchester City (2–0) – City, with the finest attack in the country, going on to win the League Championship with 107 goals.

Millwall's hero was Dave Mangnall, who scored ten goals in their run, and is pictured scoring his second against Manchester City in front of a crowd of 43,000. Frank Swift, City's goalkeeper, has misjudged a centre by McCartney, leaving Mangnall with an easy header.

In the semi-final at Huddersfield, Millwall even took the lead (Mangnall, of course) before Sunderland rallied to produce winners from Bob Gurney and Patsy Gallacher. The dream over, Millwall finished the season eighth in the Third Division (South).

Below Millwall became the first Third Division club to reach the semi-finals of the FA Cup and even went near to ruining Sunderland's long-awaited moment. Millwall began their remarkable run by winning 6–1 at Aldershot and then, in the Lions' Den, they overcame Gateshead (7–0), Fulham (2–0), Chelsea (3–0), Derby County (2–1) and, magnifi-

1938

30 April at Wembley   Att 93,497

Preston North End 1 (Mutch
  (pen))

Huddersfield Town 0   aet

Preston North End: Holdcroft,
  Gallimore, A. Beattie, Shankly,
  Smith, Batey, Watmough, Mutch,
  Maxwell, R. Beattie, H. O'Donnell.

Huddersfield Town: Hesford, Craig,
  Mountford, Willingham, Young,
  Boot, Hulme, Isaac, McFadyen,
  Barclay, Beasley.

Referee: A. J. Jewell

Right 'The Mutch penalty' in the last minute of extra-time – and for the first time a Wembley final is decided from the spot. George Mutch of Scotland wins the Cup for Preston North End with a penalty kick that sends the ball into Huddersfield Town's net via the underside of a square crossbar.

It was the controversial last act of a poor but balanced final, which was shown in full by BBC Television for the first time (estimated viewers 10,000). Mutch himself had been brought down by Alf Young, Huddersfield's captain and centre-half, but was it a foul? And was it inside the area? The Preston inside-right, dazed by his fall, had no answers. He said afterwards he was unaware a penalty had been given, unsure why he was handed the ball and couldn't even remember aiming at goal. Bill Shankly was one of the Preston players who urged him to 'just hit the ruddy thing'.

It was Preston's first Cup triumph since that of the 'Invincibles' forty-nine years before, and compensation for Huddersfield's victory over Preston in the 1922 final – again settled by a controversial penalty.

Left Joe Hulme: the 1938 final was his last first-class game – and his fifth Wembley final. He played in four for Arsenal (winner in 1930 and 1936, runner-up in 1927 and 1932) before joining Huddersfield in January 1938. He was an England international, one of the fastest wingers in football, and also a Middlesex cricketer. He later managed Tottenham Hotspur.

Above Seaweed bath for non-League Scarborough as they prepare for a first-round tie with Darlington of the Third Division (North). It was a much publicised routine (with 'secret' benefits), introduced by trainer Arthur Price. Scarborough won 2–0 and reached the third round (and a replay) before losing to Luton Town, their best run in the Cup. *Left to right* – Fieldsend, Varty, Nichol, Agar, Robinson, Sharp, Jolly and Heelbeck.

Below Wolverhampton Wanderers, 5 to 1 on favourites, finished 4 to 1 down in one of the Cup final's biggest shocks. Wolves were strong and talented, with the majestic Stan Cullis at centre-half, and had the best defence in Division One (thirty-nine goals conceded in forty-two games). They finished runners-up to Everton (whom they beat 7–0 in the League and 2–0 in the Cup) and reached Wembley with a goal balance of 19–3. Portsmouth just avoided relegation and had the First Division's poorest scoring record (forty-seven in forty-two).

Yet Portsmouth won as they pleased with goals from Bert Barlow (a Wolves player only two months before), John Anderson and Cliff Parker (two). The goal most remembered came just after half-time. Bob Scott, Wolves' goalkeeper, fumbled a shot by Barlow and had to dive towards his own line, left arm fully stretched, to retrieve the ball. But, before he could gather safely, Parker (left of picture) moved in from the left wing to force Portsmouth's third. 'I'll be back with another one, Scotty,' said Parker. And he was.

1939

29 April at Wembley   Att 99,370

Portsmouth 4 (Barlow, Anderson, Parker 2)

Wolverhampton Wanderers 1 (Dorsett)

Portsmouth: Walker, Morgan, Rochford, Guthrie, Rowe, Wharton, Worrall, McAlinden, Anderson, Barlow, Parker.

Wolverhampton Wanderers: Scott, Morris, Taylor, Galley, Cullis, Gardiner, Burton, McIntosh, Westcott, Dorsett, Maguire.

Referee: T. Thompson

Above How can such a surprise be explained? Jack Tinn's lucky white spats, of course! The Portsmouth manager shows them to his team in their Wembley dressing-room before the final. They were always clipped on, left foot first, by right-winger Fred Worrall, who is on the far left of the picture with hat on knee. The game was watched by the biggest Wembley crowd (99,370) since the White Horse final of 1923.

Below William King, a railway porter at Blackburn, finishing his own special invitation, crayon on blackboard, to the quarter-final between Blackburn Rovers and Huddersfield Town at Leeds Road. His work was locally renowned.

Chapter Seven

A Light to Follow
1946–1950

'I shall never forget the night I dropped the FA Cup – and smashed it! Charlton won this most envied of all Soccer trophies in 1947 and I planned to take it myself to the Welcome Home reception. But while opening the door of my car and, at the same time, balancing the Cup, I dropped the lid and found to my horror that the top had broken off. There was little time to spare so I called at a garage and explained my predicament. The mechanics were soon working with their soldering irons and, at the reception, not a soul apart from myself knew about the accident. Next day I arranged for a silversmith to do a really first-class job on it.'

Jimmy Seed (Cup winner with Spurs 1921 and manager of Charlton Athletic 1933–56) in *The Jimmy Seed Story* (1957).

The lean years after World War Two are often described as the golden age of football, and in some ways they were. The country was weary of sacrifice and saw the game as an exciting symbol of freedom and normality, a light to follow in days of austerity and wavering hope. Football did much more to raise the spirit of the nation than Government posters which solemnly urged people to be cheerful. The cinema played its part and so did the wireless and dance halls; but millions of men, with a lusty desire to make up for six lost years, found that the simple game of football was as intoxicating as their favourite ale. Absenteeism on match days became a problem and many employers quickly plumped for staggered hours.

The first four seasons of League football after Hitler's war attracted an aggregate attendance of 157 million with a high point in 1948–49 of 41,271,414. The FA Cup was even more popular but, although book after book is now filled with illuminating statistics, we are left to guess at the number of people who stood beside the road to Wembley in the late 1940s. The tingle was back.

The old trophy itself survived the war in good shape. Portsmouth, its winners in 1939, looked after it with due pride and attention, giving it regular airings at Fratton Park and allowing it to make public appearances in aid of charity. Once the Cup was moved on just before its caring bank was bombed and destroyed. Jack Tinn, Portsmouth's manager, spent the night of the blitz nursing it beneath the stairs of his home.

League football's boom began in 1946–47, but by then the first Cup tournament had already been completed, in a format that broke with tradition and embraced tragedy as well as triumph. For just one season, 1945–46, the format was changed. Every tie from the first round proper to the sixth was played on a home-and-away basis, with the second leg ploughing on to a finish if there was no outcome after extra-time. The reason given for the change in formula was 'special circumstances' – in other words, an urgent need for cash. There were some marathon ties and many huge crowds, one of which led to disaster.

Sixty-five thousand spectators squeezed into Burnden Park for the second leg of Bolton Wanderers' sixth-round tie with Stoke City on 9 March 1946. However, thousands more outside were determined to see Bolton build on their 2–0 victory in the first leg and to witness at first hand the magic of Stanley Matthews on Stoke's right-wing. Fences were pushed over, a brick wall toppled and a lock on a gate was broken; and quickly, horribly, a crush developed which killed thirty-three people and injured five hundred others. Bolton grieved, but it was a tragedy that could well have happened on many other old grounds that were unsafe after six years of neglect.

The Home Office described it as 'the first example of serious casualties inflicted by a crowd upon itself' and recommended measures such as limited crowds and licensed grounds. Football authorities protested against official interference and high costs, but the FA did begin a system of voluntary licensing for bigger stadiums. A new Labour Government, in any case, had other things on its mind. Its Welfare State quickly took shape and there were signal developments in health, education, homes and social justice.

Football, too, was moving forward. Players began their long trawl towards equitable contracts and their idea of a decent wage. The FA addressed itself seriously to a national coaching system. Walter Winterbottom, a promising defender with Manchester United in the late 1930s, a man of vision and a natural teacher, became director of coaching and, soon afterwards, the first manager of England's national team. England, having stood loftily apart at times between the wars, rejoined FIFA and the global family of football – and continued to lord it at international level. Holland were beaten 8–2 in 1946, Portugal by 10–0 in Lisbon in 1947 and Italy by 4–0 in Turin in 1948.

The game was studded with honest heroes: Stanley Matthews, the waltzing maestro who moved from Stoke City to Blackpool in 1947; Tommy Lawton, sleek and lethal, the archetypal English centre-forward; Tom Finney and Wilf Mannion, consummate artists; Raich Carter, Peter Doherty and Len Shackleton, brilliant conductors; Johnny Carey and Joe Mercer, born leaders; and so many others who are remembered, still, fifty years on, with veneration.

A golden age, perhaps, but the general standard of football for a season or two was variable. While the stars shone brightly, around them were many more ordinary players whose best years had been stolen from them and many tenderfoots whose best years were still to come. The transfer market was giddily busy and, in search of winning combinations, clubs built up top-heavy and costly squads of players.

The pleasure given by the Cup, on its return to active service after the war, was extraordinary. Its home-and-away format for 1945–46 gave everyone a chance to welcome it back. A crowd of 80,407, for example, a record for a mid-week game outside Wembley, saw Derby County overcome Birmingham City 4–0 in their semi-final replay at Maine Road; and Derby, duly inspired, went on to beat Charlton Athletic 4–1 after extra-time in a memorable final. Carter and Doherty sparkled on a dull day, burly Jack Stamps scored twice, as did Charlton's right-half Bert Turner – with one for each side in the space of a minute. And the ball burst.

Charlton, spiritedly, survived the long and wicked winter of 1946–47 to return to Wembley and beat Second Division Burnley with a late goal by Chris Duffy. The ball burst again, too. More significantly, Matt Busby and Stan Cullis made their first mark as managers on the Cup and Wembley. Busby, a dignified Scot with implacable faith in the virtue of talent, guided Manchester United to a 4–2 victory over Blackpool in 1948 in one of the Cup's most scintillating finals. Then in 1949 Cullis, a martinet committed to pace, stamina and the long ball, led Wolverhampton Wanderers to a 3–1 triumph over Leicester City, who were fighting relegation at the bottom of the Second Division. Busby and Cullis: here were two men who would make an indelible impression on the 1950s.

Below The first Cup final goal after World War Two – scored by Charlton Athletic's Bert Turner on behalf of Derby County. Charlton's right-half (centre, on ground) has just deflected a shot by Dally Duncan into his own net to give Derby a 1–0 lead. Less than sixty seconds later, though, Turner had earned another line in the record books by becoming the first man to score for both sides in a Cup final. He immediately drove a free-kick through a thicket of Derby defenders to equalise. His shot found the net via the right shin of Peter Doherty (who believed he, too, had managed an own goal), but Turner was given the credit.

It was a better story.

Soon after, the ball burst in a ripping final that gave the Wembley crowd a warm welcome back to normality. The score after ninety minutes was 1–1, but extra-time belonged to Derby. The flame-haired Doherty of Ireland and Raich Carter, Sunderland's hero in 1937, were in match-winning harmony and Derby took the Cup for the first time with goals by Jack Stamps (two) and Doherty himself.

Ties up to the semi-finals were two-legged, home and away, in this first season after the war, and Charlton reached the final despite losing one of their games, away to Fulham, in the third round.

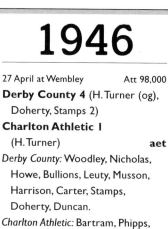

1946

27 April at Wembley   Att 98,000

Derby County 4 (H. Turner (og),
  Doherty, Stamps 2)

Charlton Athletic 1
  (H. Turner)   aet

Derby County: Woodley, Nicholas,
  Howe, Bullions, Leuty, Musson,
  Harrison, Carter, Stamps,
  Doherty, Duncan.

Charlton Athletic: Bartram, Phipps,
  Shreeve, H. Turner, Oakes,
  Johnson, Fell, Brown, A. A. Turner,
  Welsh, Duffy.

Referee: E. D. Smith

Above The start of the crush in the Railway Embankment enclosure which led to the Burnden Park disaster on 9 March 1946, in which thirty-three people were killed and five hundred injured at the start of a quarter-final between Bolton Wanderers and Stoke City. Intruders can be seen, top left, tearing down the fence and forcing their way on to a full terrace. Fans in distress were already being passed over heads and, soon after, the mass was pushed forward with such violence that a wall was broken down, steel barriers were bent and men, women and children were trampled underfoot.

Right The alternative game. Fans without tickets listening to Raymond Glendenning's commentary on the 1946 final on BBC Radio.

Above Charlton Athletic became the tenth club to lose a final one year and return to win it the next – their first Cup triumph. Their final against Burnley was a dull and defensive affair, illuminated only by Chris Duffy's spectacular winner – scored with only six minutes of extra-time left and everyone resigned to the first replay since 1912. The ball also burst again.

Alan Brown, captain of Burnley who also won promotion from Division Two, is one of the first to congratulate Don Welsh of Charlton after the game. Welsh later managed Brighton and Hove Albion, Liverpool, Bournemouth and Wycombe Wanderers. Brown went on to manage Burnley, Sunderland and Sheffield Wednesday.

1947

26 April at Wembley Att 99,000
Charlton Athletic 1 (Duffy)
Burnley 0 aet
Charlton Athletic: Bartram, Croker, Shreeve, Johnson, Phipps, Whittaker, Hurst, Dawson, Robinson, Welsh, Duffy.
Burnley: Strong, Woodruff, Mather, Attwell, Brown, Bray, Chew, Morris, Harrison, Potts, Kippax.
Referee: J. M. Wiltshire

Below The final was played on a hot and humid day, a severe contrast to the Big Freeze which had gripped the country from January to March. It forced nearly 150 postponements, and obliged the season to run until mid-June, the longest on record. With snow, ice, sleet, slush, wind and sub-zero temperatures for nearly three months, and an industrial crisis complicating things still further, the Government banned mid-week sport for a while in an attempt to boost production. Charlton practise on a frozen pitch at the Valley, while German prisoners-of-war clear snow and ice.

NEWS OF THE WORLD, April 25, 1948

THIS WAS WEMBLEY'S FINEST FINAL

Six-Goal Thriller

By HARRY J. DITTON

MANCHESTER UNITED 4, BLACKPOOL 2

What a magnificent Cup Final! It really was terrific. It had every-thing—intense drama, including six thrilling goals and some of the most delightful ball play Wembley has ever seen.

Above all, it was contested in a grand sporting spirit in spite of the fact that fouls preceded both of Blackpool's goals.

Yes, this was a game that will leave an imperishable memory with all who saw it—a classic exhibition which reflected nothing but the highest credit on every one of the 22 players.

A vintage summer for Wembley: the Olympic Games and, a few weeks before, one of the finest FA Cup finals of all. It was the sort of game the occasion deserves every season – a refined and adventurous affair with an exciting story line, outstanding players and six goals. Blackpool, with Stanley Matthews (just named as the first Footballer of the Year) and the dynamic Stan Mortensen, who scored in every round, led 2–1 with twenty-one minutes left. But then Manchester United, managed by Matt Busby and captained by the immaculate Johnny Carey, scored three times to win their first final since 1909 and the old days at Crystal Palace. Was there ever a more deserved triumph? United faced First Division opposition in every round: Aston Villa (United a goal down after fourteen seconds at Villa Park but 6–4 winners), Liverpool, Charlton Athletic, Preston North End, Derby County and Blackpool.

The pictures show two FA Cup goals, taken from a similar angle but with very different backcloths.

Left Jack Rowley walks Manchester United's first equaliser into the net in the final. He has beaten Blackpool's goalkeeper, Joe Robinson, in a race for the ball, flicked it over his head and scored with a tap.

Above Bob Curry, captain and inside-right of little Colchester United, scores one of his two goals in their 3–2 win over Bradford Park Avenue of the Second Division in the fourth round. The Southern League club had already beaten Huddersfield Town of the First Division and, with their diet of local oysters and secret F and M plan, they were the darlings of the media and public. The season belonged to them as much as Manchester United.

1948

24 April at Wembley   Att 99,000

Manchester United 4 (Rowley 2, Pearson, Anderson)

Blackpool 2 (Shimwell (pen), Mortensen)

Manchester United: Crompton, Carey, Aston, Anderson, Chilton, Cockburn, Delaney, Morris, Rowley, Pearson, Mitten.

Blackpool: Robinson, Shimwell, Crosland, Johnston, Hayward, Kelly, Matthews, Munro, Mortensen, Dick, Rickett.

Referee: C. J. Barrick

Opposite top Stan Cullis's Wolves, 1949. Cullis had an undentable belief in direct football: 'We insist that every player in possession of the ball makes rapid progress towards the business of launching an attack, our forwards are not encouraged to parade their skills in ostentatious fashion.' The method worked well. Wolves were too hungry, too strong, for Leicester City (who were fighting against relegation from Division Two) in the 1949 final and went on to three League Championships in the 1950s.

Wolverhampton Wanderers: *Back row (left to right)* – Billy Crook, Roy Pritchard, Bert Williams, Bill Shorthouse, Terry Springthorpe. *Seated* – Johnny Hancocks, Sammy Smyth, Stan Cullis, Billy Wright, Jesse Pye, Jimmy Dunn, Jimmy Mullen.

Opposite bottom Wolverhampton Wanderers won the Cup in 1949, but it was Yeovil Town's year. The Somerset club have scalped more big names in the Cup than any other non-League unit, but it was in this, their finest season, that they fired the imagination of the whole nation.

Yeovil were nowhere much in the Southern League and risibly quoted at 5,000 to 1 for the Cup, yet they beat Bury of the Second Division 3–1 in the third round and then Sunderland of the First by 2–1 in the fourth, a victory which has become the stuff of legend. Sunderland, League champions six times, were known as 'The Bank of England' club and had Len Shackleton of England – celebrity, showman, rebel, eccentric and brilliant inside-forward – as their star of stars. The publicity was immense and, on the day, a big overflow of reporters squeezed into little desks borrowed from a local school. Yeovil obliged them all. They made the most of their dramatically sloping pitch, scored through Alec Stock and Eric Bryant and then frustrated Sunderland by humping the ball towards most corners of the West Country. Yeovil were drawn away to Manchester United in the fifth round – and lost 8–0 in front of an 81,565 crowd.

Alec Stock, player-manager of

1949

30 April at Wembley   Att 99,500

Wolverhampton Wanderers 3
(Pye 2, Smyth)

Leicester City 1 (Griffiths)

Wolverhampton Wanderers: Williams, Pritchard, Springthorpe, Crook, Shorthouse, Wright, Hancocks, Smyth, Pye, Dunn, Mullen.

Leicester City: Bradley, Jelly, Scott, W. Harrison, Plummer, King, Griffiths, Lee, J. Harrison, Chisholm, Adam.

Referee: R. A. Mortimer

Yeovil (standing, centre) plots Sunderland's defeat. Stock, a former Royal Armoured Corps officer, played for Charlton Athletic and Queens Park Rangers and later successfully managed a variety of League clubs. He was popular, intelligent, articulate and an expert in the transfer market. 'Player-managership,' he would say, 'is violent exercise on top of a pile of worries.'

'General Alec' led Yeovil to finest win

SUNDERLAND SHATTERED

HANG out the flags! Ring the joybells! Let's go gay! Crown our team king of all! That was the sentiment in this football-crazy Somerset town last night after a most dramatic 2—1 Cup victory over mighty First Division Sunderland, who, in every department were outmanœuvred, outpaced and outclassed.

Never once did Sunderland settle down. The tackling of the Yeovil defence was the deciding factor. And once the attack, ever ticking like a time-bomb, finally burst, it blew Sunderland right out of the Cup.

After 28 minutes, manager and inside-right, Alec Stock, picked up a loose ball from a Keeton free-kick and scored with his left foot to send the crowd wild with ecstasy

Sunderland were worried and timid. Individually, they looked like a Test cricketer playing on a bumpy country pitch. It was no surprise that the Yeovil superiority carried on till half-time.

But Sunderland were to have their purple patch. Dyke, the young goalkeeper brought in at the eleventh hour, who had played superbly throughout, made his first blunder, and Ronnie Turnbull tapped home a mis-catch to level the score

To the end it was a riotous whirlwind of Cup-tie Soccer, neither side giving way in their dire efforts to settle the day. Yeovil were tiring, and it looked as if the sands of ambition were running out. But Alec Stock's generalship carried the day, and close marking and first-time tackling made for extra time.

Then came the great climax. Len Shackleton dallied with the ball in defence and was robbed by the magnificent Stock, who put through for Bryant to put the Glovers in the next round.

Sunderland can have no alibi. Yeovil had heaps more power and precision. A pat on the back to all their players who, each individually, played better than ever before in their lives

Yeovil: Dyke; Hickman, Davis; Keeton, Blizard, Collins; Hamilton, Stock, Bryant, Wright, Hargreaves.

Sunderland.—Mapson; Stelling, Ramsden; Watson, Hall, Wright; Duns, Robinson, Turnbull, Shackleton, Reynolds.

Sunday People.

1950

29 April at Wembley   Att 100,000

Arsenal 2 (Lewis 2)

Liverpool 0

Arsenal: Swindin, Scott, Barnes, Forbes, L. Compton, Mercer, Cox, Logie, Goring, Lewis, D. Compton.

Liverpool: Sidlow, Lambert, Spicer, Taylor, Hughes, Jones, Payne, Baron, Stubbins, Fagan, Liddell.

Referee: H. Pearce

Below The Compton brothers, centre-half Leslie (standing) and left-winger Denis, reading early telegrams of congratulation after Arsenal's comfortable victory over Liverpool. The Cup has a rest on the treatment table of the North dressing-room.

Denis, then approaching thirty-two, was nearing the end of his last season as a footballer and, during the interval after an indifferent first half, he was given a stiff brandy. He went back out to play at his best and to have a major part in the sparkling movement which led to Reg Lewis's second goal. Leslie, later that year, became England's oldest debutant (v Wales) at the age of thirty-eight years and sixty-five days.

Denis and Leslie were also Middlesex cricketers – but Denis was more than a first-class player. He was an England batsman of unconventional brilliance who scored 123 centuries and was described by the great Don Bradman as 'a glorious natural cricketer… he does things which nobody else can copy'. Denis was every schoolboy's hero.

Brothers have played together in a Cup final on more than a dozen occasions. In 1876 brothers even appeared on opposing sides, Hubert and Frank Heron playing for the Wanderers and Alfred and Edward Lyttelton for the Old Etonians. The most recent example is Phil and Gary Neville (Gary an eighty-ninth-minute substitute) for Manchester United in 1996.

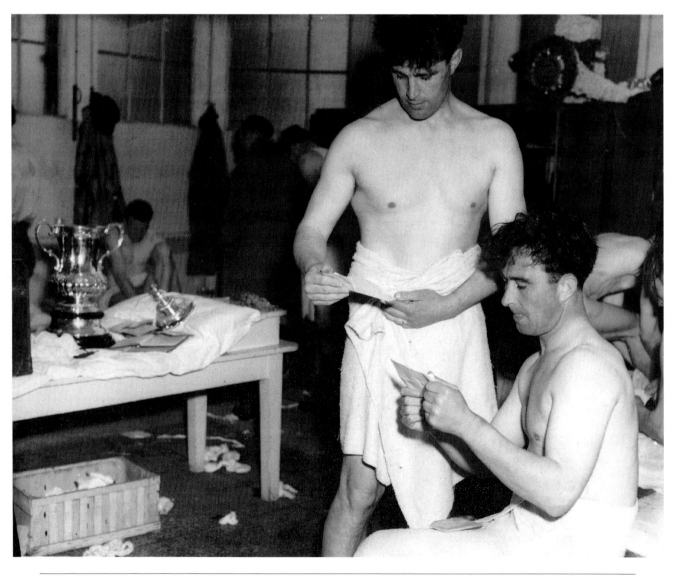

So the Story Goes...

'Is't that t'Coop? Why, 'tis nowt but a teapot,' observed a voice from the crowd after Blackburn Olympic had become the first Northern club to win the FA Cup by beating the Old Etonians 2–1 at Kennington Oval in 1883. Sam Warburton, the Olympic captain, replied: 'Ey, lad, it does, but it's very welcome in Lancashire. It'll have a good home and it'll never go back to London.' And it never did. Northern or Midlands clubs won the original trophy for the next twelve years – and then it was stolen and lost forever.

Nottingham Forest posted bills in Sheffield in 1883 offering a £20 reward for proof that one of Sheffield Wednesday's players was not properly qualified. Wednesday beat Forest 3–2 in a third-round replay.

After a tie in the 1880s, Long Eaton Rangers handed Sheffield Wednesday their £4 share of the gate money in two bags containing nearly a thousand old pennies. Wednesday refused and, after a heated argument, they were paid in silver.

Preston North End confidently asked to be photographed with the Cup before the 1888 final, but Major Francis Marindin, president of the Football Association, replied: 'Hadn't you better win it first?' Preston lost 2–1.

Aston Villa and Everton each booked into a 'secret' hotel for the 1897 final, only to discover they were staying at the same place. Villa won 3–2.

With the score 0–0, Derby County began the second half of a second-round tie at Lincoln in 1902 by surrounding the ball. They prevented any opponent getting near it, steered the ball into Lincoln's area, scored and went on to win 3–1.

Barnsley, without tickets, were refused entry to Crystal Palace before their 1910 final with Newcastle United. A passing Football League official eventually persuaded the stubborn commissionaire that unless he changed his mind there would be no final. That game was drawn 1–1 and Newcastle won the replay 2–0.

Arsenal made no arrangements for a dinner, celebratory or otherwise, after the 1927 final. They were beaten 1–0 by Cardiff City and, straight after the match, were taken by bus to Marylebone. Before making their own way home from there, though, they were treated to a drink in a nearby pub by captain Charles Buchan.

Portsmouth received £20 a man and shared a bonus of £550 for beating Wolverhampton Wanderers 4–1 in the 1939 final. It was then reported that the massed bands at Wembley were paid more and Ted (later Lord) Castle wrote an article in *Tribune* entitled, 'They would have been better off playing the cornet.'

Referee E. D. Smith of Sunderland said on BBC Radio before the 1946 final (Derby County 4 Charlton Athletic 1) that the odds against the ball bursting were a million to one. The ball burst then and again the following year when Charlton beat Burnley 1–0.

Derby County had not won the Cup before 1946 because, it was said, gypsies had put a curse on them long ago for training on their encampment. A Fleet Street reporter, however, had a bright idea. He persuaded Jack Nicholas, the Derby captain, to visit a gypsy camp near London during the week before the final. The curse was lifted in return for silver and Derby duly won the Cup for the first time.

Manchester United had a flap before leaving their dressing-room to face Leicester City in the 1963 final. Pat Crerand, their Scottish international wing-half, was missing! He was discovered in the tunnel, wearing only a jock-strap, singing 'Abide With Me'.

Chapter Eight

Day and Knight
1951–1960

'Suddenly there is a hush. Every cap and hat is removed as the band begins playing the most moving of all hymns, "Abide With Me". Then women and children from the grimy streets of the industrial town at last are on common ground with those from the stately homes of England. What does it matter if they are off key or are not quite sure of the words? Who takes notice if a few tears are shed? Who need be ashamed of keeping silent because emotion will not allow otherwise? I think it is a wonderful thing, and one for which British sports-lovers, regardless of politics and creed, are to be respected.'

Bert Trautmann, Manchester City's goalkeeper against Newcastle United in the 1955 FA Cup final and the first German to play in a final at Wembley.

From *Steppes to Wembley* (1956).

No argument about who is the greatest English footballer of them all will end in happy accord; but any such debate must begin with Stanley Matthews. Since the dawn of the game there has only been one like him. The songs of praise which followed Matthews along his right touchline for more than thirty years tell us little about this winger of middling height, impassive face and slightly bowed legs. They do, however, help confirm his uniqueness.

Matthews was the acknowledged 'Wizard of Dribble' and, by way of good measure, the 'Ageless Wonder', the 'King of Soccer', the 'Sorcerer', the 'Prince of the Potteries' and 'Knight of the Round Ball'. He was also, more substantially, the first and only professional footballer to be knighted while still playing, the first man to be named Footballer of the Year by England's football writers (an award which he won again fifteen years later) and the first to be named European Footballer of the Year.

His career of thirty-three years began at Stoke City in 1932 and ended five days after his fiftieth birthday in 1965. He played in nearly eight hundred League and Cup games for Stoke and Blackpool (including three FA Cup finals) and represented England on 84 occasions, including War and Victory internationals, between 1934 when he was nineteen and 1957 when he was forty-two.

The essence of the man was his ability to dribble past opponents. It does not sound much, put like that, but Matthews with a ball at his feet was a work of art – and the personality of art beggars description. This Merlin, with shuffle and sway, sleight of head, body and feet, severe control, exquisite balance and stunning change of pace, mesmerised opponents, sometimes confused team-mates and delighted spectators. His repertoire of tricks never changed yet nor were they ever rumbled. He was, at once, a destroyer and a charmer. His presence added thousands to gates.

The FA Cup, properly, decided the man was worth something special. Twice it frustrated him: he was in the Blackpool side which lost to Manchester United in the brilliant final of 1948 and who were bettered again by Jackie Milburn and Newcastle in 1951. But in 1953 Blackpool overcame such doughty opponents as Arsenal and Tottenham Hotspur to reach the final once more, and this time the script was both different and imaginative. It was Coronation year, after all, and the year in which Everest was conquered, Gordon Richards won the Derby for the first time at his twenty-eighth and final attempt, England regained the Ashes after twenty years and the Korean War ended.

Matthews was then thirty-eight and a treasured national institution. Bolton Wanderers were Blackpool's opponents at Wembley but, outside the walls of that worthy old cotton town, the nation shared Matthews's hopes and anxieties as he prepared for his third tilt at a winner's medal. The country was with him but Bolton, once the game started, proved able to look after themselves. They went ahead after 75 seconds, led by 2–1 at half-time and by 3–1 with little more than half an hour to go. But Bolton had a limping passenger in Eric Bell whom they switched from left-half to left-wing; and, slowly, dramatically, the balance of power changed. Matthews provided the teasing cross, high to the far post, from which Stan Mortensen made the score 3–2 and then, with less than three minutes left, Mortensen thundered home a free-kick from the edge of the penalty area.

An extra half-hour beckoned until, a minute into time added for injuries, Matthews received a pass from Ernie Taylor, flickered past Bolton's left-back Ralph Banks on the outside and – his final contribution to the match – cut the ball back along the ground, perfectly, for Bill Perry to score. Blackpool 4 Bolton 3 – and the new young Queen handed Matthews his medal.

No other final has left such a mark on the tournament. Such drama, such heroes! Mortensen, the 'Electric Eel' with his razing speed and nose for gaps before they opened, the first player to score a hat-trick in a Wembley final; Taylor with his lucid distribution; Perry with his last-breath winner; and Matthews, in his familiar number seven shirt, the high executioner.

Does it matter that Mortensen managed his first goal only with the help of a ninety-degree deflection by Bolton's Harold Hassall? Kenneth Wolstenholme, the BBC's television commentator, immediately described it as an own goal, later changing his mind. And does it matter if Matthews, on his own admission, had often played better?

There were thirty-five minutes left when Bolton established their 3–1 lead, and in that time Matthews had possession twenty-five times. He passed or centred the ball without first beating a man on fourteen occasions and beat a defender (but never two) ten times. He was dispossessed once (and fouled at the same time) and he also took four corners. What mattered most, of course, was that he twice unlocked Bolton's defence. It was, forever, the Matthews final – with some precious help from Mortensen.

It says much about the Cup that it glittered as brightly as ever during the tensions of the fifties. Newcastle United became the first club in the twentieth century to win the trophy two years running (1951 and 1952) as they triumphed three times in five seasons. 'You have to be a Geordie to understand what the Cup means in these parts,' said Jackie Milburn, a Tyneside folk hero and the arrowhead of that thoroughbred Newcastle side. 'It means glory, glamour, excitement and, above all, it is instant.' This passion for the Cup was certainly shared by three Third Division clubs – Port Vale (1954), York City (1955) and Norwich City (1959) – who beat a path to the very gates of Wembley, failing by just a finger-snap to win their semi-finals.

Yet the Cup was only one bold dimension of football in the fifties. England were even obliged to realise that they were no longer the masters of the game they had devised and exported around the world. They lost 1–0 to the United States, a collection of international tenderfoots, during their first shot at the World Cup in Brazil in 1950; and, not long after the Matthews final, they were twice overwhelmed by Hungary, whose designs and symmetry lifted the game on to a higher plateau.

The World Cup defeat was hugely embarrassing but quickly attributed to rotten luck. No adjustment of fact was possible, though, after Hungary had beaten England by 6–3 at Wembley on 25 November 1953 and, six months later, by 7–1 in Budapest. There was much anguished debate and analysis as, for a few months at least, English football seemed to accept that it had something to learn. Then it was back to old beliefs and routines.

Matt Busby and Stan Cullis governed the domestic game for most of the fifties. Busby led Manchester United to three Championships (1952, 1956 and 1957), while Cullis did the same for Wolverhampton Wanderers (1954, 1958 and 1959). Significantly, they also had a hand in the creation and acceptance of the European Cup for League champions.

Wolves advanced the birth of the European Cup by beating Moscow Spartak and Honved, the champions-elect of Hungary, in two memorable friendlies in 1954; and it was Manchester United who led English football into Europe in the 1956–57 season – a year after Chelsea had been advised not to take part in the European Cup because it was 'not in the best interests' of the Football League.

Busby's 'Babes' might have dominated English football for years but, still champions and still pursuing the European Cup, they and their dreams perished in the slush and ice of a West German airport on 6 February 1958. Their chartered aircraft crashed during take-off, after stopping at Munich to refuel on their way back from a game in Belgrade, and in a few dreadful moments the heart of a brilliant team was destroyed. Twenty-three people died, including eight players, but among the survivors were Busby himself and Bobby Charlton.

Manchester United had lost to Aston Villa in the 1957 Cup final; and now, after Munich, they clawed their way towards Wembley again on a high tide of emotion. They made one or two hasty signings, among them Ernie Taylor from Blackpool, filled in with a few reserves and, fired by the will of the nation, they overcame Sheffield Wednesday, West Bromwich Albion and Fulham to reach the final. But there the fairy-tale ended. Bolton Wanderers, as ever a strong and uncomplicated side, won with two goals by the dauntless Nat Lofthouse. United's exit from the old stadium was so poignant that thousands cried.

The Cup has never been obsessed by justice or merit. The Matthews final should, by rights, have been followed by the 'Finney final'. Tom Finney was one of English football's finest ambassadors, who spent the whole of his career playing with wonderful skill and selfless loyalty for Preston North End. He was at Wembley with his club in 1954, against West Bromwich Albion, but on his own admission he had a poor game. He was a runner-up that day, and retired in 1960 without a major domestic honour to his name.

There are times, too, when the Cup is positively cruel. Witness the number of players who sustained serious injuries in a Wembley final during the fifties and sixties: Walley Barnes of Arsenal in 1952, Jimmy Meadows of Manchester City in 1955, Bert Trautmann of Manchester City with a broken neck in 1956, Ray Wood of Manchester United in 1957, Roy Dwight of Nottingham Forest in 1959, Dave Whelan of Blackburn in 1960, Len Chalmers of Leicester City in 1961 and Gerry Byrne of Liverpool in 1965. There was talk of a Wembley hoodoo but the injuries were attributable to everyday reasons – collisions, over-zealous tackles and, in one or two cases, the lushness of the turf which caught studs and tore muscles and ligaments. The use of substitutes was approved by the Football Association on 3 July 1965.

The fifties moved the game robustly forward. Floodlights popped up on grounds all over the country and mid-week football after dark gave the season new shape and clubs a fresh source of income; undersoil heating was used for the first time; managers and coaches experimented with formats and strategies; training methods became more scientific; and players even looked different in lightweight strips and cutaway boots. The pace was quickening.

Above Jackie Milburn, 'Wor Jackie' to all Tyneside, scored twice to win the Cup for Newcastle United – but this famous clearance off the line by Bobby Cowell was the key moment of the 1951 final. Stan Mortensen's header (twenty-one minutes, 0–0) looked certain to give Blackpool the lead until Cowell, Newcastle's right-back, somehow nudged the ball upwards from right under the cross-bar. Stanley Matthews said after-wards: 'If we had got that goal I think we would have won.'

Right Newcastle steered an erratic course to Wembley, with several frights and replays, but they were worthy winners with Milburn, that dashing buccaneer, the hero. His first goal was a beauty; his second (pictured), four minutes later from twenty-five yards, was spectacular – one of Wembley's best. He scored in every round.

Right Is the King in? Newcastle fan at Buckingham Palace, 1951.

1951

28 April at Wembley   Att 100,000

Newcastle United 2 (Milburn 2)

Blackpool 0

Newcastle United: Fairbrother, Cowell, Corbett, Harvey, Brennan, Crowe, Walker, Taylor, Milburn, Robledo, Mitchell.

Blackpool: Farm, Shimwell, Garrett, Johnston, Hayward, Kelly, Matthews, Mudie, Mortensen, Slater, Perry.

Referee: W. Ling

1952

3 May at Wembley   Att 100,000

Newcastle United 1

(G. Robledo)

Arsenal 0

Newcastle United: Simpson, Cowell, McMichael, Harvey, Brennan, E. Robledo, Walker, Foulkes, Milburn, G. Robledo, Mitchell.

Arsenal: Swindin, Barnes, Smith, Forbes, Daniel, Mercer, Cox, Logie, Holton, Lishman, Roper.

Referee: A. Ellis

Right Newcastle United become the first club to win the Cup in successive years since Blackburn Rovers in 1890 and 1891 – but this was a final in which Arsenal's luck ran out on them. The north London side lost their Welsh international right-back Wally Barnes, injured, after thirty-five minutes, and Newcastle won with a headed goal, in off a post, by George Robledo (second right) six minutes from the end. Two brothers, again, were on a winning side: George, a Chilean international, and Ted Robledo. Arsenal, for the record, were gallant in defeat. 'We won the Cup,' said Newcastle's manager Stan Seymour, 'but Arsenal won the honours.'

Below Winston Churchill hands the Cup to Newcastle captain Joe Harvey – the only Prime Minister to have made the presentation at Wembley.

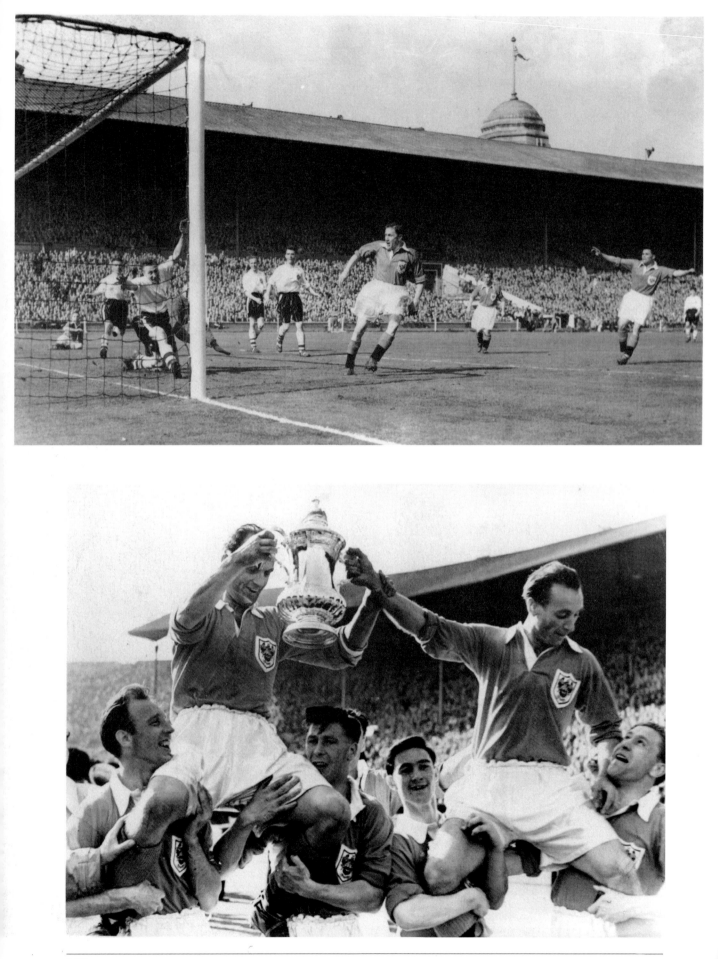

1953

2 May at Wembley   Att 100,000

Blackpool 4 (Mortensen 3, Perry)

Bolton Wanderers 3 (Lofthouse, Moir, Bell)

Blackpool: Farm, Shimwell, Garrett, Fenton, Johnston, Robinson, Matthews, Taylor, Mortensen, Mudie, Perry.

Bolton Wanderers: Hanson, Ball, Banks, Wheeler, Barass, Bell, Holden, Moir, Lofthouse, Hassall, Langton.

Referee: M. Griffiths

'The Matthews final'. The final in which the 'Wizard of Dribble', at the third attempt and at the age of thirty-eight, at last got his winner's medal. His triumph is the most familiar of all the Cup's stories: Bolton Wanderers were 3–1 up with half an hour left before Blackpool, inspired by Matthews and carrying the hopes of the nation, blazed back to win 4–3 with a last-minute goal.

Above left Bill Perry, arms outstretched, steers in Blackpool's winner with a minute left. Stanley Matthews, who provided the short centre, twenty yards, diagonal, along the ground, is on his backside on the left. Stan Mortensen, who chipped in with a hat-trick, is centre picture. The Wembley scoreboard was so confused it showed the score as Blackpool 4 Bolton 4.

Left Matthews exchanges a knowing look with Mortensen. Blackpool's captain, also aloft, called for 'three cheers for Her Majesty the Queen' after the presentation.

Right Footballer... and medal.

1954

I May at Wembley   Att 100,000

West Bromwich Albion 3 (Allen
2 (1 pen), Griffin)

Preston North End 2 (Morrison,
Wayman)

West Bromwich Albion: Sanders,
Kennedy, Millard, Dudley, Dugdale,
Barlow, Griffin, Ryan, Allen,
Nicholls, Lee.

Preston North End: Thompson,
Cunningham, Walton, Docherty,
Marston, Forbes, Finney, Foster,
Wayman, Baxter, Morrison.

Referee: A. Luty

Left Great Yarmouth Town build a
stand with fishboxes for their first-
round tie with Crystal Palace of the
Third Division (South). A winning
goal by Rackham rewarded them for
their industry, to bring their finest
result in the Cup.

Above One year on and Blackpool,
the Cup holders, are facing defeat
at Port Vale in the fifth round. Stanley
Matthews (centre of picture) is doing
his best – but, this time, it is not
enough. Port Vale won 2–0 and went
on to become the first Third
Division club to reach the semi-finals
since the war. A crowd of 68,221
at Villa Park then saw Port Vale take
the lead in their semi-final against
West Bromwich Albion, but the First
Division runners-up came back to
win 2–1, with the help of a late and
hotly disputed penalty by Ronnie
Allen. A Third Division club came
that close to Wembley! Port Vale
won the Third Division (North) by a
margin of eleven points and in fifty-
four League and Cup games they
conceded only twenty-five goals.

Right The Cup can be heartless.
After 'the Matthews final', this should
have been 'the Finney final'. Tom
Finney of England, the Preston
Plumber, played for his home-town
club with consummate skill and
versatility for fourteen years. He
was twice Footballer of the Year
(1954 and 1957) and was universally admired as a professional and
man. Here was the hero you took
your son to see, a great player by
any yardstick, but he did not win a
single major honour.

Finney, for once, had an indifferent game against West Bromwich
Albion in a defensive final which,
nonetheless, produced five goals.
Preston North End were leading
2–1 with less than half an hour left
when they conceded a penalty which
is the subject of one of football's
best pictures. Jim Sanders, Albion's
goalkeeper, dare not watch as
Ronnie Allen takes the spot-kick. A
roar told him that Allen (number
nine) had scored; and Frank Griffin
hit Albion's winner three minutes
from time.

Above Newcastle United yet again: their third triumph in five seasons, their fifth in five visits to Wembley and, in all, their sixth in ten finals. They began with another record, with the quickest goal in a Wembley final, credited at forty-five seconds, scored by Jackie Milburn from a corner by Len White. Manchester City lost their right-back Jimmy Meadows in the eighteenth minute, with an injured right knee, but clever football still earned them an equaliser by Bobby Johnstone. However, Newcastle, confident and strong despite injuries to Milburn and White, scored twice in six minutes in the second half through Bobby Mitchell and George Hannah.

Opposite top Newcastle's Cup run was nearly ended at the semi-final stage by York City – yet another Third Division club, following Port Vale's heroics the previous season, to pound on the gates of Wembley. Newcastle and York drew 1–1 at Hillsborough but Arthur Bottom (number eight) failed by just a touch to give York a perhaps decisive lead. Newcastle won the replay at Roker Park by 2–0 and Bottom, the scorer of eight of York's eighteen goals in their Cup run, joined Newcastle three years later.

1955

7 May at Wembley   Att 100,000

Newcastle United 3 (Milburn, Mitchell, Hannah)

Manchester City 1 (Johnstone)

Newcastle United: Simpson, Cowell, Batty, Scoular, Stokoe, Casey, White, Milburn, Keeble, Hannah, Mitchell.

Manchester City: Trautmann, Meadows, Little, Barnes, Ewing, Paul, Spurdle, Hayes, Revie, Johnstone, Fagan.

Referee: R. Leafe

Left Jimmy Meadows, disconsolate and holding his injured knee, sits next to Manchester City manager Les McDowall at the start of the second half. Meadows has changed into formal wear before taking his place on the bench.

1956

5 May at Wembley   Att 100,000

Manchester City 3 (Hayes, Dyson, Johnstone)

Birmingham City 1 (Kinsey)

Manchester City: Trautmann, Leivers, Little, Barnes, Ewing, Paul, Johnstone, Hayes, Revie, Dyson, Clarke.

Birmingham City: Merrick, Hall, Green, Newman, Smith, Boyd, Astall, Kinsey, Brown, Murphy, Govan.

Referee: A. Bond

Below Officials and fans of Redhill prepare to ring their council pitch with benches on the morning of their fourth qualifying round tie with the professionals of Hastings United in November 1955. Redhill, Surrey, amateurs of the Athenian League, were reported to be 'Cup crazy' – and they held their redoubtable opponents to a 2–2 draw before losing 4–0 in a replay.

Right Fred Packham, a seventy-five-year-old plater and polisher, gives the Cup a last twinkle before the 1956 final.

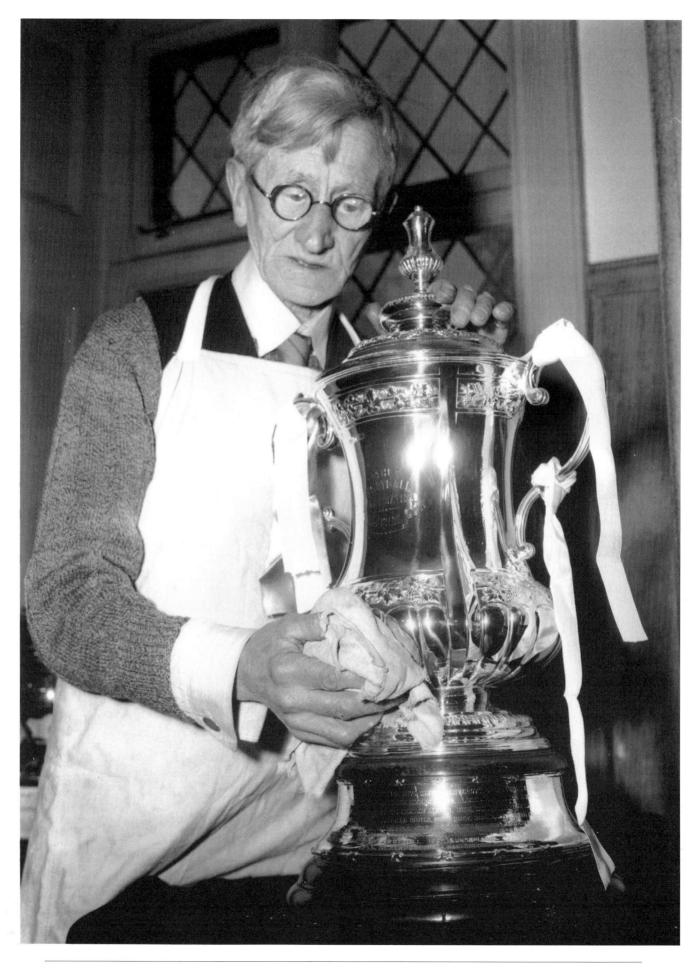

Below Bert Trautmann of Manchester City, the first German to play in a Wembley Cup final, dives at the feet of Birmingham City's Peter Murphy, fifteen minutes from the end of the 1956 final. Head met boot, but Trautmann played on in great pain and it was confirmed several days later, after an X-ray at Manchester Royal Infirmary, that the big goalkeeper had broken his neck. Birmingham, 3–1 down, were unable to capitalise on his dazed condition. Trautmann, a former paratrooper and prisoner-of-war, was immensely popular and had just been named Footballer of the Year.

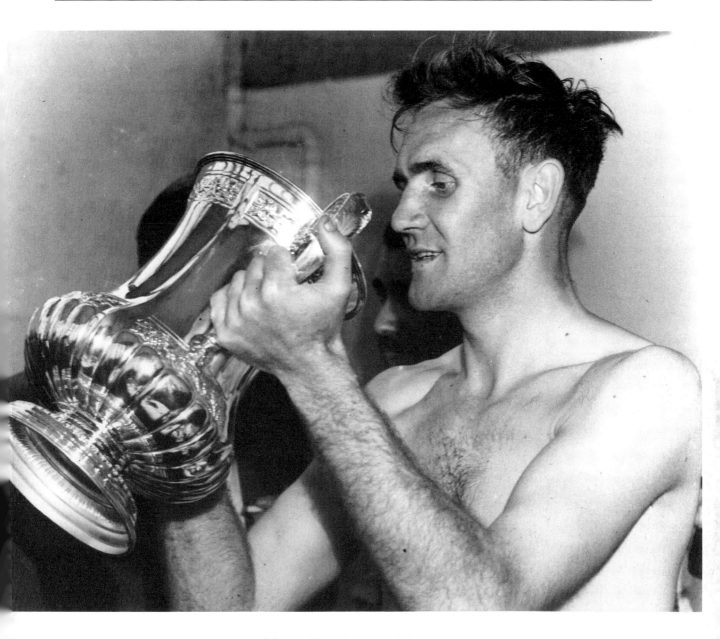

Above Don Revie celebrates Manchester City's triumph, after a final which is remembered for the 'Revie plan' as well as Trautmann's injury. Revie played as a deep-lying centre-forward, and had a hand in two of City's goals, yet he was a late selection in place of Bill Spurdle, who was suffering from an attack of boils. Revie later became a hugely successful manager of Leeds United (1961–74) and then manager of England (1974–77), before infamously taking a handsomely paid job in the United Arab Emirates, which led to a ten-year ban from domestic football. The suspension was later overruled in the High Court but the stigma remained. He died of motor neurone disease, aged sixty-one, in 1989.

Left Room at the top. Part of a crowd of 45,646 who watched Millwall of the Third Division (South) beat Newcastle United, the Cup giants of the 1950s, by 2–1 in the fourth round at the Den. Millwall's two goals were scored by Stan Anslow who, earlier in the season, had switched from full-back to centre-forward.

Below Peter McParland, Aston Villa's dashing Irish left-winger, scores the second of his Cup-winning goals from eight yards after a rebound from the bar. But injury again marred English football's big occasion when Manchester United's England goalkeeper, Ray Wood, broke his cheekbone in a barging collision with McParland himself after only six minutes. In goal, capped against the facing sun, is centre-half Jackie Blanchflower, who made some accomplished saves. Tommy Taylor scored a late goal for United but Villa's record seventh triumph denied United the double, last achieved by Villa themselves sixty years earlier. Matt Busby's champion 'Babes', all were agreed, had time on their side.

1957

4 May at Wembley   Att 100,000
Aston Villa 2 (McParland 2)
Manchester United 1 (Taylor)
Aston Villa: Sims, Lynn, Aldis, Crowther, Dugdale, Saward, Smith, Sewell, Myerscough, Dixon, McParland.
Manchester United: Wood, Foulkes, Byrne, Colman, J. Blanchflower, Edwards, Berry, Whelan, T. Taylor, Charlton, Pegg.
Referee: F. Coultas

Above Collapse at Molineux. Bournemouth of the Third Division (South) beat Wolverhampton Wanderers 1–0 in the fourth round and also brought down one of Molineux's goalposts. Reg Cutler, Bournemouth's Birmingham-born left-winger, was the destructive hero: first the goalpost, with a painful collision, and then the winning goal. Before their next tie, at home to Tottenham Hotspur, Bournemouth's manager Freddie Cox received a letter warning them 'to cut out the commando stuff you used against Wolves – or we will do the same to you and your boys'. Bournemouth, uninhibited, beat Tottenham 3–1 at Dean Court before losing 2–1 (after being a goal up against ten men) to Manchester United in the quarter-finals.

Below The programme for Manchester United's first game after the Munich disaster in which eight of the 'Busby Babes' lost their lives. It was an FA Cup fifth-round tie against Sheffield Wednesday at Old Trafford, played on 19 February 1958, thirteen days after the crash, and United's spaces were left blank because they were uncertain of their line-up. The team was announced over the tannoy system just before the kick-off, a scratch mixture of reserves, juniors, hastily imported players, and two survivors of the disaster – goalkeeper Harry Gregg and right-back Bill Foulkes, who captained the side. Stan Crowther, a hard wing-half, had been bought from Aston Villa for £23,000 and thirty-three-year-old Ernie Taylor from Blackpool for £8,000. The crowd was 60,000 and, on a night of suffocating emotion, Sheffield Wednesday must have thought they had the worst job in the world. United won 3–0 with two goals from Shay Brennan, a full-back who was making his first-team debut at outside-left. 'A Phoenix takes wing,' observed the *Guardian* and, on a wave of emotion, United went on to beat West Bromwich Albion and Fulham to reach the final.

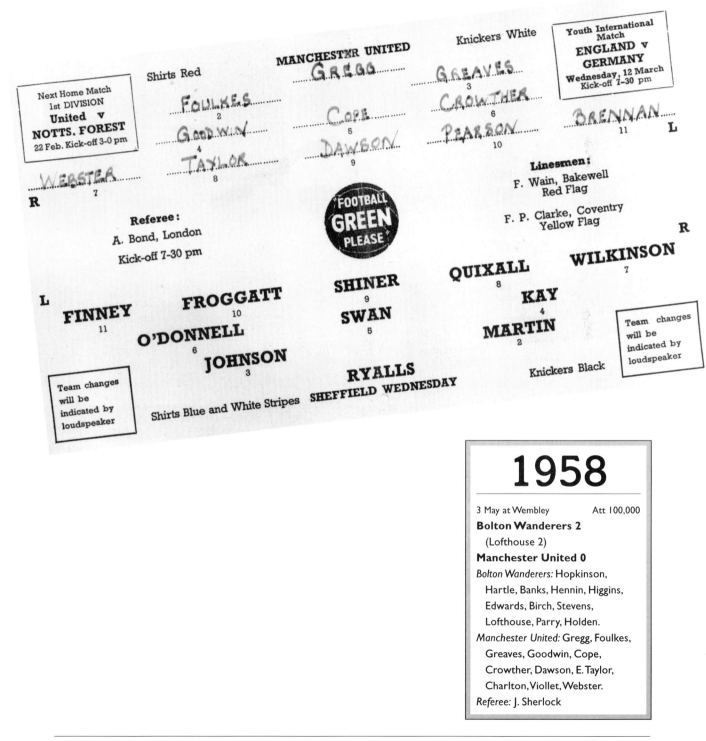

1958

3 May at Wembley — Att 100,000

Bolton Wanderers 2
(Lofthouse 2)
Manchester United 0
Bolton Wanderers: Hopkinson, Hartle, Banks, Hennin, Higgins, Edwards, Birch, Stevens, Lofthouse, Parry, Holden.
Manchester United: Gregg, Foulkes, Greaves, Goodwin, Cope, Crowther, Dawson, Charlton, Viollet, Webster.
Referee: J. Sherlock

Above Manchester United had the nation's heart in the 1958 final: their progress to Wembley had become a crusade and a fairy tale which was supposed to have a happy ending. But for the second year running United lost, beaten 2–0 by Bolton Wanderers with Nat Lofthouse scoring twice. Lofthouse of England, known as 'The Lion of Vienna' after scoring a remarkable runaway goal against Austria, was a tireless battering ram, a muscular predator. His first goal came after three minutes, a simple touch-in, but his second (pictured), ten minutes into the second half, was a hugely controversial affair. Gregg, United's goalkeeper, did well to parry a fierce drive by Dennis Stevens but, as he turned and got his hands to the ball a second time, Lofthouse charged him in the back. The ball spun out of Gregg's hands into the net and, although United protested and the crowd howled, the goal was allowed to stand. Lofthouse admitted later that he fouled Gregg.

Right Nat Lofthouse leads Bolton up Wembley's steps to receive the Cup from the Queen and the Duke of Edinburgh, while in the tunnel below, unnoticed, Matt Busby (in trilby) gives an interview. Busby was terribly injured in the Munich crash but, released from hospital only a fortnight before and still frail and uncertain on his feet, he watched the game from the touchline.

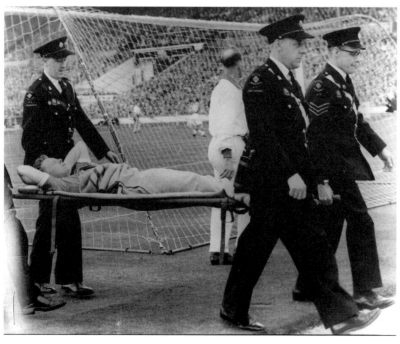

Nottingham Forest became the first club to win at Wembley with ten men – and the 'injury hoodoo' raised more heated discussion about the wisdom and morality of introducing substitutes.

Above and left Roy Dwight, an uncle of singing star Elton John, was at the heart of the drama. Forest's right-winger scored a handsome first goal in the tenth minute but, after Tommy Wilson had added a second, Dwight broke a leg in the thirtieth minute and was stretchered away to watch the rest of the game on television.

Billy Walker's Forest had played some brilliant football up to that point but, reduced to ten men, they fought a spirited rearguard action

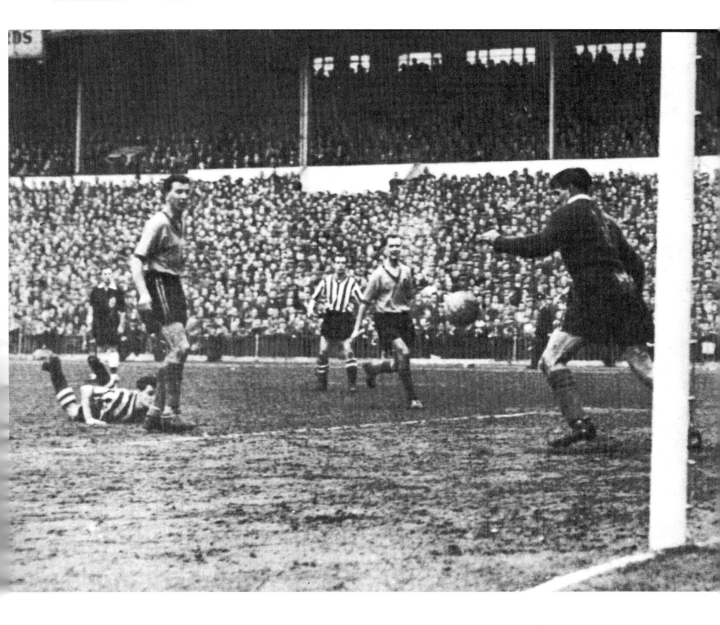

which confined Luton Town to just one goal by David Pacey.

Forest's Cup triumph was impressive and deserved. Few remembered that in the third round, away to non-League Tooting and Mitcham, they had been two goals down at half-time on a frozen and rutted pitch, equalising only by way of an own goal and a very controversial penalty.

Above A picture which does much to explain why Norwich City of the Third Division had one of the Cup's most exhilarating runs in 1959. They were a talented and well-organised side but, above all, their team spirit was tremendous. Here Ken Nethercott, their goalkeeper, defies Sheffield United in a quarter-final at Bramall

Lane, even though his right shoulder is dislocated and his arm hangs uselessly by his side. He got along by using his body and good arm – part folly, part heroism – and Norwich equalised after being a goal down. They went on to win the replay 3–2 and reach the semi-finals where, despite dominating another replay, they lost to a goal by Luton's Billy Bingham.

Norwich beat four winners of the Cup – Manchester United (3–0 on an ice-covered pitch at Carrow Road), Cardiff City, Tottenham Hotspur and Sheffield United – and were centre-stage for two glorious months. The nation loved them for their bravado; and their anthem, 'On the Ball, City', was one of the sounds of the fifties.

1959

2 May at Wembley · Att 100,000
Nottingham Forest 2 (Dwight, Wilson)
Luton Town 1 (Pacey)
Nottingham Forest: Thomson, Whare, McDonald, Whitefoot, McKinlay, Burkitt, Dwight, Quigley, Wilson, Gray, Imlach.
Luton Town: Baynham, McNally, Hawkes, Groves, Owen, Pacey, Bingham, Brown, Morton, Cummins, Gregory.
Referee: J. Clough

1960

7 May at Wembley   Att 100,000

Wolverhampton Wanderers 3
  (McGrath (og), Deeley 2)

Blackburn Rovers 0

Wolverhampton Wanderers: Finlayson, Showell, Harris, Clamp, Slater, Flowers, Deeley, Stobart, Murray, Broadbent, Horne.

Blackburn Rovers: Leyland, Bray, Whelan, Clayton, Woods, McGrath, Bimpson, Dobing, Dougan, Douglas, McLeod.

Referee: K. Howley

The Cup does not deliver to order and the 1960 final was one of the poorest. 'The Dustbin Final' is how the old *Daily Sketch* trenchantly described it. The game was bitter and one-sided, especially after Blackburn Rovers had lost left-back Dave Whelan with a broken leg just before half-time, and at the end Lancashire fans pelted the Wolverhampton Wanderers players with rubbish. Derek Dougan, Blackburn's centre-forward, with an opportunist sense of timing, even chose Cup final day to announce that he wanted a transfer, providing more evidence of a debilitating lack of harmony behind the scenes.

Below Mick McGrath, Blackburn's left-half, on knees, deflects a low centre by Barry Stobart into his own net for Wolves' first goal in the forty-first minute. Two minutes later Whelan was carried off and the day was won and lost. Norman Deeley, right of post, scored Wolves' other two goals in the second half.

Chapter Nine

Sons of the Cup
1961–1970

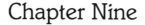

'It was a wet day, raining and splashing, and my shoes and pants were covered in white from the chalk of the pitch as I walked up to the end of the ground where our supporters were massed. We had beaten Leeds United and our players had the arena, but I took off my coat and went to our fans because they had got the Cup for the first time. Grown men were crying and it was the greatest feeling any human being could have to see what we had done. There have been many proud moments. Wonderful, fantastic moments. But that was the greatest day.'

Bill Shankly on Liverpool's first FA Cup triumph in 1965.

From *Shankly* (1976).

English football, for all its patriarchal airs and graces, reached the sixties without a decent decoration or formal battle honour to its name... apart, that is, from the good old British Championship and the Olympic titles of 1908 and 1912 when England's amateurs represented Great Britain. The home of the game then made up for lost time and won almost everything worth winning: the World Cup, the European Cup, the European Cup-Winners' Cup and the Inter-Cities Fairs Cup which later became the UEFA Cup. The FA Cup, the daddy of all tournaments, was thus obliged to share centre-stage with some of its progeny.

The Cup was even faced by a domestic rival. The Football League launched the League Cup in 1960, a money maker for its own members, and seemed surprised when it was immediately condemned as a cardboard replica of the FA Cup, a small-time pretender, an ugly duckling and a mammoth irrelevancy. It had a difficult birth and early problems, but once its final moved to Wembley in 1967 and the winner was offered an automatic place in Europe, it was granted respectability.

The tone and confidence of English football in the sixties were established by an outstanding club side. Tottenham Hotspur were the stuff of dreams for a few seasons, beautifully balanced, cleverly integrated, a sweet harmony of artists and craftsmen with a perceptible air of superiority. Bill Nicholson, Spurs' reserved but hugely respected manager, built the side with infinite care. At the heart of his formula were players of the quality of Danny Blanchflower and Dave Mackay, Irish charm and Scottish fire in midfield; John White, a phantom at inside-forward; Bobby Smith, a heavyweight warrior at the sharp end; and Cliff Jones, with his waspish speed and sting on the wing. Soon, too, they were joined by Jimmy Greaves, back from a short spell in Italy, who was one of the greatest finishers the English game has known: more than half his 491 goals were scored for Spurs.

In 1961 Spurs became the first club to complete the League and Cup double in the twentieth century; they retained the Cup and reached the semi-final of the European Cup a year later; and in 1963 became the first British club to win a major European trophy when they won the Cup-Winners' Cup.

Spurs' double was the first since Preston (1889) and Aston Villa (1897) managed it in a formative and less cluttered age of organised professional football. Eleven sides had come near to winning both trophies in a season in the next sixty or so years, including Manchester United (League champions and Cup runners-up in 1956–57) and Wolverhampton Wanderers (League runners-up and Cup winners in 1959–60), but fixture congestion, vagaries of form and tension all conspired to make victory in both tournaments an increasingly tall order.

Spurs, however, always believed in themselves. 'Our conviction was the key to everything,' said Danny Blanchflower, their captain, after collecting the two pots. It helped, too, that Spurs had range in ability, depth in reserve and wonderful support – a total of 2,512,034 (average 51,000) watched their 49 games. They scored 136 goals (115 in 42 League games, 21 in seven Cup ties) and created a handsome set of new records along the way. Their superiority was matched by their popularity.

Spurs' starry image helped to launch a new age for the professional footballer. In the early 1960s, following talk of strike action, intelligent use of the media and a celebrated judgment in the High Court, players at last got their 'freedom'. The maximum wage and the old retain-and-transfer system passed into history – and players looked forward to a more affluent life-style.

Outstanding sides took their turn to make a mark on the sixties. West Ham followed Spurs by winning the Cup in 1964 and the European Cup-Winners' Cup a year later by beating Munich 1860 2–0 at Wembley with a performance of admirable style and variety. What Bobby Moore, Geoff Hurst and Martin Peters did for West Ham, they also proved perfectly capable of doing for England during the high summer of 1966.

The winning of the World Cup did more for English football than anything since the birth of the FA Cup nearly a hundred years before. Possession of the Jules Rimet trophy – held aloft by captain Bobby Moore at 5.15 on 30 July 1966 – gave England's players the right to regard themselves as the best in the world for four years. Hurst contributed a hat-trick to England's 4–2 victory over West Germany in the final – and, just to keep things tidy, Peters scored their other goal. Alf Ramsey, England's manager, had said: 'England will win the World Cup.' This strong and complex man was always true to his word.

English football's self-esteem had never been higher and its momentum was maintained by some other redoubtable managers. Bill Shankly of Liverpool, a gravel-voiced Scot who turned a game of sweat and muscle into a faith, and Don Revie of Leeds, the professional's professional, guided their clubs expertly towards their most successful years, which included, remarkably, their very first Cup triumphs, Liverpool winning in 1965 and Leeds in 1972.

The grand and ugly city of Manchester, too, made its contribution. Manchester City, under the joint stewardship of Joe Mercer and Malcolm Allison, won the League Championship (1968), the FA Cup (1969) and the League Cup and Cup-Winners' Cup (1970). Yet no club's achievement counted for more than Manchester United's brilliant victory in the European Cup in 1968.

Manchester United were the first English club to win the champions' trophy, but their 4–1 victory over Benfica in the final at Wembley was much more than just another handsome line in the record books. It was a night of fulfilment and a tribute to the Busby Babes who lost their lives in Munich ten years before. Bobby Charlton and Bill Foulkes, two Munich survivors, were at the heart of United's triumph on that May evening in 1968, and Matt Busby himself described it as 'the most wonderful thing in my life'.

The Luck of the Draw

One of the sublime charms of the FA Cup is that its most important element cannot be bought, taught, rehearsed or even easily defined. It is that abstruse yet profound thing we call luck.

Luck has many faces. There is the kind of luck which has to do with lucky boots, lucky people to touch, lucky hotels, lucky positions in which to run onto the field and, although it doesn't work for rabbits, lucky rabbits' feet. Luck, good or bad, can be half the width of a goalpost or a moment's lunacy by an opponent. There is also the luck which is deserved: 'We make our own luck, lads.'

Perhaps the most significant luck of all is freely dispensed at the time of the draws for each round, when numbered balls are paired together and pure chance plots the road to Wembley. Herbert Chapman of Arsenal, the high priest of managers, wrote in the 1930s: 'To succeed in the Cup you want luck, a deal of it, not so much on the field as in the Council Chamber where ties are fortuitously arranged. There are times, especially when it goes against you, when you are inclined to believe that too much luck enters the tournament. Personally, however, I would not have the conditions altered. Indeed, to tinker with them would rob the event of much of its fascination.'

The ritual has changed now. The draws for the later rounds are shown on television, rather than relayed by radio, which means the old and simple formula has been decorated by personalities, interviews, film-clips and a studio audience. The balls are drawn from a plastic bowl instead of a velvet bag. Before the 1990s, however, the draws for every round were made by the venerables of the FA's Challenge Cup committee, the guarantors of the honesty of it all, and the simplicity of the format seemed only to heighten the excitement.

The draw for the third round proper is the richest theatre of all. It is then that the Bigtime Uniteds and Superior Cities are coupled with the sturdy survivors of a ragtime army from every urban and rural corner of the country, who have sharp-elbowed their way through from the early rounds.

Peer will often be drawn against peer, but Liverpool versus Manchester United versus Newcastle United versus Tottenham Hotspur are handsome yet standard roses which can be enjoyed at any time of the season. It is something else the country is waiting for, something which sounds like this: 'Number forty-two … Walsall … will play number five … Arsenal.'

The significance of the draw ripples across the land as small, lucky clubs begin to realise that the Cup has pushed them under a national spotlight. Players who, between matches, may deliver letters, drive buses or sell double glazing know they will be celebrities for at least a week or two. They know, too, that their good fortune in the draw may never mean wealth of a more tangible kind. But much more than money is involved. The Cup is important for its own sake.

The draw, once, was a strictly private affair. J. Harwood Lee, writing in a magazine called *Penny Pictorial*, had this to say about the draw for the second round in 1921: 'When I arrived in the basement press-room at the Football Association's offices in Russell Square, a little platoon of scribblers was already assembled, with sharpened pencils in front of them, and sheets of thin paper with pieces of carbon in between. They are exasperating people, though, these officers of the Football Association. They assemble immediately after lunch, yet do all sorts of footling things before they come to the real business of the day.

'At length, however, there comes a hint that the draw is actually being made, so we make sure that our pencils are really sharp. Funnily enough, on the day the draw for the second round was made the electric light in that basement

room failed about five minutes before the important news came along. Fortunately, by drawing the blind a little higher, we could just see to write. Outside, peering into the press-room, were a score or more of London boys and girls. Probably not one of them had ever seen a Cup tie, but they knew that the draw for the second round was being made.

'At last the "returning" officer arrived with his sheet of paper. In he came, and locked the door, mysteriously, silently. "Are you ready, gentlemen?" he asked. We were. And then the door was unlocked, and hot-footed messenger boys dashed off with the news to the offices of the London newspapers and the news agencies. But

I have never seen the draw made – no man has who is not an officer of the Football Association. The Council Chamber, in which the draw is made, is bolted and barred against all unofficial comers.'

Folded and numbered scraps of paper, not wooden balls, were used in the early days. They were put into a top-hat which was then covered by a handkerchief. An official carefully lifted up a corner so that the councillors making the draw could, one by one, pull out a slip.

The draw for the third round on 16 December 1935 was the first to be broadcast on BBC Radio, although it was done with misgivings on both sides and despite outright opposition from the newspapers. Sir Stanley Rous, secretary of the FA, was requested to 'ensure that the bag is shaken for a few seconds to produce a distinctive and suitable sound'. The BBC added: 'This broadcast is an experiment which we have no intention of making a regular feature.'

The experiment lasted more than fifty years on BBC Radio – a regular and traditional spot some time after noon on a Monday – until television acquired the rights as part of its mega-deal with football in the late 1980s. The placing of the draw then became variable, appearing on Saturday nights, Sunday evenings or even late on Monday; but it remains, steadfastly, a compelling piece of drama.

Sometimes, humanly, things go wrong. Once, after all the other clubs had been paired, a single ball was left in the bag. Middlesbrough, it was discovered, had been allocated two opponents.

Nervous fingers have also dropped a ball – indeed, one was dropped just before the second draw to be broadcast. All the balls were poured out of the bag and frantically counted, only a minute or so before transmission. In 1974–75 a dropped ball had an effect, perhaps, on the destination of the Cup. An 'away' ball (belonging to West Ham) bounced across the floor and, when it was retrieved, it was absent-mindedly popped back into the bag. Another club, Wimbledon of the Southern League, were pulled out and sent to their inevitable doom against Leeds, who were a formidable power. Wimbledon gallantly managed a replay before they went down – and West Ham went on to win the Cup.

As Herbert Chapman said, 'You need a deal of luck in the Cup.'

Left Monday lunch-time draw, third round, December 1958. David Wiseman (left), chairman of the FA Challenge Cup Committee, Arthur Drewry, chairman of the FA Council and, behind, BBC Radio commentator Raymond Glendenning. Mr Drewry is holding number 58 – the ball of Tooting and Mitcham United, the only amateurs left, who lost in a replay to the eventual Cup-winners Nottingham Forest.

Below Sunday tea-time draw, third round, December 1995. Denis Law, Terry Venables and Graham Kelly, chief executive of the FA – a show for BBC Television.

1961

6 May at Wembley   Att 100,000

Tottenham Hotspur 2 (Smith, Dyson)

Leicester City 0

Tottenham Hotspur: Brown, Baker, Henry, Blanchflower, Norman, Mackay, Jones, White, Smith, Allen, Dyson.

Leicester City: Banks, Chalmers, Norman, McLintock, King, Appleton, Riley, Walsh, McIlmoyle, Keyworth, Cheesebrough.

Referee: J. Kelly

The first League and Cup double of the twentieth century, the high peak of English football, was managed by Tottenham Hotspur with a knowing air of superiority. They were, simply, the best. Spurs clinched the League title by eight points, nineteen days before the final, and then at Wembley they bettered Leicester City by 2–0 without playing at their best. Leicester were an accomplished side but Len Chalmers, their right-back, was injured after eighteen minutes. Although it was the seventh final in nine seasons in which a player had been injured, substitutes in the final were still six years away.

Below Gordon Banks, Leicester's goalkeeper, fails to stop Terry Dyson (not in picture) heading Tottenham's second goal. Bobby Smith, who scored the first, a beauty from fifteen yards, is behind the far goal-post and Cliff Jones, second right, smiles approvingly.

Right Arc de Triomphe. Danny Blanchflower and Bobby Smith are uplifting... Terry Dyson checks the maker's name.

Above Players' view of Wembley:
Tottenham Hotspur and Burnley
enter the arena. Time: 2.50 p.m. The
Queen and the Duke of Edinburgh
are waiting.

1962

5 May at Wembley   Att 100,000

Tottenham Hotspur 3 (Greaves, Smith, Blanchflower (pen))

Burnley 1 (Robson)

Tottenham Hotspur: Brown, Baker, Henry, Blanchflower, Norman, Mackay, Medwin, White, Smith, Greaves, Jones.

Burnley: Blacklaw, Angus, Elder, Adamson, Cummings, Miller, Connelly, McIlroy, Pointer, Robson, Harris.

Referee: J. Finney

Above Jimmy Greaves predicted in Spurs' dressing-room that he would score in the fourth minute against Burnley. He was wrong: he was early by sixty seconds. It was a remarkable opener in a cultured final. Greaves suddenly stopped in mid-gallop, wrong-footed the desperately braking Burnley defence and, left-footed from sixteen yards, cut the ball along the ground past a queue of friend and foe. He remembers it like this: 'I darted through to Bobby Smith's header and thought I'd got a clear run. But the defenders were quick on the cover. I checked to go left to find a better shooting angle. I couldn't see the goal or Blacklaw the goalkeeper, because I cracked the ball on the turn and I think I hit it as well as any shot I'd taken. I just saw it go into the net as I was falling.'

Jimmy Robson equalised for Burnley just after half-time (Wembley's hundredth Cup final goal), but Smith and Danny Blanchflower, with a penalty, then scored for Spurs to earn them the Cup for the second year running – a feat accomplished in the twentieth century only by Newcastle United (1951 and 1952) and, later, Tottenham again (1981 and 1982).

Above Tottenham supporters demonstrating outside Lancaster Gate for a bigger share of Cup final tickets for 'real fans', 1962. At one time the share for the two clubs in the final was only around 8,000 each.

By 1962 this had risen to 15,000 each. Now a 'swing factor' is used, with allocation depending on a club's average gates over a number of seasons. In 1994, for example, Manchester United received 26,000

and Chelsea 19,000. In 1996 Manchester United and Liverpool had an equal share – with all-seater Wembley's capacity reduced to just under 80,000.

1963

25 May at Wembley   Att 100,000

Manchester United 3 (Law, Herd 2)

Leicester City 1 (Keyworth)

Manchester United: Gaskell, Dunne, Cantwell, Crerand, Foulkes, Setters, Giles, Quixall, Herd, Law, Charlton.

Leicester City: Banks, Sjoberg, Norman, McLintock, King, Appleton, Riley, Cross, Keyworth, Gibson, Stringfellow.

Referee: K. Aston

Below Manchester United turned on the style to help the Football Association celebrate their centenary with Denis Law, above all, contributing a virtuoso performance. Law, number ten, on ground, scores the opening goal in the thirtieth minute after an electric change of direction. David Herd, who scored United's other two goals in the second half, is on the right. Ken Keyworth, with a spectacular header, making contact only a foot from the ground, replied for Leicester City. Yet while United fielded one of the costliest sides in Cup final history, their victory was a surprise. Leicester finished fourth in Division One and began as clear favourites against a United side which had struggled to avoid relegation. It was, however, the start of a splendidly successful age for United.

Above Noel Cantwell, Manchester United's captain, takes a liberty. The rest are apprehensive: *(left to right)* – Tony Dunne, Bobby Charlton, Pat Crerand, Albert Quixall and David Herd.

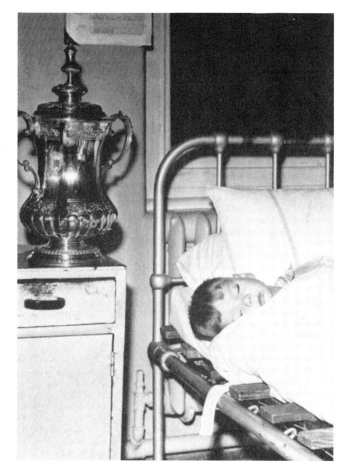

Left Cup of dreams. Four-year-old David Hodgson was asleep when United's players visited Booth Hall Hospital, Manchester. Players and Cup had gone when he woke, but Bobby Charlton left a piece of paper with his autograph on David's locker.

Below Gloomy scene typifying the frustration and chaos caused by the Big Freeze of 1963, which was even worse than the one in 1947. Football was almost at a standstill for two months and Gillingham versus Port Vale was one of fourteen third-round ties that were postponed ten times or more.

The third round took sixty-six days to complete, making it the longest round in the history of the Cup, and altogether more than four hundred Cup and League games were postponed. The Cup final had to be put back three weeks and the Pools panel was introduced to guess the results of games not played.

1964

2 May at Wembley   Att 100,000

West Ham United 3 (Sissons, Hurst, Boyce)

Preston North End 2 (Holden, Dawson)

West Ham United: Standen, Bond, Burkett, Bovington, Brown, Moore, Brabrook, Boyce, Byrne, Hurst, Sissons.

Preston North End: Kelly, Ross, Smith, Lawton, Singleton, Kendall, Wilson, Ashworth, Dawson, Spavin, Holden.

Referee: A. Holland

Below Two minutes into injury time and Ronnie Boyce wins the Cup for the first time for West Ham United with a header between George Ross and goalkeeper Alan Kelly. It was the only time West Ham had been in front against Preston North End of the Second Division, whose confident skills made this a memorable final. Howard Kendall, Preston's left-half, was the youngest player to appear in a Wembley final (17 years 345 days).

Right Bobby Moore and skylarks. The following year he lifted the European Cup-Winners' Cup for West Ham and, a year after that, the World Cup for England.

Below Under suspicion. A vigilant lady wonders about an object under wraps at Tottenham Court Road tube station, while West Ham manager Ron Greenwood looks innocent. He was on his way, with the FA Cup, to a film of the 1964 final at a West End cinema.

Above Ron Atkinson, Oxford United's captain and right-half, otherwise known as 'The Tank', is at the heart of Manor Ground celebrations after the Fourth Division club had beaten Blackburn Rovers in the fifth round. Oxford had been a League club for only two years, but they triumphed 3–1 over Blackburn, Cup favourites and second in Division One, to become the first Fourth Division club to reach the quarter-finals. The celebrations were led by a fan (probably a woman) with orange hair, orange blouse and socks, blue skirt and a wealth of gold and black ribbons. Police looked on like happy uncles. Atkinson was to achieve fame as a manager with clubs such as Manchester United and Aston Villa – but did he ever have a better moment than this?

1965

1 May at Wembley   Att 100,000

Liverpool 2 (Hunt, St John)

Leeds United 1 (Bremner)   **aet**

Liverpool: Lawrence, Lawler, Byrne, Strong, Yeats, Stevenson, Callaghan, Hunt, St John, Smith, Thompson.

Leeds United: Sprake, Reaney, Bell, Bremner, J. Charlton, Hunter, Giles, Storrie, Peacock, Collins, Johanneson.

Referee: W. Clements

Below Liverpool's Cup for the first time. It was the era of the Beatles, Gerry and the Pacemakers and other Merseyside songsters, and Wembley was filled with the sound of 'You'll Never Walk Alone'. In a tense and clinical final in which all the goals were scored in extra-time, the winner was a bullet of a header by Ian St John of Scotland from a centre by Ian Callaghan who, by the time he retired, had played in a record eighty-eight Cup ties. Bill Shankly's Liverpool had won the League Championship the year before and were nearing the time when they would dominate English football for nearly two decades. Leeds, too, under Don Revie, were shaping into the best side in the club's history.

Right Denis Law, after Manchester United and Leeds United had drawn 0–0 in a frenzied semi-final at Hillsborough in 1965. Leeds won the replay 1–0 at the City Ground, Nottingham.

Law's talent and style were arrestingly distinctive. His interpretation of the game was theatrical. He seemed to exaggerate every movement, especially his bicycle kick, a whirl of body and legs, and his heading. He shamelessly milked the applause of the terraces and his salute, right arm and index finger pointing heavenwards, was something he left to generations to come. Old Trafford called him 'The King'.

Law scored forty-one goals in the FA Cup and would have had more but for the British weather. He scored six for Manchester City against Luton Town in the fourth round in 1961, but his goals were wiped from the record after the game was abandoned because of a waterlogged pitch with twenty minutes left. Luton won the replay 3–1, with Law scoring for City. Seven goals – and he finished a loser! Eighteen months later, after a spell in Italy, he joined Manchester United.

Below One of the most dramatic finals of all, in which a twenty-one-year-old from Gunnislake in Cornwall had five minutes of fame to help Everton win the Cup for the first time in thirty-three years. Mike Trebilcock (pronounced Tre-bil-co) was such a late choice that he did not appear in the programme. He had been signed from Plymouth Argyle on New Year's Eve 1965; the final was only his second Cup game; and, just a handful of first team appearances later, he moved to Portsmouth. The 1966 final, however, gave him a place in history.

Sheffield Wednesday were two goals up with little more than half an hour left. The game was seemingly won and lost: until Trebilcock scored twice in five minutes, each handsomely struck with his right foot, and Everton went on to snatch a winner ten minutes from the end. Trebilcock (dark shirt, turning away) strikes his second goal from sixteen yards to make the score 2–2. Left-winger Derek Temple pilfered the late winner.

1966

14 May at Wembley   Att 100,000

Everton 3 (Trebilcock 2, Temple)

Sheffield Wednesday 2
(McCalliog, Ford)

Everton: West, Wright, Wilson,
Gabriel, Labone, Harris, Scott,
Trebilcock, Young, Harvey, Temple.

Sheffield Wednesday: Springett, Smith,
Megson, Eustace, Ellis, Young, Pugh,
Fantham, McCalliog, Ford, Quinn.

Referee: J. K. Taylor

Above Wembley's finest chase. This fan had run on to the pitch to congratulate Trebilcock and gave the Law a run for its money. One policeman has dived, missed and lost his helmet. Another gives chase and eventually (with the funster being cheered all the way) succeeds with a rugby tackle. Several other policemen were required to persuade him off the pitch.

1967

20 May at Wembley Att 100,000

Tottenham Hotspur 2
(Robertson, Saul)

Chelsea 1 (Tambling)

Tottenham Hotspur: Jennings,
 Kinnear, Knowles, Mullery,
 England, Mackay, Robertson,
 Greaves, Gilzean, Venables, Saul.

Chelsea: Bonetti, A. Harris,
 McCreadie, Hollins, Hinton, R.
 Harris, Cooke, Baldwin, Hateley,
 Tambling, Boyle.

Referee: K. Dagnall

Above The first all-London final of the twentieth century and Tottenham Hotspur's third Cup triumph of the 1960s. They were a better coordinated and more flexible side than Chelsea and, without being flamboyant, they sauntered to victory. They scored through Jimmy Robertson and Frank Saul, with Bobby Tambling replying for Chelsea four minutes from the end.

Spurs celebrate: (*left to right*) – Cyril Knowles, Pat Jennings, Terry Venables, Jimmy Greaves, Mike England and Joe Kinnear. The man in a suit? Just a Spurs fan who wanted to share the moment.

Right Remembered with relish: a great quarter-final which came to a head in the last half-hour. Jimmy Husband gave Everton, the holders, the lead; Nottingham Forest's left-winger Ian Storey-Moore ('Please call me Moore') scored twice in three minutes; Husband equalised in the eightieth minute; and then Storey-Moore completed his hat-trick with Forest's winner two minutes from the end. Storey-Moore's winner was remarkable. He had a shot blocked by Andy Rankin, headed the rebound against the bar and, finally, headed a second rebound into the net. All this against a back-cloth of confusion. A barrier collapsed and policemen resorted to rugby tackles and even arm-locks to restore order. At the end Forest fans loitered as if reluctant to leave the stage.

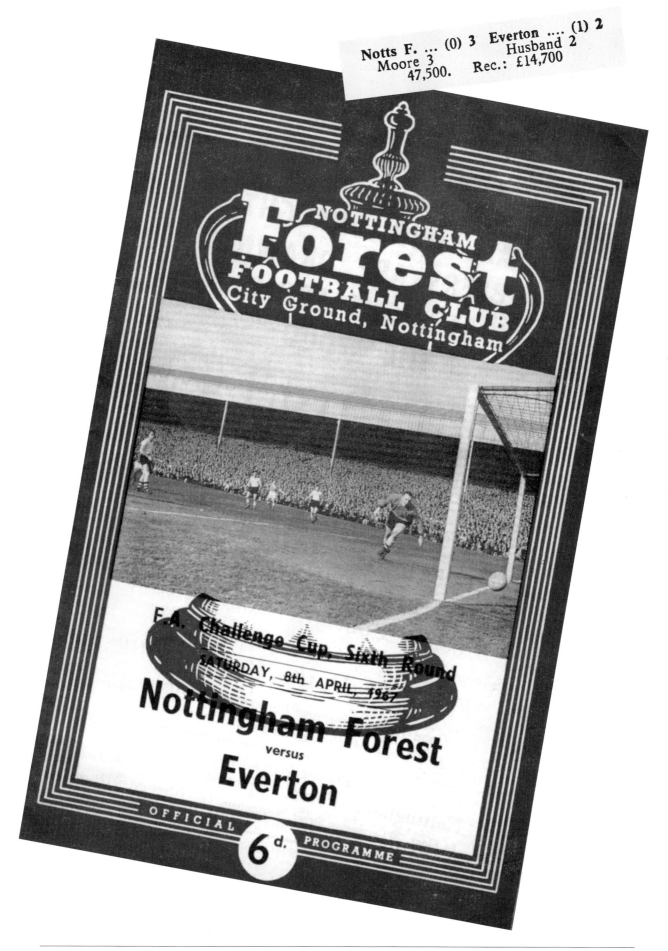

Notts F. ... (0) 3   Everton .... (1) 2
Moore 3   Husband 2
47,500.   Rec.: £14,700

Left Jeff Astle, West Bromwich Albion's centre-forward, quietly examines his winner's medal after scoring the goal which beat Everton, the strong favourites, in a final ruled by defence and littered with fouls. Everton looked the better side, but Astle won the Cup in the third minute of extra-time.

Astle, who scored in every round, described his goal like this: 'The ball came to my right foot at the edge of the box. I had a bash and duffed it. But this was my lucky, lovely day. It bounced back from Colin Harvey's knee and I met it with my left foot – that's the dummy leg, the one that's just for standing on. I saw this huge gap, the white net and the yellow ball streaking for the corner.'

It was West Bromwich's tenth final, and their fifth victory, yet only twelve months before they had been beaten 3–2 by Third Division Queens Park Rangers in the first League Cup final to be played at Wembley.

1968

18 May at Wembley · · · · · · · · · Att 100,000

West Bromwich Albion 1
 (Astle)
Everton 0 · · · · · · · · · · · · · · · · · · aet

West Bromwich Albion: Osborne, Fraser, Williams, Brown, Talbut, Kaye (Clarke), Lovett, Collard, Astle, Hope, Clark.

Everton: West, Wright, Wilson, Kendall, Labone, Harvey, Husband, Ball, Royle, Hurst, Morrissey.

Referee: L. Callaghan

Below Wembley's best-known and most photographed commission-aire, sixty-nine-year-old Fred 'Tiny' Pragnall, attempts to marshal a crest-fallen and weary Everton before collecting their losers' medals. Pragnall had been on the Wembley staff for twenty-three years and was one of three hundred commission-aires (among a total staff of 1,470) on duty.

1969

26 April at Wembley   Att 100,000

Manchester City 1 (Young)
Leicester City 0

Manchester City: Dowd, Book, Pardoe, Doyle, Booth, Oakes, Summerbee, Bell, Lee, Young, Coleman.

Leicester City: Shilton, Rodrigues, Nish, Roberts, Woollett, Cross, Fern, Gibson, Lochhead, Clarke, Glover (Manley).

Referee: G. McCabe

Salad days for Manchester City: League champions in 1968, FA Cup winners for the fourth time in 1969 and then first to a handsome double in 1970 with the League Cup and European Cup-Winners' Cup. Poor Leicester City: it was their fourth FA Cup final, their fourth defeat, and they were also relegated from Division One.

Yet only a first-half goal by Neil Young separated them at Wembley in a bright and open final. Leicester, moreover, squandered four clear chances and Manchester City's goalkeeper Harry Dowd made the save of the match from Allan Clarke who, despite being on the losing side, was named as Player of the Match.

Left Tony Book, Manchester City's thirty-four-year-old captain, a former Bath City player, leads his team back to earth. Five places behind him, looking concerned, is England forward Francis Lee who, twenty-five years later, would become Manchester City's chairman.

Right Joe Mercer, hat aloft, and Malcolm Allison – the partnership that revitalised Manchester City. Manager Mercer, a Cup-winner with Arsenal, was infinitely experienced, spirited, caring, popular and an ideal father figure. Coach Allison was imaginative, daring, outspoken and sometimes outrageous. It was an ideal marriage which produced bonny teams – until an acrimonious divorce in 1972.

1970

11 April at Wembley   Att 100,000

Chelsea 2 (Houseman, Hutchinson)

Leeds United 2 (Charlton, Jones)   **aet**

Chelsea: Bonetti, Webb, McCreadie, Hollins, Dempsey, Harris (Hinton), Baldwin, Houseman, Osgood, Hutchinson, Cooke.

Leeds United: Sprake, Madeley, Cooper, Bremner, Charlton, Hunter, Lorimer, Clarke, Jones, Giles, Gray.

Referee: E. Jennings

Replay: 29 April at Old Trafford   Att 62,078

Chelsea 2 (Osgood, Webb)

Leeds United 1 (Jones)   **aet**

Chelsea: Bonetti, Harris, McCreadie, Hollins, Dempsey, Webb, Baldwin, Cooke, Osgood (Hinton), Hutchinson, Houseman.

Leeds United: Harvey, Madeley, Cooper, Bremner, Charlton, Hunter, Lorimer, Clarke, Jones, Giles, Gray.

Referee: E. Jennings

An extraordinary and absorbing final: dramatic, turbulent and utterly unpredictable. The 1970 final went to the first replay since 1912 and was settled by a seventh goal in the 224th minute of a battle which ran to four hours on two grounds. And Chelsea won the Cup for the first time.

At Wembley, Leeds United were manifestly superior, Chelsea doggedly defiant. At Old Trafford eighteen days later, Leeds again looked the better side, but it was Chelsea who stole the show with a goal in extra-time – the first time they had been in front.

Left Chelsea defender David Webb heads Chelsea's winner from a long throw by Ian Hutchinson in the 104th minute of the Old Trafford replay. Webb relished his last word, because at Wembley he had been run into the ground by Leeds' left-winger Eddie Gray.

Right Billy Bremner of Leeds in the losers' dressing-room at Old Trafford. The title of his autobiography, published in 1969, was *You Get Nowt For Being Second*.

Below Back to nothing at Gander Green Lane, 1970. Part of a record 14,000 crowd watching non-League Sutton United face Leeds United in the fourth round. Sutton did not enjoy being beaten 6–0 any more than Leeds enjoyed losing the final.

The Giant-killers

Nothing says more about the FA Cup than the majesty of its final, but nothing is closer to the heart of the tournament than its giant-killers. They are lustrous proof that the impossible is always possible.

The giant-killers shred the form book, bulldoze their way across rigidly defined social barriers, steal a lead role in the show from the back row of the chorus and earn the sort of headlines normally reserved for wars and pretty princesses. They are mice which roar and oblige the nation to listen. They prevail, like David, with a sling and a stone. They, above all, provide the fun.

Exactly why Gnome Rovers and Outback Wanderers can sometimes skin clubs of the weight and worth of Liverpool, Arsenal, Manchester United and Leeds United is a question which fills saloon bar hours and shortens train journeys. There are no pat answers, but there is always one certainty: every tangled road to Wembley is littered with squiffy coronets, bruised egos and dented reputations.

The Cup, however, is an exercise in equal opportunity as well as random chance. Surprises do not come to order and, more often than not, Godzilla pops Rupert Bear into his mouth and then thanks the little chap for his help and courtesy. The small clubs have to succeed the hard way, but those who dare and win join a famous roll of honour. Walsall, Yeovil Town, Colchester United, Peterborough United, Hereford United, York City, Sutton United and Woking are among names which are now recited like a litany. They illuminate our winters like nothing else.

Someone can be counted on each year to state with axiomatic wisdom that the age of the giant-killer is over, a piece of Christmas-cracker logic that has something to do with a growing gap between big and small, mind-focusing bonuses and the lure of European competition. Someone, too, can be relied on to insist that the game's little folk have no right to be in the Cup at all and

that it should be strictly the preserve of the League clubs. 'Blyth Spartans?' asked one poor soul. 'What are they ... plastic soldiers you get with the cornflakes?'

We know, immediately, that here are people with no sense of history and no real understanding of what makes the Cup such a wonderful pedlar of dreams. Our potential heroes laugh with the rest of us. They know that giant-killing is often a case of answering insult with injury.

Complacency and over confidence are often part of the equation, of course, but fear and caution may also come into it. Danny Blanchflower, whose Tottenham Hotspur were famously beaten in 1959 by Norwich City, then in the Third Division, believed that 'the little guy with no fears and responsibility goes mad and turns the game into a riot where anything can happen'. He also thought that 'the big fellow is often fighting against himself as well as the upstarts'.

The popular picture is of footballing princes travelling to the far corner of a windy moor or down-town industrial estate, and then being invited to change in a dressing-room the size of a garden shed before running out in front of native partisans, smacking their lips like flesh-eaters and squaring up to muscle-bound ruffians who are ready to die for their cause.

The reality is usually different. Our princes will probably find themselves playing on a lovingly maintained and well-equipped little ground. Their opponents, moreover, are likely to be generously stocked with ambitious and talented striplings or crafty old pros who are perfectly capable of acquiring a new heart and legs for ninety special minutes – doubtless described in the programme as 'the greatest day in our history'. The gap between big and small will be further narrowed if the referee believes there is one set of laws for Cup football and another for the League and lets the underdogs

'A great leveller, the Cup . . .

get away with serious mischief. 'Typical Cup football' is not necessarily as heroic as it sounds.

Tradition always has its say. There are small clubs whose triumphs bridge generations, one golden moment in the Cup laying seed for the next. They hear bugles and smell gunpowder when the challenge comes. They respond to the clamour of battle. Players and fans become one defiant unit, and are probably joined by their goal-posts and corner flags as well. Pride and aggression are part of their armoury.

There are enough stories of giant-killing to make it one of the enduring attractions of the Cup, but not enough to reduce it to the merely routine. It would be a surprise if any FA Cup tournament failed to produce a shock or two, but every upset tickles the fancy of the nation anew. And not only in the home of the game. Soon after Sutton United beat Coventry City of the First Division by 2–1 in 1989, they received a newspaper clipping about their triumph. It was from South China.

Chapter Ten

All in Colour
1971–1980

'We, ourselves, little old Colchester, are taking on probably the greatest team in Europe. It's going to be the match everyone will be talking about and looking at. Everybody's going to be here. Television, radio, all the papers. Now we mustn't be frightened. We must take it in our stride. We must enjoy every minute of it. We must go out of our way to make everybody welcome. We may not see them again but, between now and the game, we are going to live in a tremendous Cup atmosphere. It's going to be something you remember all your lives. No nerves, no tension. Just relax. And, you know what, I think we can win.'

> **Dick Graham, manager of Colchester United, talking to his Fourth Division team before they beat Leeds United, League leaders and Cup favourites, by 3–2 in the fifth round of the FA Cup, 13 February 1971.**

'Being chosen to referee the FA Cup final is the highest accolade any referee can receive. It means they think you are the best. In previous years the FA Cup final used to be given to the senior man on the list who was about to retire. It was a reward for services rendered. But the Football Association realised that this might not have been the correct way to go about things. My reward was fifteen guineas and a medal. Not long before, it was a fee OR a medal. Everyone chose the gold medal.'

> **Norman Burtenshaw who refereed the 1971 FA Cup final between Arsenal and Liverpool. From *Whose Side Are You On Ref?* (1973).**
>
> **A Cup final referee now receives a medal and £325.**

Arsenal followed the sovereign example of their north London rivals, Tottenham, and completed the double in 1971. Sunderland (1973), Southampton (1976) and West Ham (1980) won the Cup for the Second Division. Crystal Palace of the Third Division reached the semi-finals in 1976, Colchester United (1971) and Bradford City (1976) of the Fourth aspired to the quarter-finals and, gloriously, Hereford United (1972) and Wimbledon (1975) added their names to the Cup's roll of non-League heroes.

The Cup celebrated its centenary in 1972 but, throughout the erratic years of the seventies, it showed that its appetite for drama and relish for the unexpected were as tangible as ever. It was a steadfast factor in a decade of rapid and significant change: transfer fees soared past the million pound mark, the game took on its first sponsors, the distinction between professionals and amateurs was removed and all footballers became 'players', Sunday football was introduced and now, too, television was showing everything in colour.

There were even times when the Cup found itself at the heart of domestic wrangles between the Football Association and the Football League. During one quarrel, over television fees in 1973, a special meeting of League clubs considered boycotting the FA Cup. Alan Hardaker, the League's secretary, said: 'I can't imagine a bigger or more important story than our clubs refusing to play in the Cup. It would affect millions of people and cost the game millions of pounds. But nobody, in their hearts, wants to harm the Cup.' Another fanciful suggestion was that the FA should pay for the privilege of having League clubs in its tournament. Always, though, the clubs stopped short of denting the Cup. It mattered too much.

Arsenal's League and FA Cup double was, in some ways, more remarkable than Tottenham's masterly achievement ten years before. Tottenham won both trophies in a season, simply because they were in a class of their own. An admiring nation applauded them home. Arsenal's triumph owed more to character, resourcefulness, organisation and steely consistency. They were a prime example of collective efficiency, the whole greater than its parts, although no side with players such as Frank McLintock, George Graham, Charlie George and Ray Kennedy could ever be joyless.

They kept going over a heartless course, after being seven points behind Leeds at one stage, with their season reaching its climax in one hugely dramatic week. First, on the Monday before the Cup final, they needed to win their last League game to take the Championship. It was at Tottenham, of all places, where more than 51,000 squeezed into White Hart Lane before the gates were closed. Nearly as many again were locked outside and the referee, Kevin Howley, had to abandon his car a mile away to complete his journey on foot.

The game was taut and edgy and even; but Arsenal got there with a goal by Ray Kennedy, a header off the underside of the bar, just three minutes from the end. Bertie Mee, Arsenal's manager, an expert judge of character and talent who had been the club's physiotherapist before his appointment, lost his tie and cuff-links in the jubilant mayhem which followed.

Five days later, Arsenal faced Bill Shankly's Liverpool on an oven-hot afternoon at Wembley, and once again it was a stern and technical affair which spilled glumly into extra-time. Then, mercifully, the plot took shape. Steve Heighway put Liverpool ahead and Merseyside filled the old stadium with victory anthems. But Arsenal replied with goals by Eddie Kelly and Charlie George – the twenty-year-old George, with his stringy hair and Maypole frame, striking in his late winner from twenty-five yards. Poor game, famous victory.

Arsenal were drawn away in every round of their double season and, astonishingly, the same thing happened the following season when they reached the final again. It was their eighth FA Cup final and their fifth final of one kind or another (two FA Cup, two League Cup and one Fairs Cup) in five years. But the Cup is nothing if not democratic, and this time the trophy was held aloft by a club that had never won it before – Leeds United. The final marked the hundredth birthday of the Cup, which was also celebrated by a banquet at the Royal Garden Hotel, where guests from all around the world included nine of the clubs which had competed in the first tournament of all.

The big clubs continued to take their turn in winning the Cup: Liverpool for a second time in 1974, Manchester United for a fourth time in 1977 and Arsenal again in 1979 by way of a climax which matched even the Matthews final for drama. Arsenal led Manchester United 2–0 with only four minutes left, United equalised with goals in the eighty-sixth and eighty-eighth minutes and then Alan Sunderland snatched a winner for the Highbury club in the last sixty seconds. At the end, one policeman quietly picked up a divot from the famous turf and put it in his helmet, which he then placed back on his head.

Above all, however, the seventies will be remembered as a period which confounded the soothsayers as well as all the silly asses who predicted that the fine art of giant-killing had had its day. The gap between big and small, they kept insisting, had become unbridgeable. The Cup continued to prove that they had only candyfloss between the ears. Was there ever a greater shock than Sunderland's 1–0 victory over the sterling might of Leeds United in 1973? Don Revie's Leeds, every player an international, were within twelve months of winning the League Championship for the first time; but a first-half goal by Ian Porterfield enabled Sunderland to become the first Second Division club for 42 years to win the Cup. 'The finest heroes of all,' wrote Danny Blanchflower, 'and the most gripping, emotional final I have been to – and that includes the two in which I carried off the Cup.'

Three years later much the same thing was said about Southampton, another

Second Division club, after they had beaten Manchester United, and in 1980 it was West Ham who confirmed again that Second Division does not mean second class by beating Arsenal, the holders, with a rare headed goal by Trevor Brooking. There will be no future for the Cup when the impossible is no longer possible.

Whether a club from one of the two lower divisions of the Football League will ever reach the final is another matter. Six clubs from the old Third Division (which became the Second Division after the breakaway formation of the Premier League in 1992) have made it to the semi-finals: Millwall (1937), Port Vale (1954), York City (1955), Norwich City (1959), Crystal Palace (1976) and Plymouth Argyle (1984). But that last step, past the twitchy neutrality of a semi-final, is the toughest of all. Two Third Division clubs (Queens Park Rangers in 1967 and Swindon in 1969) may have won the League Cup – but the FA Cup is a steeper and prouder mountain.

1971

8 May at Wembley   Att 100,000

Arsenal 2 (Kelly, George)

Liverpool 1 (Heighway)   **aet**

Arsenal: Wilson, Rice, McNab, Storey (Kelly), McLintock, Simpson, Armstrong, Graham, Radford, Kennedy, George.

Liverpool: Clemence, Lawler, Lindsay, Smith, Lloyd, Hughes, Callaghan, Evans (Thompson), Heighway, Toshack, Hall.

Referee: N. Burtenshaw

Arsenal's double in 1970–71 was a triumph for collective efficiency and steely resolution. They were seven points behind Leeds United at one stage and had to win their last game, at Tottenham of all places, to take the League Championship. They were drawn away in every round of the Cup and were 2–0 down in their semi-final with Stoke City, before equalising with a controversial penalty in the last minute. But, step by step, they climbed every mountain.

Below Charlie George, twenty years old, Islington-born, hair lanky, socks fallen, hits Arsenal's Cup final winner from twenty-five yards in the twenty-first minute of extra-time. Steve Heighway had given Liverpool the lead two minutes into extra-time, Eddie Kelly equalised (the first substitute to score in a final) and the way was clear for George's contribution to history. Then, after a somersault, he flopped to the ground.

Opposite top The FA Cup still has its ribbons. The lid of the League Championship trophy is wonky. Bertie Mee, Arsenal's manager, is the one with the smile.

Opposite bottom Ray Crawford of Colchester United, thirty-four years old, heads the first of his two goals against Leeds United in the fifth round at Layer Road – and the Fourth Division side are on their way to one of the FA Cup's mightiest acts of giant-slaying. Colchester were seventy-fifth in the Football League, a mixture of rejects, hand-me-downs and OAPs who were known, affectionately, as Grandad's Army. Leeds were a battle-hardened

unit of internationals, leaders of the First Division and strongly fancied to win both FA Cup and UEFA Cup. However, Grandad's Army fixed their bayonets and charged into a three-goal lead through Crawford in the eighteenth and twenty-fifth minutes and then Dave Simmons in the fifty-fifth. Leeds came back with fearful determination to score through Norman Hunter and Johnny Giles – but the final score, impossibly, was Colchester 3 Leeds United 2. Crawford, twice capped by England, had been a member of the Ipswich Town side which Alf Ramsey led to the Championships of the Second and First Divisions in successive seasons a decade before. Yet Colchester's success belonged, most of all, to their manager Dick Graham, a distinctive man of football who knew how to recognise and make the most of talent. Six of his team were free transfers.

Opposite inset The reserved opinion of the *Colchester Express*.

A day to remember
by BERNARD WEBBER

REMEMBER it well, Saturday, February 13, 1971. Forget Walsall's defeat of Arsenal in the 1930's and Colchester's 1949 triumph over Huddersfield Town. This conclusively, exclusively was the most incredible result in soccer history.

1972

6 May at Wembley   Att 100,000

Leeds United 1 (Clarke)

Arsenal 0

Leeds United: Harvey, Reaney, Madeley, Bremner, Charlton, Hunter, Lorimer, Clarke, Jones, Giles, Gray.

Arsenal: Barnett, Rice, McNab, Storey, McLintock, Simpson, Armstrong, Ball, George, Radford (Kennedy), Graham.

Referee: D. W. Smith

Below Allan 'Sniffer' Clarke, centre, is already turning away as the ball crosses the line to give Leeds United the Cup for the first time. Clarke was a losing finalist with Leicester City in 1969 and (after a record £165,000 transfer) with Leeds in 1970 – but this time his stooping header in the fifty-third minute proved too much for a disappointing Arsenal. It should have been the first stage of another double, for Leeds went to Wolverhampton forty-eight hours later needing just a draw to clinch the Championship, but they lost 2–1.

Above Flags representing past winners line the way for Arsenal and Leeds in the Wembley sunshine as the Cup celebrates its centenary – an occasion not to be confused with the hundredth Cup final, which followed in 1981. At the front of the procession is Nigel 'Dickie' Bird of the FA, a friendly and tactful man who led finalists towards the Royal Box for thirty years.

Above The Ron and Ricky show. Ron Radford (left) and Ricky George, folk heroes both, the goalscorers who enabled Hereford United of the Southern League to beat Newcastle United, six times winners of the Cup, in 1972. Hereford shocked Tyneside by drawing 2–2 at St James' Park and then amazed everyone, including themselves they admitted, by scuppering their First Division opponents by 2–1 in a much postponed third-round replay at Edgar Street.

Malcolm Macdonald gave Newcastle the lead, before Radford ploughed over a marsh of a pitch to equalise mightily from thirty yards – and, in extra-time, Radford set up substitute George for an eight-yard winner. 'The goal was somewhere near so I just tried my luck,' was George's high-tech description of that historic moment. Hereford celebrated again a few days later when they held West Ham United to a goalless draw in the fourth round, but in the replay at Upton Park they fell to a hat-trick by Geoff Hurst. The Football League had seen enough: Hereford were elected to Division Four, going on to win promotion in their first season.

The Cup marked the fiftieth anniversary of the White Horse final by proving it could still produce grand theatre. Sunderland's victory over Leeds United was one of Wembley's most improbable results – a miracle, it was generally agreed, of dishwater-into-champagne proportions. It was certainly a whopping surprise.

Leeds United's record was inhibitingly impressive. For nine seasons they had finished in the top four of the First Division, they were the Cup holders, it was their third final in four years and every one of their players was an international. Sunderland were a Second Division team who, around Christmas, had been candidates for relegation.

Yet, on the day, Sunderland scored after half an hour and with stout hearts and no more than an acceptable pinch of luck, they deflected everything Leeds could throw at them to become the first Second Division club for forty-two years to win the Cup, after West Bromwich Albion in 1931.

Few outside Yorkshire shed tears for Don Revie's Leeds. They were the most criticised as well as the most consistent side in the land, a team who stretched the laws of the game and the goodwill of others to twanging point, although they were also a team who won far fewer trophies than they should have done.

Below Ian Porterfield, perfectly balanced, drives in Sunderland's goal despite two Leeds defenders on the line. It was his first goal of the tournament.

1973

5 May at Wembley   Att 100,000

Sunderland 1 (Porterfield)
Leeds United 0

Sunderland: Montgomery, Malone, Guthrie, Horswill, Watson, Pitt, Kerr, Hughes, Halom, Porterfield, Tueart.

Leeds United: Harvey, Reaney, Cherry, Bremner, Madeley, Hunter, Lorimer, Clarke, Jones, Giles, Gray (Yorath).

Referee: K. Burns

THE SUNDAY EXPRESS London May 6 1973

32 **

'WE WANT STOKOE, WE WANT STOKOE'

Leeds............(0) 0   Sunderland............(1) 1
(Porterfield, 31 min. 31 sec.)

(at Wembley. Attendance : 100,000. Receipts : £233,800.)

IT WAS not so much the Cup Final fall of the century as a shattering CRASH which could be heard throughout the whole world of football. Soccer has never known—or seen —anything like it.

It was the Sunderland miracle . . . the Roker explosion that destroyed Leeds, the overwhelming favourites, in the biggest Wembley upset of all time.

The golden goal that sent Don Revie's white - faced men reeling to defeat, their faces choked with shock and disbelief, was scored— amid an hysterical hurri- cane of sound from the Second Division's s i d e 's supporters — in the 31st minute.

ALAN HOBY reports

Below Bob Stokoe, Sunderland's manager, hugs Jim Montgomery, who made a double save in the second half which is still remembered with reverence on Wearside. First Montgomery palmed away a diving header from Trevor Cherry and then, when Peter Lorimer, Leeds' hot-shot, powered the ball in again, the Sunderland goalkeeper turned it to safety via the underside of the crossbar. Stokoe, one of Newcastle United's winners in 1955 and the man who recharged Sunderland, provided an indelible memory of his own that famous day as he dashed on to the pitch at the end, mackin- tosh flapping, arms waving, towards his players. There was a hug for them all — and a special one for Montgomery.

1974

4 May at Wembley Att 100,000

Liverpool 3 (Keegan 2, Heighway)
Newcastle United 0

Liverpool: Clemence, Smith, Lindsay, Thompson, Cormack, Hughes, Keegan, Hall, Heighway, Toshack, Callaghan.

Newcastle United: McFaul, Clark, Kennedy, McDermott, Howard, Moncur, Smith (Gibb), Cassidy, Macdonald, Tudor, Hibbitt.

Referee: G. C. Kew

Below William Shankly of Glenbuck. A man at ease with the world, a man fulfilled, a man with nothing to prove. His Liverpool have just won the FA Cup for a second time during his fifteen years as their manager, to add to three League Championships and a UEFA Cup. Fans had kissed his shoes at Wembley and he is the idol of the Kop, a darling of the media, founder of a footballing dynasty and a legend in his own extraordinary lifetime.

Yet two months later Shankly retired – a decision he had made, with a cup of tea and a pie on his knees, back in Liverpool's dressing-room at Wembley. If his players had lost to Newcastle United he would have carried on, but he thought: 'Well, we've won the Cup and maybe it's a good time to go.' He knew he was going to finish. He was tired. He was sixty.

Above Kevin Keegan (fourth from left) begins the dismantling of Newcastle in the 1974 final. This goal, handsomely struck from sixteen yards, was his first. His simpler second, two minutes from the end, was the product of a classic movement involving a dozen passes. Liverpool were at their best, coordinated, skilful, patient and too good for Newcastle, who lost a Wembley final for the first time. Keegan had been bought from Scunthorpe United for £33,000 by Shankly and he developed quickly into a complete all-round footballer, a modern superstar and captain of England. He moved on to Hamburg, Southampton and Newcastle as a player, retired to Spain for a few years and returned to manage Newcastle in 1992.

The Cup at its most democratic. West Ham United finished thirteenth in Division One and Fulham ninth in Division Two – but these two workaday sides still picked a path to Wembley. Although the rest of the country sniffed its disapproval, enough camp followers were found in east and south-west London to fill the old stadium as usual and the occasion, if not the match, was colourful. The two managers, Alec Stock of Fulham (of earlier Yeovil fame) and Ron Greenwood of West Ham, encouraged their sides to play carefree football, neither trainer had to leave his bench and the result was a pleasant if sometimes bland

final. It also had its personalities, among them Bobby Moore (against his old club) and Alan Mullery, both of Fulham, two former England captains, who were nearing the end of distinguished careers.

Below A London festival, but it was still won by a lad from Lancashire. Alan Taylor, otherwise known as 'The Rochdale Whippet', a twenty-one-year-old who only a few months before had been playing Fourth Division football, scored both West Ham's goals… just as he had scored two against Arsenal in the quarter-finals and two more against Ipswich Town in the semi-finals.

1975

3 May at Wembley   Att 100,000
West Ham United 2 (A. Taylor 2)
Fulham 0
West Ham United: Day, McDowell,
  T. Taylor, Lock, Lampard, Bonds,
  Paddon, Brooking, Jennings,
  A. Taylor, Holland.
Fulham: Mellor, Cutbush, Lacy,
  Moore, Fraser, Mullery, Conway,
  Slough, Mitchell, Busby, Barrett.
Referee: P. Partridge

Above Chris Kelly scores a third-round winner for Leatherhead of the Isthmian League against Third Division Brighton and Hove Albion at the Goldstone Ground. Kelly, alias 'The Leatherhead Lip', a loquacious chap who was not above a bit of self-promotion, also scored against Leicester City in the fourth round – but, after leading 2–0, the Surrey club went down 3–2 to their First Division opponents at Filbert Street. It was a good year for giant-killers, with Wimbledon of the Southern League giving notice of their ambitions by beating First Division Burnley 1–0 at Turf Moor and then gallantly taking Leeds United to a replay.

Below Players and playboys. Trevor Brooking of West Ham (left) and Alan Mullery, Fulham's captain, training for the final at London's Playboy Club.

What a fine final it might have been if Manchester United and Derby County, who finished third and fourth in the First Division, had met at Wembley in 1976! They reached the semi-finals and needed only a pinch of luck to keep them apart in the draw. They didn't get it. United and County were paired to play at Hillsborough, leaving Southampton of the Second Division and Crystal Palace of the Third to meet in the other semi-final at Stamford Bridge.

'This,' said United's manager Tommy Docherty, 'is the first time a Cup final will be played at Hillsborough. The other semi-final is a bit of a joke, really.'

One month later his words came home to roost. Manchester United and Southampton, each having won their semi-final 2–0, met at Wembley; and Southampton – good old, homely old Southampton – won the first major honour in their history with an eighty-third-minute goal by left-winger Bobby Stokes. United were young and vibrant but missed their chances. Southampton, built with care and perception by Lawrie McMenemy, were more experienced and replete with characters such as Mike Channon, Peter Osgood, Jim McCalliog and Peter Rodrigues. They did a sounder job.

Below Tommy Docherty, left, realises the joke in his jibe is now on him. Peter Rodrigues, Southampton's captain, has the last laugh.

1976

1 May at Wembley   Att 100,000

Southampton 1 (Stokes)

Manchester United 0

Southampton: Turner, Rodrigues, Peach, Holmes, Blyth, Steele, Gilchrist, Channon, Osgood, McCalliog, Stokes.

Manchester United: Stepney, Forsyth, Houston, Daly, B. Greenhoff, Buchan, Coppell, McIlroy, Pearson, Macari, Hill (McCreery).

Referee: C. Thomas

Above Bobby Stokes, the match-winning Saint, with halo. He played more than two hundred games for Southampton from 1968 to 1977 and then joined Portsmouth, his home-town club, before spending four years with the Washington Diplomats in the USA. He died from natural causes, aged forty-four, in May 1995.

1977

21 May at Wembley   Att 100,000

Manchester United 2 (Pearson, J. Greenhoff)

Liverpool 1 (Case)

Manchester United: Stepney, Nicholl, Albiston, McIlroy, B. Greenhoff, Buchan, Coppell, J. Greenhoff, Pearson, Macari, Hill (McCreery).

Liverpool: Clemence, Neal, Jones, Smith, Kennedy, Hughes, Keegan, Case, Heighway, Johnson (Callaghan), McDermott.

Referee: R. Matthewson

Below Sometimes a final lives up to the ballyhoo. This was one of them. It was exciting, skilful, sporting and decided in a twinkling, just after half-time, when three goals were scored in five minutes: Stuart Pearson for Manchester United, Jimmy Case for Liverpool and then, involuntarily, Jimmy Greenhoff for United. A mis-hit shot by Lou Macari struck Greenhoff on the chest and spun wickedly wide of Liverpool's goalkeeper Ray Clemence and left-back Joey Jones. Greenhoff, far right in picture, holds his arms high. Macari is in front of him.

Liverpool had to be satisfied with winning the League Championship and European Cup while Manchester United's triumph gained flavour from their defeat (but only after a replay) of Southampton in the fifth round.

Above Tommy Docherty is crowned by the Cup for the first time in his roller-coaster career, after failing in the final as a player with Preston North End (1954) and as a manager with Chelsea (1967) and Manchester United (1976).

He was not to know, at this moment of elation, that it was his last game in charge of United. Two months later he was sacked after publicly revealing that he was having an affair with Mary Brown, the wife of the club's physiotherapist Laurie Brown. There was talk of a breach of contract and a moral code. Docherty immediately claimed another record: 'I am the first manager,' he said, 'to be sacked for falling in love.'

1978

6 May at Wembley   Att 100,000

Ipswich Town 1 (Osborne)

Arsenal 0

Ipswich Town: Cooper, Burley, Mills, Osborne (Lambert), Hunter, Beattie, Talbot, Wark, Mariner, Geddis, Woods.

Arsenal: Jennings, Rice, Nelson, Price, Young, O'Leary, Brady (Rix), Hudson, Macdonald, Stapleton, Sunderland.

Referee: D. R. G. Nippard

The fiftieth final at Wembley deserved something special and Ipswich Town, in their first final, provided it with delightful football and impeccable behaviour. They scored only once, but they hit post or bar three times and Arsenal, the favourites, never had much more than a supporting role. It was an attractive climax to a tournament in which form and pedigree counted for little. Six non-League clubs reached the third round, and Blyth Spartans, those doughty north-easterners, even became the first non-League club since Yeovil Town in 1949 to reach the fifth round.

Below Roger Osborne hits Ipswich's winner in the seventy-sixth minute. David Geddis made a buccaneering run on the right before centring,

Arsenal's Willie Young (tea-cosy haircut, centre picture) only quarter-cleared and Osborne (right) hammered the ball past Pat Jennings (number one) and Pat Rice (two) on the line. Osborne, a local boy and a loyal clubman, was so overcome that he had to leave the field immediately. 'Exhaustion and all the excitement were just too much for me,' he said later. In ten First Division seasons (1973–82), Bobby Robson's Ipswich were out of the top six only once – the year they won the Cup.

Right Margaret Barrett, one of Ipswich's blue-and-white army of supporters, displaying a £2.50 ticket, a level of standing ticket for which touts were asking ten times face value. The Suffolk fans made a big contribution to a memorable day.

'The Five Minute Final'... a routine heavyweight bout with a finish that matched even 'the Matthews final' for raw excitement. Arsenal led 2–0 with less than five minutes left and some Manchester United fans, unwilling to witness the last rites, had already left the stadium. Then, in 115 seconds, officially timed, United scored twice: Gordon McQueen's long left leg made it 2–1 and Sammy McIlroy filtered through Arsenal's defence to equalise. Arsenal's fans swallowed their victory songs. The sun shone just for United. Extra-time looked inevitable until Liam Brady, Arsenal's mainspring, the Irish architect of their first two goals and undoubtedly the man of the match, ran at United's defence straight from the restart. He gave Graham Rix, on the left, time and space to centre, and Alan Sunderland slid the ball into the net at the far post.

Terry Neill, Arsenal's manager, took the Cup home with him next day. 'Oh, that's a grubby old Cup,' said his daughters – and a few minutes later they were giving it a clean in a neighbour's pool.

Opposite top Liam Brady, possessively round-shouldered, deceptively relaxed and policed by four United players, begins his winning run for Arsenal in the last minute of the 1979 final. 'It was vital in those remaining seconds to catch United while they were still mentally celebrating,' he wrote in his autobiography *So Far So Good.* 'Right up to the moment of defeat I doubt if United realised the danger.'

Opposite bottom Sunderland slides in at the far post, past Arthur Albiston's tackle, to score Arsenal's winner. It is timed at 89 minutes 10 seconds.

1979

12 May at Wembley   Att 100,000

Arsenal 3 (Talbot, Stapleton, Sunderland)

Manchester United 2 (McQueen, McIlroy)

Arsenal: Jennings, Rice, Nelson, Talbot, O'Leary, Young, Brady, Sunderland, Stapleton, Price (Walford), Rix.

Manchester United: Bailey, Nicholl, Albiston, McIlroy, McQueen, Buchan, Coppell, J. Greenhoff, Jordan, Macari, Thomas.

Referee: R. Challis

Master Gunner

THE SUNDAY EXPRESS May 13 1979

HAS THERE EVER BEEN A FINAL LIKE THIS!

ARSENAL (2) 3   MANCHESTER UTD (0) 2
Talbot (scored in 12 min 2 sec)
Stapleton (43 min 28 sec)   McQueen (86 min 20 sec)
Sunderland (89 min 10 sec)   McIlroy(88 min 15 sec)
Attendance: 100,000   Receipts: £500,000

SOCKS TUMBLING around his ankles, the sweat of effort darkening his shirt, Liam Brady stood in the centre of Wembley's vast stage and took his share of the applause at the end of a Cup Final that will be written into history because of its sensational climax.

Above Victory rock by Brady and Sunderland. 'God knows,' wrote Brady, 'I didn't know whether to laugh or cry. It was the most emotional and satisfying moment of my career.' Nobody at this point was remembering how Arsenal's Cup run had begun – a third-round tie with Sheffield Wednesday that ran to five games (1–1, 1–1, 2–2, 3–3, 2–0). A marathon at the start... a sprint at the end.

There is no end to the Cup's facts and figures and records. It produces them, infinitely, like the seeds and leaves of nature. The 1980 final had its quota: Arsenal were the first side to appear in three successive finals this century; Pat Rice of Arsenal was the first player to appear in five finals for one club; Paul Allen of West Ham United, at 17 years and 256 days, was the youngest player to appear in a Wembley final; Arsenal equalled Newcastle United's record of eleven finals; it was only Wembley's third all-London final; Arsenal and Liverpool had met in the Cup's longest semi-final (0–0, 1–1, 1–1, 1–0, 420 minutes in all); and West Ham's victory was the Second Division's third in eight seasons.

But, above all, a fact verified by himself, Trevor Brooking's winning nod in the thirteenth minute was only the third time in his distinguished career that he had scored a goal with his head.

Below Brooking, having stooped to head a wayward shot by Stuart Pearson, takes a seat to admire his handiwork. John Devine and David Price guard the Arsenal line, either side of Pat Jennings, but the ball still finds a path into the net.

1980

10 May at Wembley — Att 100,000

West Ham United 1 (Brooking)
Arsenal 0

West Ham United: Parkes, Stewart, Lampard, Bonds, Martin, Devonshire, Allen, Pearson, Cross, Brooking, Pike.

Arsenal: Jennings, Rice, Devine (Nelson), Talbot, O'Leary, Young, Brady, Sunderland, Stapleton, Price, Rix.

Referee: G. Courtney

Below Maidenhead United have competed in every Cup tournament except one, and here they receive ecstatic but lone tribute from a lady fan (top of picture) as they score their winner against Metropolitan Police in the third qualifying round on 3 November 1979. Maidenhead fell to Merthyr Tydfil in the next round but, if luck had been with them all the way, they would have overcome Fareham Town, Chesham United, Cambridge United, Aston Villa, Blackburn Rovers, West Ham United and Everton before pulverising Arsenal at Wembley.

First Cup Firsts

First FA Cup goal

Jarvis Kenrick of Clapham Rovers (3–0 v Upton Park) 11 November 1871

First FA Cup final goal

Morton Peto Betts of the Wanderers (1–0 v Royal Engineers) 1872

First FA Cup final replay

Royal Engineers v Old Etonians (1–1, 2–0) 1875

First League club to lose to non-League club

Stoke (lost 1–2 to Warwick County) 1888–89

First hat-trick in FA Cup final

Billy Townley of Blackburn Rovers (6–1 v The Wednesday) 1890

First Division Two club to win FA Cup

Notts County (4–1 v Bolton Wanderers) 1894

First player to score in every round

Alex (Sandy) Brown of Tottenham Hotspur, 15 goals (a record) 1900–01

First (and only) non-League club to win FA Cup since formation of Football League

Tottenham Hotspur 1901

First penalty goal in FA Cup final

Albert Shepherd of Newcastle United (2–0 v Barnsley in replay) 1910

First reigning monarch to attend FA Cup final

King George V (Burnley v Liverpool, 1–0) 1914

First FA Cup final at Wembley

Bolton Wanderers v West Ham United (2–0) 1923

First Wembley goal

David Jack of Bolton Wanderers (two minutes) 1923

First all-ticket FA Cup final

Newcastle United v Aston Villa (2–0) 1924

First (and only) non-English club to win FA Cup

Cardiff City (1–0 v Arsenal) 1927

First radio public broadcast of FA Cup final

Cardiff City v Arsenal 1927

First time players wore numbered shirts in FA Cup final

Everton v Manchester City (3–0), numbered 1–22, 1933

First TV live broadcast of FA Cup final

Preston North End v Huddersfield Town (1–0) 1938

First floodlit FA Cup tie

Kidderminster Harriers v Brierley Hill Alliance (4–2 preliminary round replay) 14 September 1955

First substitute to be used in FA Cup final

Derek Clarke of West Bromwich Albion (1–0 v Everton) 1968

First FA Cup tie on a Sunday

Cambridge United v Oldham Athletic (2–2) 6 January 1974

First player sent off in FA Cup final

Kevin Moran of Manchester United (1–0 v Everton) 1985

First FA Cup tie, under new regulations, to be decided by a penalty shoot-out

Rotherham United v Scunthorpe United (first round, 7–6 on penalties after two drawn games finished 1–1 and 3–3) 26 November 1991

Chapter Eleven

A Choirboy Sang
1981–1990

'It was the Centenary Cup Final and it is true to say that the Queen Mother received the greatest reception that anybody has ever had at Wembley, and when I heard 100,000 rough and ready football fans from Manchester and London singing, "There's only one Queen Mother, one Queen Mother", to the tune of one of football's most famous chanting songs, it brought a lump even to a cynical throat like mine.'

Peter Swales, chairman of Manchester City who played Tottenham Hotspur in the hundredth Cup final, 1981. From *What a Game!* (1983).

English football sank to the lowest point in its history during the 1980s. There were times when the ritual of winning championships and cups seemed irrelevant. 'The game has gone,' declared a portentous editorial in *The Times*. Here were the years of Heysel, Bradford and Hillsborough, hellish disasters in which 190 people died and more than 800 were injured, chilling obscenities born of complacency, inefficiency and, in the case of Heysel, the ulcer of hooliganism. They wounded the heart and conscience of the nation.

Fifty-six people perished and more than two hundred suffered burns in the fire disaster during Bradford City's Third Division game with Lincoln City at Valley Parade on 11 May 1985. The cause: a lighted match or cigarette dropped on to the debris beneath the floorboards of a seventy-six-year-old wooden stand. Unburned rubbish found afterwards included a local paper with a 1968 dateline.

Thirty-nine people were killed – most of them Italian – and more than four hundred injured in a riot shortly before the kick-off of the European Cup final between Liverpool and Juventus at the Heysel Stadium, in a northern suburb of Brussels, on 29 May 1985. 'It was like a war,' said one observer. Drunkenness, muddled supervision, poor segregation and frail barriers were among the reasons. English clubs were banned from European competition, and remained in the cold for five years.

The FA Cup itself was the hapless agent of the worst disaster in the history of British sport on 15 April 1989. Ninety-five Liverpool supporters lost their lives and more than two hundred were injured in a crush at the start of the Anfield club's semi-final with Nottingham Forest at Hillsborough. Fans were squashed against wire fences at the front of pens at the Leppings Lane end of Sheffield Wednesday's ground. Steel was twisted by the pressure and, as ambulance men and women cried as they did what they could, the gymnasium became a mortuary.

Liverpool was united in its sorrow. Anfield became a place of mourning. The Shankly gates were draped with wreaths, scarves, hats and precious mementoes. The pitch was covered in red, white and blue flowers. A queue of people, half a million and more, moved silently and endlessly around its edge. A chain of scarves, a mile long, linked the grounds of Liverpool and Everton. Masses were held and a choirboy sang, beautifully, 'You'll Never Walk Alone'.

Football became a political issue. Prime Minister Margaret Thatcher gave the impression that the game was something worse than a nasty infection, a succession of Sports Ministers squeaked obediently on the sidelines and the Government announced that its main plank of reform was a national membership scheme which would require every fan to produce an identity card before being allowed into a ground. Police, several working parties, the FA and the Football League strongly opposed the plan.

Hillsborough, however, changed everything. Lord Justice Peter Taylor, who had supported Newcastle United as a boy, was appointed to inquire into the tragedy; and his seventy-one page report, the ninth covering crowd control and safety since the White Horse final in 1923, pointed English football in a new direction. It identified failure of police control as the main reason for the Hillsborough disaster and, on a broader front, he called for 'a totally new approach across the whole field of football'. His plans for radical modernisation included all-seater stadiums for big clubs by 1994 and the rest by 1999, which signalled the beginning of the end for the old standing terraces. He also rejected the plan for a national membership scheme. The Government was impressed and accepted his recommendations. Tragedy had ushered in a new age.

The Hillsborough disaster confronted the FA with the hypersensitive question of whether the 1988–89 FA Cup should be allowed to continue. There were even suggestions that the final should be played at the start of the following season and that the trophy itself should be presented to Merseyside. Newspaper polls, however, indicated that a big majority of people believed the tournament should continue and Graham Kelly, the FA's chief executive, agreed. He said it would be a fitting memorial to carry on.

Liverpool overcame a subdued Nottingham Forest when their semi-final was played, at Old Trafford this time, a fortnight after the tragedy; and as Everton had already beaten Norwich City in the other semi-final at Villa Park, it meant that Wembley would belong to Merseyside. It was described as the 'Requiem Cup final', perhaps the most private final of all, and Liverpool won a stylish match by 3–2 with the help of two goals by Ian Rush, who had come on as a substitute. They were confirmed again as the most successful club in English football's history, standard bearers and standard setters, an obsession and a cause inside the family circle, an impossible lot for the rest of mankind.

Manager followed manager: Shankly the Messiah, the sage and avuncular Bob Paisley, good old Joe Fagan and, moving easily from dressing-room to boss's office, Kenny Dalglish. In eighteen seasons between 1972 and 1990, Liverpool won the League Championship eleven times. In 1984, they won the European Cup (for the fourth time), the Championship (for a third season running, equalling the record of Huddersfield Town and Arsenal) and the League Cup (for the fourth year in a row) – the only time an English club has won three major trophies in a season. And in 1986 they became the fifth club to complete the precious League and Cup double.

Liverpool's secret confounded everyone, but this, Paisley insisted, was because there was no secret. The real answer, he would say, was 'good players – and simplicity'. One thing was certain, though: a lesser club might have been destroyed by the tragedies of Heysel and Hillsborough.

Not that Liverpool were allowed to think of themselves as more than mere mortals. They reached the Cup final three times in the eighties, twice beating Everton, but in

1988 they were victims of one of the Cup's most extraordinary upsets. The noble tradition of giant-killing was embellished at Wembley itself.

Liverpool lost by 1–0 to Wimbledon, scallywags from London's southern outback, who had climbed from non-League football to the First Division in only nine seasons (1977–86) and whose combative, aerial style had few admirers. Liverpool were the hottest tips since the war; but Lawrie Sanchez scored for Wimbledon in the first half and Dave Beasant, their 6ft 4in goalkeeper, saved a penalty by John Aldridge in the second – the first missed penalty in a Wembley Cup final. Liverpool had just won the League Championship for the seventeenth time and victory over Wimbledon would have made them the first club to complete the double twice.

It was a remarkable period in which the Cup opened its heart to half a dozen clubs who had served it well without enjoying a final outing in London Town. Queens Park Rangers (1982), Brighton and Hove Albion (1983), Watford (1984), Coventry City (1987), Crystal Palace (1990) and, of course, Wimbledon all reached the final for the first time – and Coventry were even permitted to win the first major trophy in their 104-year history. Everton stylishly aspired to four finals during the eighties, including three in a row, but won only one. Tottenham Hotspur reached Wembley three times and, just as Bill Nicholson's team had done twenty years before, they won two in succession. The Cup may nod towards one of its supporting cast from time to time, but it never forgets its favourites.

There is also a symmetry about the Cup, amid its random tracery, and Tottenham, in one curious way, were a natural choice to be at Wembley in 1981 to celebrate the hundredth final. The north London club won the Cup in 1901, 1921 and 1961 – and would win it again in 1991. They also, for the record, won the League Championship in 1951 and 1961 and the League Cup in 1971.

Nearly thirty Cup final captains, going all the way back to 1930, were introduced to a warmly responsive crowd before the start of the hundredth final, and then Tottenham and Manchester City rose handsomely to the challenge of producing something special for this historic party. It stretched to two matches, the tenth final to need a replay but the first in which the second game was also played at Wembley. As always, the Cup selected its heroes with a sense of occasion and drama.

The oldest player on the pitch, thirty-three-year-old Tommy Hutchison, Manchester City's angular Scottish international forward, scored for both sides in the first game, which was drawn 1–1. Five days later, Spurs won a replay of quality and rising tension by 3–2, with two goals by Ricardo Villa, a bearded Argentine, who had trudged forlornly back to the dressing-room – and, for all he knew, out of the story of the FA Cup – after being substituted in the first meeting. His winner, moreover, was one of Wembley's finest. He spun past three defenders before scoring with calculated ease. It was a perfect postscript for the hundredth final.

There was also a banquet, of course, a sumptuous affair at the Royal Garden Hotel in West London which was attended by six hundred guests from every county and nearly thirty countries. Was a good knees-up ever more deserved?

The hundredth Cup final had the kind of script it deserved: two full houses at Wembley, seven goals, heroes and anti-heroes, mercurial twists in the plot and a last flourish, a final memory, that was positively golden.

Tommy Hutchison, Manchester City's thirty-three-year-old Scottish international forward, scored twice in the first game, one for his own side and an equalising own goal for Tottenham Hotspur – the first man to score for both teams in a final since Bert Turner (also the oldest man afield) back in 1946.

The following Thursday the full cast reassembled at Wembley for the replay and this time it was a Tottenham man who scored twice. He was Ricardo Villa, a black-bearded Argentine, who, together with Osvaldo Ardiles, a high-stepping, endlessly inventive midfield player, had been imported by Spurs after the 1978 World Cup. Villa was substituted in the drawn final but now, given a second chance, he scored the first and last goals of the replay – his second a gem under the Wembley floodlights and a winner.

Above Ricardo Villa (number five) settles the hundredth Cup final with one of Wembley's finest goals. He ran thirty yards, beating three City defenders, one of them twice, before gliding the ball past Manchester City's goalkeeper Joe Corrigan. The press box, high above, prepares to pen his praises.

Above Sutton United 2 Coventry City 1, third round 1989. Sutton of the Vauxhall Conference are on their way to beating Coventry of the First Division and Cup winners only two years before – and the view from the bungalow kitchens at Gander Green Lane is excellent. Tony Rains, leading the celebrations, has just scored the Surrey club's first goal.

Right Wrexham 2 Arsenal 1, third round 1992. Wrexham, bottom of the Fourth Division the season before, have just beaten Arsenal, the League champions, at the Racecourse Ground. They are feeling pleased.

The Cup is full to the brim with memories but will always find room for more. Thirty Cup-winning captains were at Wembley on 9 May 1981 to mark the hundredth final. It took David Barber of the FA more than a month to trace them.

Above *(left to right)* – Dave Mackay (Tottenham Hotspur 1967), Danny Blanchflower (Tottenham Hotspur 1961 and 1962), Dick Pym (Bolton Wanderers 1923, 1926 and 1929, aged eighty-eight, not captain but one of the oldest surviving finalists), Pat Rice (Arsenal 1979), Peter Rodrigues (Southampton 1976), Bobby Kerr (Sunderland 1973), Graham Williams (West Bromwich Albion 1968), Ron Yeats (Liverpool 1965), Noel Cantwell (Manchester United 1963), Jack Burkitt (Nottingham Forest 1959), Johnny Dixon (Aston Villa 1957), Jimmy Scoular (Newcastle United 1955), Joe Mercer (Arsenal 1950), Johnny Carey (Manchester United 1948), Tom Smith (Preston North End 1938), Ronnie Starling (Sheffield Wednesday 1935).

Opposite top *(left to right)* – Tom Parker (Arsenal 1930), Jack Swann (Huddersfield Town 1920, aged eighty-eight, not captain but played in first final after World War One), Raich Carter (Sunderland 1937), Don Welsh (Charlton Athletic 1947), Billy Wright (Wolverhampton Wanderers 1949), Joe Harvey (Newcastle United 1951 and 1952), Len Millard (West Bromwich Albion 1954), Nat Lofthouse (Bolton Wanderers 1958), Bill Slater (Wolverhampton Wanderers 1960), Bobby Moore (West Ham United 1964), Brian Labone (Everton 1966), Frank McLintock (Arsenal 1971), Emlyn Hughes (Liverpool 1974), Mick Mills (Ipswich Town 1978), Roy Paul (Manchester City 1956), Tony Book (Manchester City 1969).

Right The Centenary final 1972 – and the Royal Engineers, who took part in the first final in 1872, are properly on parade.

Anfield in the spring of 1989.

Above Wimbledon's 1988 Cup
heroes are welcomed home by
25,000 people – many more than
watched them week by week in the
League. Three years later they left
Plough Lane, their home for
seventy-nine years, to share Crystal
Palace's home at Selhurst Park near
Croydon.

Left Diss Town v Sudbury Town, FA Cup first qualifying round, September 1994. Eddie Maze of Sudbury looks for the ball – but, in the background, help is at hand.

Right Blue headgear, red rosette and something to wave at the venue of legends. A winner, he hopes, whatever happens inside Maine Road. Oldham Athletic v Manchester United, semi-final 1990.

Below Ruud Gullit may be a former European and World Footballer of the Year – but the FA Cup is still hair-raising. Chelsea have just beaten Newcastle United in a third round penalty shoot-out, 1996.

Above Manchester United celebrate the double, Wembley 1994. Paul Ince takes it lying down. The neatly framed head (top centre) belongs to Adrian Titcombe, the FA Head of Competitions and Regulations.

Left Eric Cantona has just scored the late winner which completes the double double for Manchester United, Wembley 1996 – and manager Alex Ferguson (above the W in Littlewoods) leads the songs of praise.

Below White Horse final. Tottenham fans, queuing at Wembley for tickets for the replay, are marshalled by a policeman on a white horse – just as the first Wembley crowd had been fifty-eight years before.

1981

9 May at Wembley   Att 100,000
Tottenham Hotspur 1 (Hutchison (og))
Manchester City 1 (Hutchison)   **aet**
Tottenham Hotspur: Aleksic, Hughton, Miller, Roberts, Perryman, Villa (Brooke), Ardiles, Archibald, Galvin, Hoddle, Crooks.
Manchester City: Corrigan, Ranson, McDonald, Reid, Power, Caton, Bennett, Gow, MacKenzie, Hutchison (Henry), Reeves.
Referee: K. Hackett
Replay: 14 May at Wembley   Att 92,000
Tottenham Hotspur 3 (Villa 2, Crooks)
Manchester City 2 (MacKenzie, Reeves (pen))
Tottenham Hotspur: Aleksic, Hughton, Miller, Roberts, Perryman, Villa, Ardiles, Archibald, Galvin, Hoddle, Crooks.
Manchester City: Corrigan, Ranson, McDonald (Tueart), Caton, Reid, Gow, Power, MacKenzie, Reeves, Bennett, Hutchison.
Referee: K. Hackett

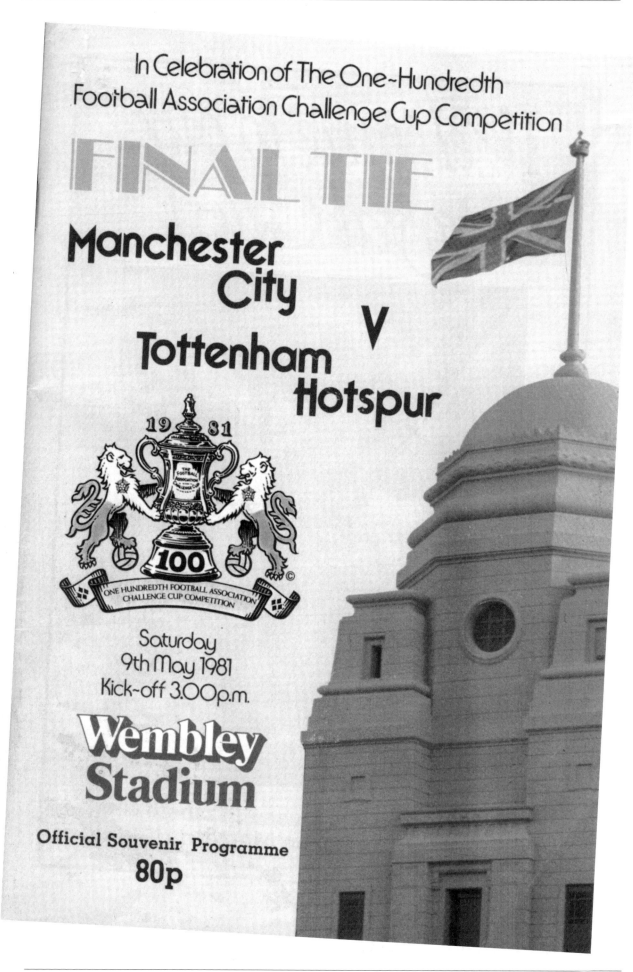

Tottenham Hotspur, in their centenary year, had a brave tilt at the FA Cup, the League Championship, the League Cup and the European Cup-Winners' Cup. They finished with the FA Cup, their seventh win in seven finals, but only after they were taken to another replay by Second Division Queens Park Rangers, who were managed by Tottenham old boy Terry Venables. The Falklands War had started – so no Ossie Ardiles or Ricky Villa.

Below A Queens Park Rangers banner politely suggests that Tony Currie will get the better of Tottenham's Glenn Hoddle in midfield.

1982

22 May at Wembley   Att 100,000
Tottenham Hotspur 1 (Hoddle)
Queens Park Rangers 1 (Fenwick)   **aet**
Tottenham Hotspur: Clemence, Hughton, Miller, Price, Hazard (Brooke), Perryman, Roberts, Archibald, Galvin, Hoddle, Crooks.
QPR: Hucker, Fenwick, Gillard, Waddock, Hazell, Roeder, Currie, Flanagan, Allen (Micklewhite), Stainrod, Gregory.
Referee: C. White
Replay: 27 May at Wembley   Att 90,000
Tottenham Hotspur 1 (Hoddle (pen))
Queens Park Rangers 0
Tottenham Hotspur: Clemence, Hughton, Miller, Price, Hazard (Brooke), Perryman, Roberts, Archibald, Galvin, Hoddle, Crooks.
QPR: Hucker, Fenwick, Gillard, Waddock, Hazell, Neill, Currie, Flanagan, Micklewhite (Burke), Stainrod, Gregory.
Referee: C. White

Below What happened was that Currie (left, grounded) gave Tottenham a penalty by fouling Graham Roberts (right, grounded) in only the sixth minute of the replay – and Hoddle scored Spurs' winner from the spot.

Right No ticket... no seat. Not even for a Tottenham cockerel.

1983

21 May at Wembley   Att 100,000

Manchester United 2 (Stapleton, Wilkins)

Brighton and Hove Albion 2 (Smith, Stevens)   **aet**

Manchester United: Bailey, Duxbury, Moran, McQueen, Albiston, Davies, Wilkins, Robson, Muhren, Stapleton, Whiteside.

Brighton and Hove Albion: Moseley, Ramsey (Ryan), Stevens, Gatting, Pearce, Smillie, Case, Grealish, Howlett, Robinson, Smith.

Referee: A. W. Grey

Replay: 26 May at Wembley   Att 92,000

Manchester United 4 (Robson 2, Whiteside, Muhren (pen))

Brighton and Hove Albion 0

Manchester United: Bailey, Duxbury, Albiston, Wilkins, Moran, McQueen, Robson, Muhren, Stapleton, Whiteside, Davies.

Brighton and Hove Albion: Moseley, Gatting, Pearce, Grealish, Foster, Stevens, Case, Howlett, Robinson, Smith, Smillie.

Referee: A. W. Grey

Above The last minute of extra-time, the score 2–2, and Gordon Smith of Brighton and Hove Albion has the chance of all chances to win the Cup in 1983. 'And Smith must score,' Peter Jones, BBC Radio's commentator, told the world.

But Smith missed. 'Mike Robinson pushed the ball across to me,' he would remember, 'and I took a touch to control it. I wanted to send it in hard and low, first time, but Manchester United's goalkeeper Gary Bailey spread himself well and the ball stuck between his legs. People say it was an open goal, but how can that be when the keeper made a save? If time travel ever becomes a reality, I'll be the first to volunteer. I'll go back and score that goal.'

The moment passed in a blink; but not the memory. Smith became instantly famous for a failure. A Brighton fanzine called itself *And*

Smith must score and the south coast playground will never forget that he didn't.

Yet Smith *did* score. The Scot gave Brighton the lead after fourteen minutes – but his miss meant a replay and Manchester United, third in Division One, were in no mood for further alarms five days later. They won 4–0 on Sir Matt Busby's seventy-fourth birthday.

Brighton were relegated from Division One that season, rock bottom and out of their class, but in the Cup they were virile dreadnoughts. They reached Wembley by beating Newcastle United (in a replay at St James' Park), Manchester City (4–0), Liverpool (League champions and League Cup winners, away), Norwich City and Sheffield Wednesday.

Below Norman Whiteside (number ten) heads Manchester United's second goal in the replay to become the youngest player to score in a Cup final. Whiteside, strong, aggressive and precociously talented, was 18 years 19 days old – and already a Northern Ireland international.

Above Jimmy Melia (right) will always be part of Brighton's memory of their wonderful failure. Melia, a clever inside-forward in his day and an England international, had managed Aldershot, Crewe Alexandra and Southport before his brief but exhilarating spell as manager at the Goldstone Ground. He was a showman who disco-danced in white shoes and loved publicity and acclaim.

1984

19 May at Wembley   Att 100,000
Everton 2 (Sharp, Gray)
Watford 0
Everton: Southall, Stevens, Bailey, Ratcliffe, Mountfield, Reid, Steven, Heath, Sharp, Gray, Richardson.
Watford: Sherwood, Bardsley, Price (Atkinson), Taylor, Terry, Sinnott, Callaghan, Johnston, Reilly, Jackett, Barnes.
Referee: J. Hunting

A softening of the heart, a new generosity, was apparent in the character of the Cup in the 1980s. It allowed Queens Park Rangers and Brighton and Hove Albion to enjoy the Wembley experience for the first time and, later in the decade, there would be similar invitations to Coventry City, Wimbledon and Crystal Palace. They were loyal servants of the game, never its masters, but taking part in the final did wonders for their self-esteem. Watford's turn came in 1984.

Watford, part of the heart of Hertfordshire, had climbed from Fourth Division to First in five seasons under chairman Elton John and manager Graham Taylor, who would one day lead England. Their direct and uncompromising style saw them finish as League runners-up to Liverpool in 1983 and then, a year later, they reached the Cup final – their road to Wembley eased, perhaps, by a universal disregard for status and pedigree in the earlier rounds. Nine First Division clubs fell in the third round (four to clubs of lower order), Brighton beat Liverpool (again), Bournemouth bettered Manchester United and non-League Telford United reached the fourth round. Watford, the luck of the draw with them, beat Luton Town, Charlton Athletic, Brighton, Birmingham City and, in the semi-finals, Plymouth Argyle from the muddy end of the Third Division. It was that sort of season.

Left Elton John, born Reginald Kenneth Dwight, nephew of 1959 Cup-winner Roy Dwight, chairman of Watford, pop and rock musician. First a salute… then a tear. The superstar was back at Wembley six weeks later for a pop concert.

Below Andy Gray, having beaten Watford's goalkeeper Steve Sherwood to a centre (he might even have headed the ball *out* of the keeper's hands), watches the ball cross the line for Everton's second goal. Gray, a Scottish warrior, had joined Everton from Wolverhampton Wanderers earlier in the season – and his arrival set them alight.

Season 1984–85 might have been remembered for many good things: Everton's stylish double of League Championship and European Cup-Winners' Cup; the FA Cup exploits of York City (who beat Arsenal) and non-League Telford United; Norwich City's League Cup triumph; Oxford United's promotion to the First Division; and the opening of the FA National School at Lilleshall. But it is recalled, sadly, as the season of the Bradford fire, the Heysel disaster, the Millwall riot and the first sending-off of a player in an FA Cup final.

Above Luton v Millwall, sixth round of the FA Cup, 13 March 1985. Police confusion as Millwall fans riot at Kenilworth Road. There were pitch invasions during the game, which was stopped for twenty-five minutes, and at its end, the mob tore out seats to use as weapons and the pitch became a battleground. Television viewers watched as the police (thirty-one injured) bravely restored order. Luton won 1–0.

1985

18 May at Wembley   Att 100,000

Manchester United 1
  (Whiteside)

Everton 0   aet

Manchester United: Bailey, Gidman,
  Albiston (Duxbury), Whiteside,
  McGrath, Moran, Robson,
  Strachan, Hughes, Stapleton,
  Olsen.

Everton: Southall, Stevens, Van Den
  Hauwe, Ratcliffe, Mountfield, Reid,
  Steven, Gray, Sharp, Bracewell,
  Sheedy.

Referee: P. Willis

Below Kevin Moran of Manchester United and the Republic of Ireland becomes the first player to be sent off in an FA Cup final – the 104th. Moran protests aggressively, team-mate Frank Stapleton restrains him and other United players have their say. But referee Peter Willis, a police-man from Meadowfield, County Durham, is adamant that Moran must go for his 'professional' foul. Manchester United, with ten men, won with an extra-time goal by Norman Whiteside.

Below Liverpool's League and Cup double… Merseyside's Wembley… and, in its own special way, a blessing for English football. An excellent final in front of an audience that was mixed and mellow yet divided and passionate as only a Merseyside crowd could have been. Hooliganism, Europe believed, was an English disease, but there was no sign of contagion here.

It was the first all-Mersey FA Cup final and its timing was perfect. Liverpool were the new 1986 League champions; Everton were the runners-up and 1985 champions. Everton were playing in their third successive final, Liverpool in the first of three in four years.

Merseyside turned its back on the rest of football and produced a final that looked to be going Everton's way for nearly an hour, but which Liverpool then hijacked and eventually dominated. Two goals by Ian Rush of Wales made all the difference.

Liverpool's double was the third of the century and the fifth in all, a triumph for Kenny Dalglish in his first season as Liverpool's player-manager.

The full Liverpool cast: *standing (left to right)* – Bruce Grobbelaar, Kenny Dalglish, Gary Gillespie, Jan Molby, Paul Walsh, Mike Hooper, Sammy Lee, Mark Lawrenson, Ian Rush, Kevin MacDonald, Ronnie Whelan, John Wark. *Squatting* – Steve McMahon, Craig Johnston, Jim Beglin, Alan Hansen, Steve Nicol.

1986

10 May at Wembley   Att 98,000

Liverpool 3 (Rush 2, Johnston)
Everton 1 (Lineker)
Liverpool: Grobbelaar, Lawrenson, Beglin, Nicol, Whelan, Hansen, Dalglish, Johnston, Rush, Molby, MacDonald.
Everton: Mimms, Stevens (Heath), Van Den Hauwe, Ratcliffe, Mountfield, Reid, Steven, Lineker, Sharp, Bracewell, Sheedy.
Referee: A. Robinson

Gallaher's Cigarettes.

Above The last of the old Corinthians: Benjamin Howard Baker – England international goalkeeper, Olympic high-jumper, hurdler and discus-thrower, cricketer, swimmer and tennis player, Liverpool born, an Everton and Liverpool player – pictured in 1986, Merseyside's year, at the age of ninety-four. He also assisted Blackburn Rovers, Preston North End, Chelsea and Oldham Athletic. A brilliant but unorthodox goalkeeper who was noted for his long kicking, he died in 1987.

Above This card, interestingly, shows Howard Baker in action for the Corinthians in one of their greatest FA Cup ties, against Newcastle United (soon to be League champions) in the fourth round in 1927. The small figure of the great Hughie Gallacher is to the right of Howard Baker. The Corinthians lost 3–1 at Crystal Palace after leading until fifteen minutes from the end.

Coventry City: formed 1883; highest League position sixth in Division One (once); best in FA Cup sixth round (four times). Nice people, nice club, who began their 104th year without a major honour and knowing exactly what the poet Rupert Brooke meant when he wrote about 'the long littleness of life'.

Their time arrived in 1987. They beat Bolton Wanderers, Manchester United (at Old Trafford), Stoke City, Sheffield Wednesday and Leeds United to reach Wembley and there, in an absorbing match, they became the first club to beat Tottenham Hotspur, seven times winners, in an FA Cup final. Spurs had an international sweet trolley of a team

(including Glenn Hoddle, Chris Waddle, Ossie Ardiles and goal-keeper Ray Clemence, once of Liverpool, who was playing in his fifth final), while Coventry were essentially a team without stars. Twice Coventry were a goal down, but the spirit and confidence built up during their rousing Cup run enabled them to push the match into extra-time – and there an own goal by Tottenham defender Gary Mabbutt gave Coventry their precious Cup.

Above The most remembered moment of the 1987 final. A spectacular header by Keith Houchen, from a centre by Dave Bennett, gives Coventry their second equaliser.

1987

16 May at Wembley   Att 98,000
Coventry City 3 (Bennett, Houchen, Mabbutt (og))
Tottenham Hotspur 2 (C. Allen, Mabbutt)   **aet**
Coventry City: Ogrizovic, Phillips, Downs, McGrath, Kilcline (Rodger), Peake, Bennett, Gynn, Regis, Houchen, Pickering.
Tottenham Hotspur: Clemence, Hughton (Claesen), M. Thomas, Hodge, Gough, Mabbutt, C. Allen, P. Allen, Waddle, Hoddle, Ardiles (Stevens).
Referee: N. Midgley

Below An open-topped bus from Coventry's Transport Museum carried the Cup and its new winners along the city's Corporation Street. It had been a long wait.

A strong case can be made for recognising Wimbledon's triumph in 1988 as the most remarkable in the history of the Cup. There are other candidates, of course, but Wimbledon's story is unique. Only eleven years earlier, they had been a Southern League club with few resources and supporters. Then, without noticeable gain in wealth or sympathy, they rose from the bottom of the pond to a place amid the stars of the First Division. They were muscular opportunists whose Battle of Britain style, aerial forays and dauntless pursuit appalled those who saw football as 'a beautiful game'. Wimbledon were neither understood nor admired and were given considerably less than no chance when they met Liverpool at Wembley. Liverpool, after all, had just won the League Championship for the seventeenth time (by a margin of nine points) and were hell-bent on a second League and Cup double.

But Wimbledon's nerve and verve won them their first major trophy. Lawrie Sanchez, with a nicely angled header, scored in the first half, and (below) Dave Beasant, Wimbledon's captain and goal-keeper, made history by saving John Aldridge's penalty in the second. It was the first time a penalty had been missed in a Wembley final and Beasant duly became the first goal-keeper to receive the Cup.

Above The most successful gang of pirates in the Cup's history. Dave Beasant lifts manager Bobby Gould (left) watched by coach Don Howe (fourth from right). They knew how to celebrate.

1988

14 May at Wembley   Att 98,203

Wimbledon I (Sanchez)

Liverpool 0

Wimbledon: Beasant, Goodyear, Phelan, Jones, Young, Thorn, Gibson (Scales), Cork (Cunningham), Fashanu, Sanchez, Wise.

Liverpool: Grobbelaar, Gillespie, Ablett, Nicol, Spackman (Molby), Hansen, Beardsley, Aldridge (Johnston), Houghton, Barnes, McMahon.

Referee: B. Hill

1989

20 May at Wembley   Att 82,500

Liverpool 3 (Aldridge, Rush 2)

Everton 2 (McCall 2)   **aet**

Liverpool: Grobbelaar, Ablett, Staunton (Venison), Nicol, Whelan, Hansen, Beardsley, Aldridge (Rush), Houghton, Barnes, McMahon.

Everton: Southall, McDonald, Van Den Hauwe, Ratcliffe, Watson, Bracewell (McCall), Nevin, Steven, Sharp, Cottee, Sheedy (Wilson).

Referee: J. Worrall

Seven days after the Hillsborough disaster: Anfield at six minutes past three. The only sound is that of the wind tugging at the wrapping on the flowers and wreaths. It sounds, eerily, like distant applause. In the city, traffic has stopped and shoppers bow their heads as Merseyside observes a minute's silence.

The Cup went ahead and Liverpool met Everton in 'the Requiem final'. Thirty-seven thousand tickets went to each club and the Merseyside crowd sang 'You'll Never Walk Alone' as it had never been sung before. Then Liverpool won a stylish and dramatic game by 3–2 with Ian Rush, who had come on as a substitute, scoring twice in extra-time.

Above Rush, perfectly balanced, drops low to head a centre from John Barnes past Everton's goalkeeper Neville Southall. It was Liverpool's winner and the final tribute their players had set their hearts on. The double, however, proved just beyond them. Liverpool lost the Championship to Arsenal at Anfield, when Michael Thomas scored for the north London club in the last minute of the last match of the season, the most dramatic finish in League history.

Palm Sunday, 8 April 1990. Was there ever a semi-final day like this? Thirteen goals were scored at Villa Park and Maine Road, with extra-time at both, as Crystal Palace beat Liverpool 4–3 and Oldham Athletic and Manchester United drew 3–3.

Below Alan Pardew of Crystal Palace celebrates his winning goal against Liverpool in the 109th minute of their Villa Park semi-final. Liverpool, the Cup holders and League leaders, had beaten Palace 9–0 in the League earlier in the season. But Palace, threatened by relegation, undermined by injuries and twice a goal down, dismantled the Anfield defence with their punchy directness to reach the final for the first time.

1990

12 May at Wembley   Att 80,000

Manchester United 3 (Robson, Hughes 2)

Crystal Palace 3 (O'Reilly, Wright 2)   **aet**

Manchester United: Leighton, Ince, Martin (Blackmore), Bruce, Phelan, Pallister (Robins), Robson, Webb, McClair, Hughes, Wallace.

Crystal Palace: Martyn, Pemberton, Shaw, Gray (Madden), O'Reilly, Thorn, Barber (Wright), Thomas, Bright, Salako, Pardew.

Referee: A. Gunn

Replay: 17 May at Wembley   Att 80,000

Manchester United 1 (Martin)

Crystal Palace 0

Manchester United: Sealey, Ince, Martin, Bruce, Phelan, Pallister, Robson, Webb, McClair, Hughes, Wallace.

Crystal Palace: Martyn, Pemberton, Shaw, Gray, O'Reilly, Thorn, Barber (Wright), Thomas, Bright, Salako (Madden), Pardew.

Referee: A. Gunn

Above Roger Palmer, right, earns a replay in extra-time against Manchester United at Maine Road after coming on as a substitute for Oldham in their first semi-final for seventy-seven years. Oldham lost the replay, again after extra-time, by 2–1 and so just failed to reach both domestic finals. They had lost 1–0 to Nottingham Forest in the League Cup final.

Below Lee Martin (third from left), a twenty-two-year-old defender, scores his only goal of the season to win the Cup for Manchester United in their final replay with an oddly negative Crystal Palace. The first game, in front of Wembley's first all-seated crowd, had been much better, with Ian Wright (back in action after breaking a leg twice that season) coming on as a substitute to score two memorable goals for Palace in a 3–3 draw. United had a poor League season and their Cup success probably saved the job of their manager Alex Ferguson.

Chapter Twelve

Into the Fast Lane
1991–1996

'The FA Cup final is the greatest single match outside the World Cup final – and it's ours.'

Bobby Robson, manager of Ipswich Town when they won the FA Cup in 1978, and manager of England for the World Cups of 1986 and 1990. Speaking at the annual dinner of the Football Writers' Association, May 1995.

A new FA Cup, the fourth in 120 years, was played for in 1992. The third, bless its silver soul, had become weary after eighty years of being held aloft by jubilant captains, carted roughly around Wembley by winning teams, humped up and down the country in aid of good causes, polished with such love and vigour that it lost weight, and occasionally, unforgivably, even ill treated. It is now in happy retirement but still doing valuable promotional work. The new trophy is a faithful replica, complete with bunches of grapes, vine leaves and pinched waist, which had been waiting patiently as a standby for more than ten years. And, indeed, in case of theft or accident, there is a third Cup which is also identical. It was made in 1993 by John Taylor's of London at a cost of £12,403 (and thirty pence) and is kept in a bank vault. The old and familiar shape is guaranteed until well into the twenty-first century.

Imagine what the latest trophy might look like, however, if it had been considered desirable to commission a new design in keeping with the changing face of the tournament as well as modern taste. It would be a different and maddening creation because the format of the Cup lost some of its comely shape and sweet innocence in the nineties. It was assailed by television, money, expediency, legislation and the Law.

The police requested that, for logistical reasons, there should be a minimum of ten days between a Cup tie and its replay. This meant the end of unlimited replays and, in the 1991–92 season, led to the introduction of penalty shoot-outs if a first and only replay was not settled by the end of extra-time. Scunthorpe, Colchester, Newcastle and Manchester United were the first clubs to lose by way of this dramatic lottery, but the barbarity of it really sank in when Portsmouth of the Second Division lost their semi-final with Liverpool in a shoot-out. Portsmouth had had the better of two absorbing games and many agreed with Jim Smith, their manager, when he said shoot-outs trivialised the competition.

Cup ties in some rounds were played on every day of the week – a spread contributed to by the demands of television – which meant the tournament forfeited some of its simple and natural rhythm. Draws for the Cup, too, for a while, were treated with an irritating lack of respect. No more Monday lunchtimes on BBC Radio. They popped up randomly on the box, anywhere and any time between Saturday (once after midnight) and Monday evening.

Semi-finals also became moveable feasts. They were, traditionally, Saturday fixtures on neutral grounds, until the Hillsborough disaster changed everything. The control and safety of crowds became a paramount consideration. Semi-finals were switched to Sundays or staggered over a weekend – sometimes with a lunchtime kick-off. Sunday semi-finals, indeed, are now the norm.

No harm has been done by switching days, but there was a critical howl when some semi-finals were moved to Wembley. This, it was claimed, was greed mugging tradition, a studied insult to everything the old stadium stood for and one more step towards the destruction of the greatest competition in club football. How could Wembley, it was asked, be just another bus-stop on the way to Wembley?

The first time a semi-final was played at Wembley was in 1991, when Arsenal and Tottenham were drawn together for the first time at this stage. It made sense to send the two north London clubs' big and passionate army of supporters a few miles down the road to play at the national stadium. 'Our priority is the convenience and safety of the watching public,' said Graham Kelly. It also enabled nearly 78,000 people to watch the game which, quite incidentally of course, was very good business. But there was no intention of repeating the move. It was unique encounter, a one-off solution.

Two years later, however, Arsenal and Spurs were drawn together again in the semi-finals. It was perfectly logical to send them back to Wembley; but the situation this time was complicated by the coincidental and historic pairing of Sheffield United and Sheffield Wednesday in the other semi-final. The two South Yorkshire clubs were invited to play at Elland Road, the home of Leeds United, but they argued strongly that they should have the same chance of rehearsal time at Wembley as the London clubs. They were also very conscious, post-Hillsborough, of the issue of safety. The FA agreed with their argument and so the City of Sheffield on Grand National Day and then north London on Palm Sunday sent a total of more than 150,000 to Wembley over one exhilarating and momentous weekend. Arsenal and Sheffield Wednesday survived, just a fortnight before they were also due to meet in the final of the League Cup. In the end it proved to be Arsenal's year – the first club to win both domestic cups in one season.

There was again a double booking of Wembley for the 1993–94 semi-finals but criticism of the practice reached new heights and Elland Road and Villa Park were selected the following season. Venues in future will depend on circumstances and demand. The FA will take each game as it comes.

Few issues involving the FA Cup have inspired more emotive debate than sponsorship. The popular attitude to this was expressed by Ted Croker, the Football Association's secretary from 1973 to 1989, who wrote, a few years before his retirement: 'The Cup is above sponsorship. It sells itself. FA policy is against the whole concept.'

Football's marketplace was changing, however, and so were attitudes. This was reflected by the FA's willingness to consider sponsorship of the Cup in 1987, a change of mind prompted by an offer from Elders, the Australian brewing company, who wanted to use the Cup to promote their Fosters lager. There were immediate reservations about linking the tournament with alcohol but, given so many pressing needs for funds, Elders' offer of £20 million over five years was undoubtedly attractive. In the end, the deal foundered on the negotiating table. Elders wanted the FA Cup to be known as the Fosters

Cup which provoked a coast-to-coast scream of horror. The Australian stock market then took a nasty fall and Elders' offer suddenly became £10.5 million over four years. This was rejected, and so was an offer from another brewer of £18.5 million over five years. Croker announced the FA had 'insufficient common ground' with the would-be sponsors.

Sir Bert Millichip, chairman of the Football Association, declared they had 'a duty to explore every commercial avenue', but the search for the right kind of sponsor for the Cup, with the right kind of money, was stalled by a frosty contractual row with Wembley Stadium Ltd. Wembley claimed they were entitled to twenty-five per cent of any Cup sponsorship which, together with other rights and charges, meant that football's corner of any such income would be damagingly reduced. Trevor Phillips, the FA's commercial director, who had previously held a similar post with the Football League, decided that no progress could be made until the contract with Wembley was renegotiated. This took more than twenty months of frustration, bitterness, stalemate, veiled threats and expensive arbitration – but the solution, when it was reached in 1994, was original and pragmatic.

All the FA's rights and all Wembley's rights were put into one basket in a major enterprise called Total Football. Financial guarantees and splits were agreed and sponsorship was shared among a number of companies, one of which, it was announced, would be expected to pay more – considerably more – for the privilege of underwriting the FA Cup.

Enter Littlewoods Pools. Their offer of £14 million, rising to £20 million with 'direct support expenditure', was accepted by the FA. And so, after 123 years of financial self-sufficiency, the full and proper title of the world's oldest football tournament became 'The Football Association Challenge Cup, sponsored by Littlewoods Pools'.

There were discordant rumblings about tradition, the amount of money that would find its way to the grass-roots of the game and even about the total size of the 'jackpot'. The FA conceded they could have made more by dealing with a tobacco company and also by selling title-sponsorship. As Barry Dale, Littlewoods chief executive, admitted: 'We would have liked it to be called Littlewoods Pools FA Cup, but this was never really on the agenda.'

Littlewoods Pools, a Liverpool-based empire with the same birth year as the White Horse final at Wembley, fitted the bill admirably. Their retail arm had backed the League Cup for four seasons (1986–90) and they valued the traditions of football, as well as understanding the broad and sometimes complex responsibilities of sponsorship. Lord Aberdare, chairman of the Football Trust, said: 'This cements the relationship between football and Littlewoods Pools, who are among the game's most generous benefactors.' The Football Trust, a respected body experienced in funding the game at all levels, receives nearly £40 million a year from pools competitions.

English football had now moved into the fast lane. The twenty-two clubs of the First Division divorced themselves from the Football League, with the imperial warrant and active support of the Football Association, and set up shop as the Premier League in

1992. They did a deal with Sky Sports, the satellite channel, and the BBC that was worth, all told, £304 million over five years. Sponsorship, advertising and merchandising helped the game move into overdrive, and wealthy benefactors threw their pennies into the ring. Jack Walker spent £30 million on buying players to secure the Premier League title for Blackburn Rovers in 1995. Crowds overall, despite rising admission prices, increased for ten successive seasons from 1986–87 onwards.

The push for success and status became manic. Transfer fees and wage bills soared alarmingly. There was a major influx of foreign players, decorative imports from almost every corner of the globe. Astrakhaned agents became significant figures in the marketplace. And the morality of the game trembled: there were headlines about drugs, match-fixing and 'bungs'.

The picture, on face value, was depressing; but, against logic and expectation, the game's profile was higher than ever. Improved facilities and stadiums, exciting entertainment, a decline in hooliganism inside grounds and brightly wrapped projection on television, radio and the back pages all helped to claw back ground lost in the early eighties. A simple playground game was once again popular theatre.

The Cup rose buoyantly above all the turbulence like a good ship riding a storm. But, if it continued to offer hope and glamour to the needy and small, it still reserved its final favours for those of rank. The first six finals of the nineties were won by the clubs sometimes referred to as the Big Five – Spurs, Liverpool (in their centenary year), Arsenal, Everton and, toweringly, Manchester United who completed the double in both 1994 and 1996 – the awesome and historic 'double double'. Manchester United were simply a cut above their contemporaries, expensively, imaginatively and boldly constructed by their manager Alex Ferguson whose record with Aberdeen and Manchester United (including the double with both) gives him a singular place among all his kind. Why have so many great managers been Scottish?

The cities of London, Manchester and Liverpool have dominated things since 1961 when the ceiling on wages was removed. Twenty different clubs, including just five from these three cities, won the tournament between 1923 and 1960. But only sixteen clubs won it during the thirty-six seasons between 1961 and 1996 – and on thirty occasions the Cup finished in London, Manchester or Liverpool. It is a record hardly befitting such a staunch democrat.

Cup minnows go out in style

WO-KINGS!

WOKING TALL! Skipper Adie Cowler leads his players on a lap of honour. *Picture: ALBERT COOPER*

Even Everton join in the cheers

IT WAS party time for Woking's part-timers at Goodison Park yesterday as 34,724 fans saluted their tremendous FA Cup fourth-round performance.

Above Royal tribute by the *Daily Mirror* to Woking, the non-League part-timers from Surrey, who beat West Bromwich Albion by 4–2 at the Hawthorns in the third round, and then lost by just a single goal to Everton at Goodison Park in the fourth. Woking skipper Adie Cowler said afterwards: 'We had 10,000 fans here, young lads were asking for an autograph and old men wanted to shake me by the hand – who the hell am I?'

1991

18 May at Wembley   Att 80,000
Tottenham Hotspur 2 (Stewart, Walker (og))
Nottingham Forest 1
(Pearce)   **aet**
Tottenham Hotspur: Thorstvedt, Edinburgh, Van Den Hauwe, Sedgley, Howells, Mabbutt, Stewart, Gascoigne (Nayim), Samways (Walsh), Lineker, Allen.
Nottingham Forest: Crossley, Charles, Pearce, Walker, Chettle, Keane, Crosby, Parker, Clough, Glover (Laws), Woan (Hodge).
Referee: R. Milford

Contrast in kicks: different days but same end, same ground, by Paul Gascoigne (number eight) of Tottenham Hotspur.

Below Hero Gascoigne audaciously swerves a thirty-five-yard free-kick into the top right corner of Arsenal's net, a glorious goal after only five minutes of the first semi-final to be played at Wembley, on Sunday 14 April 1991. Gary Lineker, back in England from Barcelona after leaving Everton, scored two more for Tottenham, who won 3–1.

Opposite top Villain Gascoigne recklessly tackles Gary Charles of Nottingham Forest after only fifteen minutes of the final on 18 May 1991. But it was Gascoigne and Tottenham who paid an immediate price. Gascoigne was carried off, with a badly injured knee, and from the free-kick Stuart Pearce gave Forest the lead. The year ended in one, however, so it had to be Tottenham's year. Paul Stewart equalised and an own goal by Forest's Des Walker in extra-time gave Tottenham the Cup for the eighth time (including 1901, 1921, 1961 and 1981).

Opposite bottom Gascoigne cried after England's semi-final defeat by Germany in the 1990 World Cup… and he is close to tears again before being stretchered off at Wembley. It was his last game for Tottenham. Gazza, brilliant footballer, social sinner, later joined Lazio of Rome before returning to British football with Glasgow Rangers.

1992

9 May at Wembley   Att 79,544
Liverpool 2 (Thomas, Rush)
Sunderland 0

Liverpool: Grobbelaar, R. Jones,
  Burrows, Nicol, Molby, Wright,
  Saunders, Houghton, I. Rush,
  McManaman, Thomas.

Sunderland: Norman, Owers, Ball,
  Bennett, Rogan, D. Rush
  (Hardyman), Bracewell,
  Davenport, Armstrong, Byrne,
  Atkinson (Hawke).

Referee: P. Don

Above Another contrast. John Beresford of Second Division Portsmouth has just failed from the spot in the first semi-final penalty shoot-out. Liverpool and Portsmouth drew 0–0 in their replay at Villa Park and Liverpool won 3–1 on penalties. Portsmouth's manager Jim Smith said shoot-outs trivialised the competition.

Left Michael Thomas has just scored the first of Liverpool's two winning goals in the final against Sunderland of the Second Division. Ian Rush got the second – his fifth goal, a record, in Cup finals. Thomas, of course, was the man who scored Arsenal's last-minute Championship winner at Anfield in 1989. He moved to Liverpool in December 1991 for £1.5 million.

Right New tradition and new Cup. The runners-up were first to climb the thirty-nine steps this time, and Sunderland, to their surprise and official embarrassment, were presented with the winners' medals. Then Liverpool went up to collect a brand new FA Cup, the fourth in 120 years, before returning to pitch level to swap medals with Sunderland.

The new Cup, a faithful replica of the old, is displayed by Liverpool captain Mark Wright. It was damaged, slightly, as Liverpool put it on to their team coach.

Below Andy Linighan heads Arsenal's winner against Sheffield Wednesday with less than a minute of extra-time left in the 1993 final replay – a goal which spared the Cup the indignity of its first penalty shoot-out at Wembley. Defender Linighan rose high to a corner by Paul Merson, a theatrical last act on a night of glistening puddles, to give Arsenal the distinction of being the first club to win both FA Cup and League Cup in one season. Wednesday were their opponents in both finals.

Both FA Cup semi-finals were staged at Wembley, so Arsenal and Wednesday each played there four times in six weeks – FA Cup semi-final, League Cup final, FA Cup final and replay. Perhaps familiarity with each other, and even with the stadium, were among the reasons why the four hours of the longest final of all were so greyly ordinary. The replay attracted the smallest crowd (62,267) for an FA Cup final at Wembley. The kick-off was put back half an hour because an accident on the M1 had halted thousands of Wednesday fans. It was the first time a Wembley kick-off had been delayed since the White Horse final.

Indeed, there were bigger crowds for the Wembley semi-finals. Arsenal's 1–0 victory over Tottenham Hotspur was watched by 76,263, and the Sheffield derby (Wednesday 2, United 1 after extra-time) was a happy family affair witnessed by 75,364.

1993

15 May at Wembley   Att 79,347

Arsenal 1 (Wright)

Sheffield Wednesday 1

(Hirst)   **aet**

Arsenal: Seaman, Dixon, Winterburn, Davis, Linighan, Adams, Jensen, Wright (O'Leary), Campbell, Merson, Parlour (Smith).

Sheffield Wednesday: Woods, Nilsson, Worthington, Palmer, Anderson (Hyde), Warhurst, Harkes, Waddle (Bart-Williams), Hirst, Bright, Sheridan.

Referee: K. Barratt

Replay: 20 May at Wembley   Att 62,267

Arsenal 2 (Wright, Linighan)

Sheffield Wednesday 1

(Waddle)   **aet**

Arsenal: Seaman, Dixon, Winterburn, Davis, Linighan, Adams, Jensen, Wright (O'Leary), Smith, Merson, Campbell.

Sheffield Wednesday: Woods, Nilsson (Bart-Williams), Worthington, Harkes, Palmer, Warhurst, Wilson (Hyde), Waddle, Hirst, Bright, Sheridan.

Referee: K. Barratt

Right Alan Cork gets a hug for scoring United's goal in the Sheffield semi-final, nearly fifteen years after scoring his first FA Cup goal – for Wimbledon against Gravesend, first round, November 1978. Cork, thirty-four, was one of Wimbledon's Cup-winners in 1988.

Above The ball is still billowing the net, but Eric Cantona is already receiving weighty congratulations from Roy Keane after the second of his two penalties in the 1994 final. Chelsea had beaten United twice in the League and played with authority and promise for an hour; but then United took over.

Right Victory roll by builder Delwyn Humphreys of non-League Kidderminster Harriers after scoring the goal which beat Preston North End in the fourth round, 1994.

Manchester United were back on a high column of their own again, crown and garlands in place, after a quarter of a century of under-achievement. They became the first champions of the new Premier League in 1993 and now, twelve months on, they became the sixth club to complete the League and Cup double: four-goal winners at Wembley, champions, again, by a margin of eight points and, just for good measure, League Cup runners-up. Alex Ferguson, a strong-willed Scot who had already led Aberdeen to great deeds, was given money, time and his head – and he built a team of which Old Trafford could be proud. It was a compound of flair and muscle, experience and ambi-tion and, in the modern way, different nationalities, including Eric Cantona, a many faceted French international who made more of an impression on English football than any foreigner before him. Irascible, yes, but also brilliant and intelligent, an inspira-tion and a cult figure, a champion with Leeds United and then with Manchester United after moving to Old Trafford in November 1992.

United's path to the double was not always strewn with roses. There were sendings off, blots in form and moments of high uncertainty. A late and brilliant goal by Mark Hughes, for example, got them off a nasty hook in their semi-final with Oldham Athletic. But Ferguson's team, on all important counts, were the tops.

1994

14 May at Wembley   Att 79,634

Manchester United 4 (Cantona 2 (2 pens), Hughes, McClair)

Chelsea 0

Manchester United: Schmeichel, Parker, Irwin (Sharpe), Bruce, Kanchelskis (McClair), Pallister, Cantona, Ince, Keane, Hughes, Giggs.

Chelsea: Kharine, Clarke, Sinclair, Kjeldbjerg, Johnsen, Burley (Hoddle), Spencer, Newton, Stein (Cascarino), Peacock, Wise.

Referee: D. Elleray

Below Early intimations, June 1994. The sponsorship of the FA Cup by Littlewoods Pools was formally announced three months later.

Daily Mirror.

Wembley's fiftieth post-war final was a classic reminder that League form is a poor clue to the destination of the Cup. Manchester United spent the season hunting the Championship... Everton were darkly haunted by relegation. It was Everton who won at Wembley.

Manchester United were without Eric Cantona, who had been suspended for eight months for a two-footed kung fu style kick at an abusive spectator during a League game at Selhurst Park in January 1995. His absence was critical: United finished as double runners-up.

Below Paul Rideout (second right) heads Everton's winner after a shot by Graham Stuart had hit the bar in the thirtieth minute. Then Everton's defence took over, marshalled stubbornly by captain Dave Watson, brilliantly backed by Neville Southall in goal, and United could do nothing to budge them.

1995

20 May at Wembley   Att 79,592

Everton 1 (Rideout)

Manchester United 0

Everton: Southall, Jackson, Ablett, Parkinson, Watson, Unsworth, Limpar (Amokachi), Horne, Stuart, Rideout (Ferguson), Hinchcliffe.

Manchester United: Schmeichel, G. Neville, Irwin, Bruce (Giggs), Sharpe (Scholes), Pallister, Keane, Ince, McClair, Hughes, Butt.

Referee: G. Ashby

Below Darren Anderton and Teddy Sheringham of England are pleased with Jürgen Klinsmann (underneath), who has just scored Tottenham Hotspur's winner against Liverpool at Anfield in the quarter-finals. Yet Tottenham were not even among the runners and riders when the tournament started. The FA had banned them from the 1994–95 FA Cup (among other swingeing penalties) for financial irregularities. However, they were reinstated by a tribunal in December – and went on to reach the semi-finals.

Klinsmann joined Spurs from Monaco before the start of the season and moved to Bayern Munich soon after it, but the impact the German international striker had on the north London club was enormous. He was unfailingly courteous, popular, a first-class ambassador and a consistent and spectacular scorer (twenty-nine goals) who was voted Footballer of the Year.

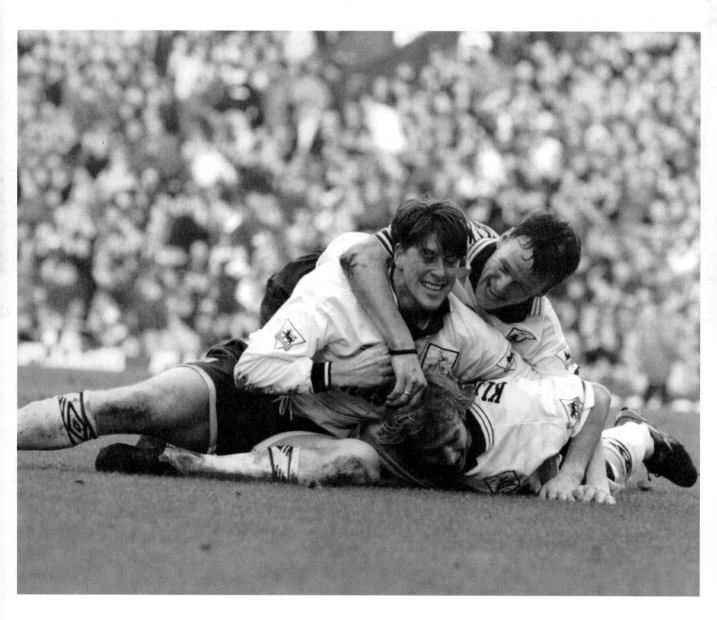

Manchester United scaled English football's Everest in 1994 by completing the double. Two years on, the mountain peak below them, they just kept on climbing. Alex Ferguson's team became League and Cup winners for the second time in three years, the sixth and seventh time it had been managed in a sovereign line going all the way back to the old 'Invincibles' of Preston.

United won the Premiership for the third time in four years, even though, at one stage, they were a dozen points behind Newcastle United. They won the Cup for a record ninth time because – in a poor final full of clutter and clatter, a disappointment at the end of a handsome season – they had a player with a divine spark. Eric Cantona struck United's winner from the edge of the area with only five minutes left, balance quickly

adjusted, short back-lift and the ball given a dipping passage into the net through a forest of Liverpool defenders. Sir Bobby Charlton, a Cup-winner under Matt Busby more than thirty years before, said of United's Frenchman: 'Exceptional ability, an inspiration, simply a great player. And you've got to put this team up there with the best of any era. It has so much talent and ambition and so many good young players coming through.'

Above Two days before the final, sixteen months after his infamous kick at Crystal Palace, Cantona received the Footballer of the Year award. Now he has received the Cup from the Duchess of Kent and he holds it aloft with goalkeeper Peter Schmeichel of Denmark, another key member of United's team, alongside him.

1996

11 May at Wembley   Att 79,007
Manchester United 1 (Cantona)
Liverpool 0

Manchester United: Schmeichel, Irwin, P. Neville, May, Keane, Pallister, Cantona, Beckham (G. Neville), Cole (Scholes), Butt, Giggs.

Liverpool: James, McAteer, Jones (Thomas), Scales, Wright, Babb, McManaman, Redknapp, Collymore (Rush), Barnes, Fowler.

Referee: D. Gallagher

Below Ian Rush scoring his forty-second FA Cup goal, Liverpool v Rochdale (7–0), third round, January 1996. The goal made him the tournament's leading post-war scorer, beating the old record of Denis Law. Rush had three winner's medals (1986, 1989 and 1992) and came on as a late substitute in the 1996 final, making his 670th appearance for Liverpool. 'It would have been tremendous to score, but Cup goals, especially in a final, don't come to order,' he said.

Above For better or worse. Neil Campbell and Joan Dowey watching Hereford United play Tottenham Hotspur at Edgar Street in the third round 1996, immediately after their marriage at St Margaret's Church, Wellington. They were chauffeured straight to the game which finished 1–1. Spurs won the replay 5–1.

The League of Cup Finalists

1872–1996

Two points for **winners**, one for losing finalists

	FINALS	POINTS
Manchester United	**1909**, **1948**, 1957, 1958, **1963**, 1976, **1977**, 1979, **1983**, **1985**, **1990**, **1994**, 1995, **1996**	23
Arsenal	1927, **1930**, 1932, **1936**, **1950**, 1952, **1971**, 1972, 1978, **1979**, 1980, **1993**	18
Everton	1893, 1897, **1906**, 1907, **1933**, **1966**, 1968, **1984**, 1985, 1986, 1989, **1995**	17
Newcastle United	1905, 1906, 1908, **1910**, 1911, **1924**, **1932**, **1951**, **1952**, **1955**, 1974	17
Tottenham Hotspur	**1901**, **1921**, **1961**, **1962**, **1967**, **1981**, **1982**, 1987, **1991**	17
Aston Villa	**1887**, 1892, **1895**, **1897**, **1905**, **1913**, **1920**, 1924, **1957**	16
Liverpool	1914, 1950, **1965**, 1971, **1974**, 1977, **1986**, 1988, **1989**, **1992**, 1996	16
West Bromwich Albion	1886, 1887, **1888**, **1892**, 1895, 1912, **1931**, 1935, **1954**, **1968**	15
Blackburn Rovers	1882, **1884**, **1885**, **1886**, **1890**, **1891**, **1928**, 1960	14
Manchester City	**1904**, 1926, 1933, **1934**, 1955, **1956**, **1969**, 1981	12
Wolverhampton W	1889, **1893**, 1896, **1908**, 1921, 1939, **1949**, **1960**	12
Bolton Wanderers	1894, 1904, **1923**, **1926**, **1929**, 1953, **1958**	11
Sheffield United	**1899**, 1901, **1902**, **1915**, **1925**, 1936	10
The Wanderers	**1872**, **1873**, **1876**, **1877**, **1878**	10
Preston North End	1888, **1889**, 1922, 1937, **1938**, 1954, 1964	9
Sheffield Wednesday	1890, **1896**, **1907**, **1935**, 1966, 1993	9
Old Etonians	1875, 1876, **1879**, 1881, **1882**, 1883	8
West Ham United	1923, **1964**, **1975**, **1980**	7
Huddersfield Town	1920, **1922**, 1928, 1930, 1938	6

Sunderland	1913, **1937**, **1973**, 1992	6
Chelsea	1915, 1967, **1970**, 1994	5
Derby County	1898, 1899, 1903, **1946**	5
Leeds United	1965, 1970, **1972**, 1973	5
Nottingham Forest	**1898**, **1959**, 1991	5
Oxford University	1873, **1874**, 1877, 1880	5
Royal Engineers	1872, 1874, **1875**, 1878	5
Blackpool	1948, 1951, **1953**	4
Burnley	**1914**, 1947, 1962	4
Bury	**1900**, **1903**	4
Leicester City	1949, 1961, 1963, 1969	4
Portsmouth	1929, 1934, **1939**	4
Southampton	1900, 1902, **1976**	4
Barnsley	1910, **1912**	3
Cardiff City	1925, **1927**	3
Charlton Athletic	1946, **1947**	3
Clapham Rovers	1879, **1880**	3
Notts County	1891, **1894**	3
Birmingham City	1931, 1956	2
Blackburn Olympic	**1883**	2
Bradford City	**1911**	2
Coventry City	**1987**	2
Ipswich Town	**1978**	2
Old Carthusians	**1881**	2
Queens Park (Glasgow)	1884, 1885	2
Wimbledon	**1988**	2
Brighton and Hove Albion	1983	1
Bristol City	1909	1
Crystal Palace	1990	1
Fulham	1975	1
Luton Town	1959	1
Queens Park Rangers	1982	1
Watford	1984	1

Index

Illustrations are indicated in **boldface**.

Picture Credits

Roman numerals refer to pages in the colour sections.

Action Images: 305; XVIb

Allsport: 106b, 280, 296, 301, 303; IXb, XIII

Bickley Park Cricket Club: 24b

British Film Institute: 52

British Newspaper Library: 32

Christie's: VIIIb

Stuart Clarke: XVt

Richard Cohen: 56t, 125

Colorsport: 48, 51, 57, 61t, 67, 69t, 77, 87, 105, 119tl, 141t, 189, 196b, 207, 214, 215, 244, 270; IXt, XIb, XII, XVIt

Gareth Davies: 68t

FA: 8, 16–17, 33, 35, 46, 49, 56b, 64, 65, 66, 75, 78, 82t, 117bl, 119r, 123, 139, 144, 151b, 155, 156, 161, 165, 170, 177, 178t, 182l, 183, 184, 185, 188, 192, 197, 198–9, 204, 208, 209, 211, 213t, 219, 221, 224, 225, 243, 246–7, 257, 258, 271t, 277l

Football Museum, Preston: 53; It

David Frith: IVt

Clynt Garnham: XIV

Hailey Sports Photographic: 276

Hulton-Deutsch Collection: 61b, 73b, 94–5, 97, 103b, 112b, 113b, 120, 122–3, 129t, 131, 137b, 141b, 145, 150, 154t, 157, 163, 166, 179b, 180, 186, 187, 191, 210, 212, 216, 218, 220, 229b, 237b, 241, 251, 256, 295t

Councillor Mrs Ruby Hunt: 24t

Illustrated London News Picture Library: 27, 55, 74, 79, 80b, 81, 83, 84t, 85b, 86, 101, 112–13t, 114–15, 124–5, 126, 127, 130, 138, 162

Lancashire Evening Telegraph: 50

Paul Macnamara: 23t, 69b, 76, 85t, 88, 118, 124

Mary Evans Picture Library: 40–41, 47, 68b, 102, 103t; III

Andy Mitchell: 26, 29, 30

Oxfordshire Photographic Archive: 31

Popperfoto: 23b, 25, 38r, 39, 54, 58b, 59, 62, 80t, 89, 96, 100, 106t, 121, 128, 136, 147, 148, 149, 151t, 152–3, 169b, 182t, 193, 194, 195, 228, 229t, 238, 250, 252, 271b, 275; II, IVb, VII, X, XIt

Press Association: 98, 99, 104, 107b, 119bl, 164, 167, 178b, 179t, 196t, 206, 217, 222, 227, 239, 240, 245, 247b, 248, 249, 253, 254b, 264, 265, 267, 268, 269, 272, 273, 274, 278, 279, 281, 282–3, 284, 285, 286, 287, 294, 295b, 297, 298, 299, 300, 304, 306, 307; XVb

Jack Rollin: 129br

Rugby Union Museum, Twickenham: 38l

Dave Shopland: 205

Graham Smith: 116–17; V, VIbl, VIIIt

Sport and General: 213b, 226, 242, 254t

Mrs Violet Stait: 63tr

Stoke Evening Sentinel: 10

Syndication International: 12, 181, 236, 237t

Gordon Wallis: 28

Ted Wilding: 190

Wolverhampton Express and Star: 60